Praise for *Death's Door*

"The souls of the innocent have finally
compassion were the keys to Lehto's succ   …….ng wnat really
happened. His tenacity and perseverance will preserve the true story of
what happened in the Copper Country's 'Hall of Horror.'"

JAY BRANDOW, REPORTER, WNEM TV-5 SAGINAW

"I learned a great deal about the Italian Hall disaster. I'm impressed
with the amount of research that Lehto has done, and his keen eye for
nuance and detail that must be considered when interpreting documents
and making historical judgments. The good news is that it's a moving,
poignant story. In any event, I enjoyed it, and I appreciate the amount of
blood, sweat and tears that Lehto has put into it."

DR. DANIEL CLARK, ASSOCIATE PROFESSOR OF HISTORY, OAKLAND UNIVERSITY

"Lehto puts events back together with the eye of a crime-scene investigator
and first-class historian."

PETER WERBE, HOST OF "NIGHTCALL," WRIF-FM 101.1 DETROIT

"Lehto deftly sets the scene of the strike and for the Italian Hall deaths.
With the tools of his professional disciplines, he adeptly dissects the
legal handling of events surrounding the strikes, the two sets of murders
preceding the tragic Christmas Eve and the investigation after the deaths
in the Italian Hall."

LAKE SUPERIOR MAGAZINE

Death's Door

The Truth Behind Michigan's Largest Mass Murder

by Steve Lehto

Bunny — I hope
you enjoy the
story.

Published by Momentum Books, L.L.C.

2145 Crooks Road, Suite 208
Troy, Michigan 48084
www.momentumbooks.com

ISBN-13: 978-1-879094-77-2
ISBN-10: 1-879094-77-0
LCCN: 2006932142

Cover photograph courtesy of David V. Tinder and the Clements Library, University of Michigan.

For my wife, Amanda ...

and the victims of the Italian Hall tragedy: the seventy-three who perished and the countless others affected by the events of December 24, 1913.

Table of Contents

1913 Massacre

By Woody Guthrie

Take a trip with me in nineteen thirteen
To Calumet, Michigan in the copper country
I'll take you to a place called Italian Hall
And the miners are having their big Christmas ball

I'll take you in a door and up a high stairs
Singing and dancing is heard ev'rywhere
I'll let you shake hands with the people you see
And watch the kids dance 'round the big Christmas tree.

There's talking and laughing and songs in the air
And the spirit of Christmas is there ev'rywhere
Before you know it you're friends with us all
And you're dancing around and around in the hall

You ask about work and you ask about pay
They'll tell you they make less than a dollar a day
Working their copper claims, risking their lives
So it's fun to spend Christmas with children and wives.

A little girl sits down by the Christmas tree lights
To play the piano so you gotta keep quiet
To hear all this fun; you would not realize
That the copper boss thug men are milling outside

The copper boss thugs stuck their heads in the door
One of them yelled and he screamed, "There's a fire"
A lady she hollered, "There's no such a thing;
Keep on with your party, there's no such a thing."

A few people rushed and there's only a few
"It's just the thugs and the scabs fooling you."
A man grabbed his daughter and he carried her down
But the thugs held the door and he could not get out.

And then others followed, about a hundred or more
But most everybody remained on the floor
The gun thugs, they laughed at their murderous joke
And the children were smothered on the stairs by the door.

Such a terrible sight I never did see
We carried our children back up to their tree
The scabs outside still laughed at their spree
And the children that died there was seventy-three

The piano played a slow funeral tune,
And the town was lit up by a cold Christmas moon
The parents, they cried and the men, they moaned,
"See what your greed for money has done?"

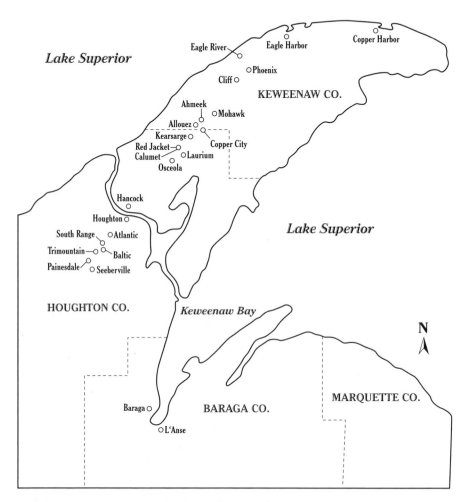

Lake Superior

Eagle River
Eagle Harbor
Copper Harbor

Phoenix
Cliff

KEWEENAW CO.

Ahmeek
Mohawk
Allouez
Kearsarge
Copper City
Red Jacket
Calumet
Laurium
Osceola

Hancock

Houghton

Lake Superior

South Range
Atlantic
Trimountain
Baltic
Painesdale
Seeberville

HOUGHTON CO.

Keweenaw Bay

N

MARQUETTE CO.

Baraga

BARAGA CO.

L'Anse

Michigan Copper Country

Introduction

If you visit Calumet near the northern edge of Michigan's Upper Peninsula, you may think the village has always been on the verge of being a ghost town. Empty buildings lean over the main streets, and it doesn't seem there are enough people around to justify the size of the place. Some two-story buildings have the false-fronted roofs of the Old West. Looks are deceiving, of course. The town has a grand history; its heyday centered on the copper industry boom that began in the late 1800s. Walking around Calumet today looking for clues to the turning point might lead you over a few blocks to a small remnant of a building—a sandstone arch, alone in the middle of a vacant lot. You have to walk beyond the arch to read an historical marker—it's too far from the road to be read from a car—and little else calls attention to the spot. The arch is a memorial and all that remains of the building that once stood on the lot: the Italian Hall. The marker—placed by the state of Michigan more than 70 years after the event it describes—tells its story in only a few sentences.

More than six dozen people were crushed to death on this spot on Christmas Eve 1913, as they scrambled to get through the doors beneath the arch after someone cried "Fire" at the top of the stairs that led to the meeting hall on the building's second floor. There was no fire, and the man who yelled "Fire" was never caught, although he had been seen by many who survived. The entire event was over in a flash, but the tragedy would scar the psyche of the region for decades. The memorial lot is too small and unremarkable to properly remember those who died and the atmosphere in which they were killed. No marker or park could ever tell the story completely, or convey the melancholy that has hung over Calumet ever since.

If you walk back toward the center of town from the arch and look for a resident of Calumet today, you could ask them about the Italian Hall and what happened there that Christmas Eve. You wouldn't need to mention the date, just the name of the building. You might hear variations on the story: The number of dead will be fluid; the doors to the street may have opened inward; someone may have been holding the doors shut from the outside. None of it will be as certain as the few words on the historical marker. What won't change are the powerful emotions the event resurrects. Some won't talk about it; others will get angry or agitated. Many will cry. All will be moved, as if being brought back to the night death swept over the town.

* * *

My family's roots trace back to this region of Michigan. My grandfather was a dean of Suomi College, where my father met my mother a few decades after the Italian Hall tragedy. Suomi is now called Finlandia and is the only Finnish college in the United States. The school was founded to serve the huge Finnish population that poured into this area around the turn of the 19th century to work in the copper mines. Both of my parents speak Finnish fluently, and the transition of family identity from Finnish to American seemed to occur somewhere closer to the arrival of my brothers and myself in the middle of the 20th century.

We vacationed in the Copper Country each summer, and I remember visiting Calumet as a child. When the Italian Hall was mentioned, conversations often shifted into hushed tones, and among the older generation, into Finnish. It bordered on the unmentionable. Most of the dead were of Finnish descent—and children, at that.

* * *

As personal as the catastrophe was for those in the area, it holds a much larger meaning to those who study it. The tragedy struck at a seam in history, a defining border between the Old World and New World in race and labor. The deaths occurred in the middle of a bitter labor dispute between the miners and the mines. Sharp cultural lines were obvious at the time of the strike: Those who spoke English were in charge, and those who spoke the funny languages of Finland or Eastern Europe were given the hardest manual labor. When the strike was called, sides were drawn from these language pools.

The event also occurred at the pre-dawn of the labor movement in America. Unions were a relatively new thing, and many people considered them un-American and socialistic. In the summer of 1913, it was considered good business to bring in hired thugs to beat up strikers. It was in this environment that the Christmas Eve party was disrupted by the man who cried "Fire."

One summer as I revisited the Calumet area, I found a book that mentioned the Italian Hall, and how the event had never been properly explained. The book had been written in 1943; surely, someone had to have figured it out by now. I began looking into it and was puzzled by the lack of work in the area because interest remains high, even as time passes. Woody Guthrie had written *1913 Massacre* to help rally labor in the 1940s; the song had been revived by Bob Dylan. More than seventy years later, local papers ran front-page stories about the calamity when unnamed sources came forward and offered solutions to the mystery without naming names. In the 1990s, an opera was staged about the event, and in 2005, filmmakers visited the town, shooting footage for a documentary about the impact the event had—and continues to have—on Calumet.

I studied history in college and eventually went to law school. I wondered what the evidence would show: I scoured archives and libraries, and located transcripts of trials and hearings from 1913 and 1914. I read newspaper articles and affidavits, and even found documents that had been misfiled and had not seen the light of day since they were first put away. The picture that emerged was very different from the stories I'd heard growing up and from those I'd read. I began to write the story as best I could, to try and show what the facts were after removing the distortion and noise of past decades. Many of my conclusions differed from accepted versions of the event, probably because I approached much of the evidence from a legal perspective.

The event was murder—not an accident or prank—and was most likely instigated by mine management. As such, it is the largest mass murder in Michigan, and it is still officially an open case. Theoretically, someone could still be charged and tried for the murders of seventy-three people at the Italian Hall, but time has probably caught up with the perpetrator.

It has been, after all, more than ninety years since the event. In a vacuum, the idea that someone could get away with causing the death of seventy-three people in front of witnesses seems incomprehensible. The event, though, did not occur in a context familiar to us. Calumet of 1913 was a different world, with different rules and rulers. In this book, I'll do my best to lead you through that world.

One important note for the reader: In the time frame of the Italian Hall tragedy, there was a glaring lack of uniformity when it came to the spellings of proper names. This becomes problematic to anyone sifting through the primary documents that describe the event. Some names are spelled so many different ways that it is impossible to guess which was correct. This issue spilled over into punctuation of official transcripts and the way organizations even spelled their own names. Here, I try to be consistent when faced with various spellings, defaulting to those used in the most official source, such as a transcript. When quoting portions of a transcript or other primary source, I try to do so verbatim. Also, be aware that a prominent character in this tale, the Citizens Alliance, spelled its own name at least three different ways: Its buttons bore no apostrophe, while some of their literature did. ("Citizens" versus "Citizens' ".) In that regard, I simply chose to use the format found on the button. After all, the button played a key part in the tragedy.

* * *

In the early afternoon of Christmas Eve 1913, most of the children in Red Jacket, Michigan, headed to the Italian Hall, a two-story brick building where a party was being thrown for them. Hundreds of children converged on the Italian Hall building and climbed the narrow flight of stairs to the meeting room on the second floor. There, they saw a stage with a piano and some meager Christmas decorations. Adults milled about with others they knew or who spoke their language. Many in the audience had come to America to work in the copper mines of northern Michigan and didn't speak English. Most of the conversations were in Finnish, Croatian or Italian. Soon, there were more than 700 people in the building, with some standing in the vestibule at the top of the stairs. Some of the adults slipped downstairs to the first floor saloon where mine workers often gathered.

Annie Clemenc directed the activities from the stage. Over six feet tall, "Big Annie" as she was known, was of Croatian descent and the wife of a striking miner. She helped lead the singing of carols and noted the size of the crowd. Annie and the others in the women's auxiliary purchased barrels of candy for the party, but she became concerned that they might run out. As the party progressed, the children in the crowd became visibly excited, pushing toward the stage. Annie decided to forego a Christmas play and announced it was time to begin handing out the presents and candy.

Many of the children ran directly toward the front of the room and began climbing up the front of the stage. Others, better behaved, went around to the right side of the stage and went up the stairs like they were told. As the children crossed the stage, the women gave them presents and candy; the gifts were inexpensive but precious to those who otherwise might not receive anything that Christmas.

After they received their presents, the children were directed off stage to the left side of the room, where they went down some steps that led to a hallway that ran parallel to the main room. Some enterprising children realized they could cut around the stage and go through the line a second time. One of the women on stage saw a face she recognized in the line and went and asked a Finn to watch the doors to make sure that children were routed all the way down the hallway so they could not go through the line twice.

The number of children was greater than anyone anticipated. Still, it looked like there might be enough treats to go around. The women on stage asked men in the kitchen—behind and below the stage—to send up more candy. Even after a couple of hundred children had crossed the stage, there seemed to be hundreds more. Although no one had taken a head count at the door, some estimated there were as many as 700 people in the main room, with perhaps 500 or 600 children.

Some children went home after getting their presents. Others stayed to see what else was on the schedule. Some families visited with friends and neighbors. A few Italians discussed the news at the top of the stairs. A group of Finns sat and chatted nearby, likewise on the landing at the top of the staircase. The noise level was remarkable. Women on stage could not hear each other speak; they worried their announcements could not be heard more than a few feet from the stage. Some men inside the building stayed in the vestibule, out of the noise. Others stood on chairs to look for their children, mixed into the crowd.

Then a flash of movement and a loud voice drew attention toward the swinging doors at the top of the stairs. A man wearing a dark coat and a hat pulled low over his eyes stepped into the main hall and yelled, "Fire!" He motioned with his hands as if trying to get the attention of people who could not hear him. On his coat was a white pin with red lettering:

CITIZENS ALLIANCE. He waited a moment to make sure his message had been heard and then he ran back through the double swinging doors and down the stairs to the street.

People nearest the door repeated his warning, crying "Fire" themselves and then heading for the stairway as well. Some repeated the cry in their native tongue, to make sure their compatriots understood. Some thought the cry had been raised because there was a fire in the saloon downstairs. Still others thought there might be a fire in the kitchen or the bar, both parts of the building's top floor that were out of sight of most of the people in attendance. People standing closer to the stage could not hear what caused the rush, but soon they saw people swarming toward the exit. Others did not recognize the cry of alarm at first because it was in English, a language they could not speak.

Within seconds, children were screaming and rushing toward the stairway. There were other ways out of the hall, but they were not well marked and everyone had come in through the front. While hundreds were rushing for the stairs, some cooler heads attempted to calm the crowd. A woman from the stage jumped down onto the main floor and grabbed a man who was yelling "Fire." She shook him and told him to stop. She jumped back onto the stage and began yelling that there was no fire. People near the stage could not make out what she was saying; some thought she was confirming the danger because of her agitated behavior. Although the cry of "Fire" had first been raised by the door, others yelling it within the hall added to the confusion.

The first few people down the staircase made it safely to the street, running through the two sets of doors at the bottom of the stairs, letting the doors shut behind them. Then, someone fell on the stairs. Whether they fell because they were pushed or if they tripped, no one knows. There were no handrails on either side of the staircase, so it would have been difficult for someone to regain their balance once they stumbled. After the first person tripped, others fell and soon, people began piling up in the stairway. Some got carried into the rush and were hauled down the stairs even though they tried to stay in the hall. Others were caught in the rush and then tried to make it to safety by climbing over those on the stairs who had fallen before them.

In less than a minute, the pile of people was several feet high. Some said it was six feet deep at its highest point, and ran from the bottom of the stairs upward a total of thirty feet. Children underneath suffocated from the weight of the people above them. People climbing through the morass stepped on the heads and chests of people who had fallen. A woman with a baby in her arms realized that she was going to die; she lifted her baby over her head and the baby was found alive, clutched in his dead mother's hands.

All the screaming and rushing in the building attracted the attention of people on the street level—inside the saloon and on the street. Dominic Vairo ran through the door between his saloon and the landing at the bottom of the stairs and realized there was nothing he could do at the bottom; he went through his saloon and into the alley behind the Hall. There, he climbed a fire escape, went into the Hall and began telling people to stop going toward the stairs. Jacob Kaiser, the assistant fire chief, was the first official on the scene. When he saw the mass on the stairs he tried unsuccessfully to pull some of the children from the pile. He ran around the back of the Hall and climbed a fire escape to get in. Other firemen followed him in and they began telling the people to stop crowding the stairs, that there was no fire, and then began the horrific task of untangling the pile of people in the stairway.

Some children familiar with the building and the neighborhood knew there was a ladder on the back of the building. As many as a hundred ran from the stage area and climbed down the ladder, while many more jumped from rear windows to a roof below.

Someone on the street called in a fire alarm when they heard the commotion; the alarm was reported at 4:45 p.m., Calumet time. Firemen appeared almost instantly—the Red Jacket fire station was less than a block away—and when they arrived, they leaned ladders against the building and began helping people out through the windows and fire escapes. They also helped clear the stairway. From the moment the man with the Citizens Alliance pin yelled "Fire," it had been only a matter of minutes. But the results were everlasting. The mayor of the town found himself among the rescuers and he pulled a young girl from the pile: "She brought her rescuer to tears with an inquiry if she would go to heaven if she died." She lived, but her mother died.

Although many of the last people to enter the stairway were not injured, or injured only slightly, there were people packed so tightly into the stairway that it took hours to remove them. The first bodies were removed from the stairway and brought back upstairs. Some survivors had fainted in the mass of people and regained consciousness inside the Hall, not knowing how they had gotten back inside. Lifeless children were laid out on tables, and those in attendance tried in vain to resuscitate them. Many bore no visible signs of injury, but were dead nonetheless.

A crowd began to gather on the street in front of the doors to Italian Hall. Rumors swirled. Was there a fire or not? Deputies and firemen on the street pushed the curious back. Some in the crowd had relatives inside the Hall and wanted to see them. They couldn't get in through the front; the stairway was still jammed with bodies. Some went around the back of the building and went up fire escapes. Others got into pushing matches with the deputies who did their best to restrain them.

As those inside the Hall saw the dead being carried in, they realized the extent of the tragedy. Some stayed to help; others left and spread the word. Soon, several thousand people from the area were crowding around the Hall. Once the stairway was cleared, rescue workers began laying the bodies out on the sidewalk in front of the building. So many were children, but adults had died, too. Many of them were related to one another; fathers and their children had died. Sisters and brothers were killed. Some would not be identified soon because their relatives had died with them. At least six dozen bodies were carried from the Hall. They were taken across the road to the Red Jacket fire hall where a temporary morgue would be set up.

One distraught woman picked up a dead child and wandered off into the darkness, crying. A few minutes later she returned and placed the child back in the row of dead. In her grief, she had misidentified the child; her child was home, safe. Some other mother's life was about to be shattered. A few children were pulled from the pile and lived. At least three were sent to local hospitals. Rumors swept through the crowd. Many had seen the man who cried "Fire" and more than half a dozen said he wore an Alliance button. In all, sixty-two children and eleven adults had died in the crush.

The confusion that began with the cry of "Fire" has never been extinguished. Sinister forces were at work in Calumet at the end of 1913. It helps to understand the Copper Country of the time: After all, the ones who ran the area and were responsible for the calamity weren't the ones burying their children.

Seeds of Discontent

"Timbering costs money while men do not cost us anything."
- C&H MINE BOSS TO A MINER -

The Copper Country

Today the Keweenaw Peninsula of upper Michigan is still called the "Copper Country." No mining activity remains; the few open mines derive their income solely from giving tours. The Keweenaw is a fascinating and beautiful area, because of its geographic isolation and low population. It seems to be at the end of the Earth because it is on a peninsula and so far from the major population centers; no one passes through while going somewhere else. Michigan has two halves—two peninsulas—the "upper" and the "lower." The bulk of the population today lives in the lower, where Detroit, Grand Rapids and the state capital of Lansing are found. Yet, just a century ago, an area in the Upper Peninsula known as Calumet had such a thriving economy and so large a population that many suggested making it the state capital.

In the mid-1800s, the Upper Peninsula was largely barren wilderness. Much of the land seemed impassable because of its rocky and swampy nature, and the few who visited there were natives who fished and

9

hunted and dug a strange red metal from the ground. The earliest white adventurers to visit the Keweenaw reported finding copper in its native form—copper nuggets. While gold and silver often occur in nature in this form, copper had always been reduced from copper ore, which required a chemical process to transform it to copper. The discovery of copper nuggets created excitement in the settled world to the south, and many began the long and troubled trek to the Keweenaw.

In 1864, a civil engineer named Edwin J. Hulbert explored the region and found a promising site for a copper mine. The land was virtually impassable, but there—about halfway up the peninsula, maybe ten miles from the town of Hancock—he found large chunks of "float" copper. These were nuggets of pure copper merely lying on the surface. Hulbert suspected they were the tip of a large deposit. He reported his find to a group of investors from Boston who quickly signed on to form a mining venture with him. They called their operation the Calumet Mining Company.

The Calumet operation purchased the huge tract of land that sat atop the copper lode, and as Hulbert's hunch proved correct, it quickly became a financial success. Miners dug copper from below while Hulbert set out to build a company town around the mine. He labeled the town Red Jacket after a famous Native American. The area provided so much copper that the same investors sank another shaft nearby—an operation they called the Hecla mine. After a few years of prosperity, they merged the two operations under one corporate name: Calumet & Hecla.

Although the area around the mines was called Calumet, and the mining operation resided in Calumet Township, the town itself was known as Red Jacket. In fact, the village was incorporated under the laws of Michigan in 1875 as "Red Jacket." This caused confusion for many who went to Calumet looking for work. One traveler famously reported back, "There is no Calumet," as he tried to explain the differences between Red Jacket the village and Calumet the mine. The area became a magnet for immigrants. Anyone hardy enough to make the trip to the Keweenaw and willing to put in a ten- or twelve-hour day moving tons of rock was welcome to work at the mines. They came from Finland, the British Isles, Canada, and from as far away as Austria and Italy. By 1870, Calumet Township was home to 3,182 people.

Once in Red Jacket, the workers adopted many American customs while still maintaining their homeland traditions. Local baseball and hockey teams dominated their sports in the region. Huge parades took place on the Fourth of July. And while many spoke English as their second language, there was a good market for newspapers in the native tongues of residents. In 1903, there were no fewer than eight foreign language newspapers serving the community, and many of the English language papers carried columns in Finnish and Italian. Secret societies and benevolent organizations for various ethnic groups prospered. The Italian Hall was built by the Italian Benevolent Society, although they often rented it to others in the community. The ground floor held two businesses and the upper floor was a large meeting hall with a stage. Down the street a bit was the Polish Society's meeting place.

Finns were the most numerous of the immigrants in the Calumet area. To people who are not familiar with Finns, their language appears and sounds incomprehensible. Finnish is not descended from the same language families as English or French, and is marked by words and names that are often long and filled with improbable—to speakers of English—letter combinations. Names like Aaltonen, Piira, and Wuolukka show the propensity for doubled letters in combinations that are uncommon elsewhere. It doesn't help that many of the names contained the letters "a" and "o" bearing umlauts—two dots above the letter denoting that it is a different letter altogether. Stories written in Finnish newspapers often contain spellings for names that are different from the spellings found in English versions of the same story.

Along with the Finns, there were Italians, Poles, Hungarians, Austrians, Croatians—the list seems endless. Visitors often remarked that Calumet was more than a melting pot; it was a virtual Tower of Babel. It would seem impossible to the average person that these various groups could all get along—let alone organize a union, which they would eventually attempt.

Although Calumet & Hecla was by far the largest mine in the Copper Country, there were many others. The Ahmeek and the Allouez to the north, the Quincy and the Isle Royale further south were just four among the more than two dozen mines that dug copper in 1913. There is no question, however, that Calumet & Hecla led the way: The other mines emulated them, and the miners were to do as they were told. The story of the Christmas Eve tragedy at the Italian Hall can only be told accurately if it includes a description of Calumet & Hecla's role in the Keweenaw.

Calumet & Hecla

Some people called Calumet & Hecla's relationship with its employees "benevolent feudalism." Not only did C&H employ most of the male population of the area, they owned the land the mines sat on as well as the surrounding area—even when they allowed workers to build homes and shopkeepers to erect stores. C&H also built many homes it rented to employees, making it the landlord that everyone in the area answered to. Rents were low, but onerous terms left the tenant-miners under the constant threat of eviction at the whims of management.

One common practice was the ground-rent lease. C&H leased land to prospective homeowners on five-year terms, with the proviso that C&H could cancel the lease on ninety days' notice if the tenant failed in any way to fulfill the terms of the lease. Upon cancellation, the tenant had ninety days to remove his home from the property; if he was unable to remove it, the home became the property of C&H without any compensation to the tenant. When the Department of Labor investigated the copper strike in 1914, they were surprised at how draconian the terms of the leases were. "It is unnecessary to comment on the drastic nature of the terms of these five-year ground-rent leases, but it seems strange that any person would build a house on land leased on such conditions, and it is most astonishing that 1,000 houses have been built on land so leased from Calumet & Hecla Mining Co."

Most shocking was that some of the leases contained provisions canceling the lease if the miner left the mine's employ, and allowing the mine to evict a tenant for any reason whatsoever. It is unclear if the tenant-mine workers fully understood the language of the leases they had signed; they were so laced with legalese that they were all but unreadable.

> *PROVIDED, That in case any rent shall be due and unpaid, or the party of the second part shall erect or maintain, or suffer to be erected or maintained, thereon, any other structure or structures than as aforesaid, or shall neglect or refuse to pay any tax or assessment, ordinary or extraordinary, levied upon said land, or upon the structure or structures to be erected thereon during the life of this lease, for the space of sixty days after the same shall become due and payable, or shall sell or suffer to be sold, upon said land any spirituous or intoxicating liquors, or shall carry on ...*

This particular sentence—from a ground-rent lease with Calumet & Hecla—continues on like that for much longer. As confusing as this is for English speakers, how well could it have been comprehended by those who didn't speak English?

In 1912, C&H owned 1,764 houses. The cost of renting a home from Calumet & Hecla—if you were a worker—was quite low. Many of the homes could be rented for as low as \$4 or \$5 a month—about two days' wages. The rental of the homes owned by the mines was also fraught with peril. The mine could evict a tenant from a company-owned home on just fifteen days' notice for any reason, and the contract stipulated that a person who ceased employment with the mine had fifteen days to vacate.

Besides the housing, Calumet & Hecla built and owned ten school buildings in the area. The local armory was built by C&H, which rented it to the state militia. The YMCA sat on C&H land, as did most of the churches. Calumet & Hecla also built and maintained the public library, a modern bathhouse and the hospital. To a miner in Red Jacket in 1913, it seemed that Calumet & Hecla owned the world. In fact, C&H was so powerful, it decreed that local time would be a half-hour faster than the rest of the state. When it was noon in nearby Hancock, it was 12:30 in Calumet. It was an early form of daylight-savings time.

In 1900 Calumet opened a grand opera house, one of the finest of its time, and hosted the biggest names in entertainment. Enrico Caruso, John Philip Sousa, Lillian Russell and Sarah Bernhardt all performed there. Although it has often been lumped in with the other civic works bestowed by Calumet & Hecla, the Calumet Theater was actually built with village funds when the council found itself with a \$50,000 surplus one year.

One of the few pieces of the Keweenaw Peninsula not owned by C&H in the Calumet area was the Lakeview Cemetery. Just two miles west of town, it was the place where the Catholics and Protestants buried their dead.

In 1901, James MacNaughton was made general manager of the Calumet & Hecla operations. He was born in 1864 in Canada, but his family moved to Hancock while he was still quite young. At the age of eleven, MacNaughton joined his father working for C&H; his father worked in a stamping mill while he earned a dollar a day as a water boy. Later, he attended Oberlin College and the University of Michigan before returning to work in the management of the mines. MacNaughton would be one of the most prominent figures in the Copper Country during the next two decades. It was said that C&H held an insurance policy on MacNaughton's life in the amount of half a million dollars. His own feelings of self-importance would become apparent throughout the strike. He was even known to embellish his life story when he felt the need to impress interviewers or reporters. In 1914, he told an interviewer that he had played football for the University of Michigan. Even then, Michigan was a powerhouse; the previous season they had outscored their opponents 175-21 with a win-loss record of six and one. MacNaughton was never on the football team.

The Unions

MacNaughton hated unions and was specifically brought to Calumet &
Hecla because the corporate bosses in Boston thought that the mine had
been getting "soft" on its employees, "coddling" the men with too many
perks. They feared that if management in Red Jacket didn't tighten the
reins, the workers might get out of control. MacNaughton was the man
for the job. The bosses back east were also concerned about rising costs
and lower productivity in the Copper Country. Recent years had seen the
mines reach new depths—some shafts at C&H were approaching a mile
in depth straight down—and the deeper the men went, the costlier the
recovery of copper became.

In 1904, MacNaughton's anti-union leanings began to show, at least to
those with whom he worked. As a strike in the mines ended out west, many
blacklisted union organizers came back east looking for jobs in the mines
on the Keweenaw. MacNaughton made it his mine's policy not to employ
anyone with a union history. As MacNaughton went, so did the rest of the
Copper Country. MacNaughton and the others also hired spies to infiltrate
the organizations that might try to bring unions to the Copper Country,
but in doing this MacNaughton was not breaking new ground. In 1887
Calumet & Hecla had hired private detectives to infiltrate the Knights of
Labor. Later, Quincy Mining Co. hired more than twenty private detectives
to pretend they were miners and report back on unionization efforts in the
mines. C&H under MacNaughton hired spies to join the Western Federation
of Miners—the union making inroads in the Copper Country in 1910.

One of the spies hired by Quincy got more than he bargained for when
he signed on. The Thiel Detective Service of Chicago sent the spy—known
only as "J.A.P."—to Hancock and told him to get a job at the Quincy mine
and report back on union activities. Once he'd been hired, he found that
working in the mines wasn't all that easy—or safe. His reports, sent via
Chicago, went to Quincy's superintendent who was baffled by the things
occupying his spy's mind. Down in the mine, J.A.P. began to wonder when
he would be crushed by falling rock. His supervisor told him, "Timbering
costs money while men do not cost us anything." Another common saying
he may have heard while trying his hand at mining was that management
ranked losing a mule as worse than losing a man in the mine. He spent
more time worrying about getting out of the mines alive at the end of the
day than he did spying on his fellow workers. All that he learned, though,
he duly reported to his bosses, who passed it along to Quincy.

J.A.P. began looking for a way out of the unsafe portions of the mine. He missed a day of work his first week because he was "sore" from the job. One day he went to see a supervisor to ask about getting moved to a safer shaft, only to find a bunch of men standing around a fresh opening in the ground. The man he'd come to see was too busy to talk—he was peering into a 400-foot deep hole where a worker had just died. Over the next few weeks, he was injured a few more times and managed a transfer to a better part of the mine. One day, another miner confided that J.A.P. seemed like a spy. Glad his cover had been blown, he quit his job and left town as fast as he could.

MacNaughton also became distrustful of the Finns in his employ. He never said why, but he was expressing a common prejudice many locals had against those with the "funny" language. At one point, he told the Commissioner of Immigration "we do not want Finlanders" at C&H. It was a large group to exclude, however. The year before MacNaughton arrived in Calumet, there were more than 7,000 foreign-born Finns in the county. The census of 1910 showed 11,500. It was easy to paint them all with the same brush. MacNaughton would often refer to people he did not like as "Socialists," so it was easy for him to dislike the Finns. Many of the recent immigrants were, indeed, Socialists. Even though the earlier immigrants were not, MacNaughton lumped them all together and disliked them as a group.

MacNaughton spent as much time as he could with the wealthier members of the community. In 1903, he and others at C&H formed a private club called the Miscowaubik—Ojibwa for "red metal." They met at a renovated home owned by the C&H, and MacNaughton was the group's first chairman. The membership was exclusive and included many of the rich and powerful of the county who gathered for fine dining and cigars—and to give each other alibis.

Patrick H. O'Brien was another local man, like MacNaughton, whose father had worked in the mines. His father worked for C&H, where he had been killed in the mine. After graduating from Calumet High, O'Brien went to law school in Indiana and eventually returned to Laurium—a town not far from Calumet—and hung out his shingle to handle personal injury cases. He specialized in suing the mines, representing injured workers or the surviving family members of miners who'd been killed. O'Brien made a name for himself with his success against the mines and helped reshape the law in the Keweenaw, particularly in the field of compensation for injured miners.

His practice flourished and he became well known as one of the few locals not intimidated by the copper barons. In 1907, there had been labor unrest at the mines near Rockland, Michigan, southwest of Calumet. In a

15

confrontation between unarmed strikers and armed and deputized mine workers, two Finnish miners were shot and killed. The local authorities arrested strikers for the killings, so they could claim they had prosecuted someone, even if they were the wrong people. The Finnish community called for help and O'Brien came down to defend the wrongfully accused Finnish defendants. O'Brien's skills in the courtroom gained acquittals for the first two defendants tried; the court dismissed the charges against the other eleven. Another Copper Country Finn was involved in the case: An attorney named Oscar Larson came down from Calumet to handle the prosecution.

Capitalizing on his fame, O'Brien ran for circuit court judge and won. If mine management hated him as an attorney, they'd hate him even more as a judge.

Although Finns had been a large percentage of all mine workers, as the 1900s progressed their percentage in the workforce dropped as mine managers hired other ethnic groups. It was so noticeable that by 1914, a mining journal reported that the mines of upper Michigan "seemed to be eliminating Finnish workers." There was little the Finns could do to combat discrimination—except hope that it didn't get worse.

The Copper Mines

The mines in the Copper Country are generally of similar type. They began where someone started digging an exposed vein of copper on the surface. From there, the hole was widened into a shaft. If the vein proved worthwhile, the shaft was shored up with timbers if necessary, and a shaft house was built near the opening. Shaft houses contained engines for raising and lowering cars or "skips" if the shaft wasn't horizontal. In a deep mine like the Red Jacket shaft, men would ride down into the mine in the skips and they would load the rock into skips to be pulled to the surface.

The shaft descended into the earth at whatever angle was necessary to reach the copper. At about every hundred feet, a level or "drift" was cut, running horizontally away from the shaft. Workers would enter the shafts and start cutting and blasting their way outward from the drifts. The areas they cut out to the sides were called "stopes." The rock was cut and blasted from the stopes, and then loaded into tramcars. The trams were pushed by hand along the drift back to the shaft where the ore was then lifted to the surface. Although copper occurs in the Keweenaw in nugget form, much of the copper being mined in this area was in much smaller form: Rock from the mines was hauled to the surface and crushed. Small copper flakes were then removed from the stamped material and smelted into ingots.

The work in the mines fell into several categories, although miners and trammers were the ones most people talked about. Miners operated drills that cut holes into the rock walls and used explosives to blast the ore loose. The job was dangerous and paid a bit better than being a trammer. The trammers loaded rock onto the tramcars, and then pushed the tramcar along a track back to the shaft. Their work was backbreaking. Most trammers hoped to work their way up to being miners. More experienced miners—like many Cornish and English—would rather be unemployed than work as a trammer.

There was a general labor shortage in the Keweenaw that began around 1910. The mines were willing to hire almost any able-bodied man available, but it seemed that employment in the area was approaching one hundred percent. During 1911 and 1912, the mines were even faced with a shortage of trammers.

The mines were lit by candle at first, then by electric lamps when the technology arrived. Even so, most mines were dimly lit. Further, the mines were generally damp and dusty, although the copper mining process did not create the airborne hazards of the coal mines. The conditions in the mines were crude as they possibly could be. There were no latrine facilities, and for the most part, the trip to the surface was far too time-consuming to be wasted on such a simple matter. Men relieved themselves where they were working, and many mines merely had rules requiring the levels "to be cleaned up occasionally."

However, no one complained about the unsanitary conditions. If anything, they worried about accidents. Statistics for the time showed that copper mining was more likely to prove fatal to the worker than any other kind of metal mining in the United States. For every thousand men employed in the copper mines, five would die on average each year. For each death, there were ten or more serious injuries and perhaps a hundred "slight" injuries. Most fell victim to falling rock, although explosions, fires and plunging down a shaft were also causes of death or injury. In 1912, forty-seven men were killed underground in the local copper mines, while 643 were seriously injured and another 3,936 were "slightly injured." Some sources placed the fatality rate in the region at closer to sixty-one per year, just a little over one death per week.

Work underground strained the men in other ways. The Keweenaw is so much closer to the Arctic Circle than the equator that it has noticeably longer summer days and longer winter nights compared to lower Michigan. Copper miners who arrived for work in the mornings often went

17

underground before sunrise and emerged after sunset. Many of the men went weeks without seeing daylight in the winter.

Although some would point out later that the mines paid relatively well and the mines provided housing and other necessities to the workers at reduced rates, the men of the area were becoming more open to the idea of organizing. As with most changes, the shift occurred gradually. The work was hard, conditions difficult. Deaths and injuries were a constant, but seemed of little importance to management. Under these conditions, union organizers would have better luck than when they had visited the Copper Country twenty years earlier and failed.

The Western Federation of Miners

In 1909, the Western Federation of Miners came to Calumet seeking to organize the workers in the Copper Country. The WFM ran into a bit of resistance at first, however. Problems with the various languages and ethnic groups kept their message from getting across. There was also a general feeling in the area that work in the copper mines wasn't all that bad. Why unionize?

The wages in the mines were fairly competitive. In 1913, most miners in the district were making around $3 per day. When the Labor Department investigated wages in the mines, the only oddity they found—which the miners had never complained about—was how the wages were often computed:

> Contracts were formerly let on the basis of cubic fathom of rock mined, but now they are usually let on the basis of tons mined. In no mines is the rock actually weighed, but the pay of contract miners is figured on the number of tramcar loads of rock which they blast out and which the trammers push to the shaft. In each mine the dimensions of the tramcars are the same, but the load, of course, depends on how fully they are filled or how much they are heaped. The miners seem to have accepted without much complaint this method of estimating their production, though it is rather surprising that such a crude method has not caused dissatisfaction.

The mines were notoriously stingy when it came to paying the men, though. Stories abounded of men who complained they were not paid as promised, and if they complained too loudly, they were fired. William MacDonald, a congressman from the area, had been an attorney before entering politics. He filed several suits against the mines for unpaid wages. The mines fought the cases tooth-and-nail, but lost. Most of his clients quit their jobs during the suit, knowing they'd be fired for filing the action. His one client who didn't quit was fired when he won.

The mines were also known to lower wages when they felt the conditions were right. Slow sales of copper might occasion lower wages. The mines out west—also the site of labor unrest—had lowered wages when new equipment made the workers more productive. The miners in the Keweenaw were well aware of the situation in the west, and watched developments there as a sign of things to come. One ugly development in Colorado was a vigilante force that called itself the "Citizens Alliance." This group opposed the unions, supported local businesses and often broke the law in doing so. Local law enforcement appeared not to care when the Alliance broke the law. When a strike was called by the Western Federation of Miners, the mine owners appealed to the Colorado governor to send in the militia. When they arrived, violence flared and escalated.

As the WFM continued recruiting in the Copper Country, the Calumet & Hecla Mining Co. continued to grow. In 1912, the company produced more than sixty-seven million pounds of copper. It paid dividends to stockholders totaling $42 per share that year. In fact, business was so good that wages were raised ten percent for all employees that year.

The company also optimistically announced the arrival of some new equipment at most of its mines: "After two years' experiments with various types of drilling machines, the Leyner-Ingersoll one-man drill has been adopted as a standard, and these machines are being introduced as fast as practicable. The results are an increase in the wages of the miners and a decrease in the cost of drifting and stoping."

By the way, calling the mine workers "men" was not a euphemism: there were no women working in the mines. In 1913 C&H had more than 4,000 men on its payroll. There were twenty-eight women employed by C&H, but all worked for the hospital, library or the company's bathhouse. At that time, C&H would not even hire women as secretaries.

The WFM slowly gained membership until 1913 when the union focused on the one-man drill. Up to this point, the drilling in the mines had been accomplished by two men operating a huge drill. The machine was so heavy and cumbersome that it kept two men busy for an entire shift. Recent technological advancements had seen the creation of a smaller and lighter drill that could be handled and set up by one man. The WFM attacked the drill: It would put half the miners out of work! What if a miner fell while drilling and was injured—with no one nearby to help him? Someone dubbed the one-man drill the "widow maker" although there was little evidence that the drill was actually killing husbands. Union membership increased dramatically, and by 1913 there were almost 9,000 unionized copper workers in the Keweenaw.

Many union critics argued that the drill was attacked only because it cut down on the number of workers needed in the mines. There is some evidence to show this is not wholly accurate. In 1913, the Isle Royale Copper Co. began using mules in its mines for tramming. Mules had been used at another mine in the district and presumably were replacing people who had done the tramming before. Throughout the entire debate over labor conditions and the one-man drill, no one ever complained about the use of mules in the mines. Some of the mines had also begun using motorized tramcars. Likewise, these eliminated jobs and no one complained about their introduction either.

Feeling they had enough clout to negotiate better working conditions with the mine owners, the WFM locals asked their members if they could approach mine management and address the pressing issues of the day. While fighting the threat of the one-man drill, the union also sought an eight-hour workday and a channel for workers to air day-to-day grievances.

The WFM explained to its members that management ought to recognize the unions, and not to do so would be the height of hypocrisy. After all, the corporations that ran the mines were owned by stockholders. Those individual stockholders did not negotiate each deal the corporation struck; they selected a board to run the business and the board chose the mine manager. The workers never refused to recognize MacNaughton's right to speak for the board or the stockholders. How could the corporation not extend the same courtesy to the workers?

A vote was held:

OFFICIAL BALLOT

Following the instructions of the convention of the copper district union held on June 29, we hereby submit the following questions for referendum vote of the members of the local unions of the Western Federation of Miners in Copper District of Michigan.

C. E. Hietala, Secretary-Treasurer

Dan Sullivan, President

Shall the miners' unions, acting through the district union, ask for a conference with the employers to adjust wages, hours, and working conditions in the copper district of Michigan?

YES [ ]

NO [ ]

Shall the executive board of the copper district union, acting in conjunction with the executive board of the Western Federation of Miners, declare a strike if the mine operators refuse to grant a conference or concessions?

YES [ ]

NO [ ]

The vote was held July 1-12, 1913, and notices were posted at the union halls and in local foreign language newspapers. Ominously, the notices were not printed in any of the three English language daily papers in Calumet, Houghton or Hancock. Later, the investigation of the strike by the Department of Labor found that these papers were "more or less indirectly controlled by the mining companies." Even so, "Without doubt all members of the federation in the district were informed that they had the opportunity of voting on the two questions."

The editorial leanings of the various newspapers in the region played an important role in how the mines and workers were perceived—and ultimately laid the groundwork for a false historical record about the Italian Hall tragedy. Downstate, the *Detroit Free Press* could be counted on for positive press coverage because C&H paid off one of its reporters. They called the money they gave him "expenses," but by today's ethical standards they were nothing less than bribes. The *Free Press* reporter wrote positive articles about the mines, interfered with negative articles— killing them if he could—and even wrote a positive editorial about C&H, all the while pretending he was neutral and accepting thousands of dollars from his news subject.

It wasn't just the bribery of reporters that created positive press coverage for the mines. The *Evening Journal* from Hancock expected to—and did—receive cash with its "Thank You" notes after each piece it wrote—positive, of course—about the Quincy mine.

The Daily Mining Gazette from Houghton went so far as to assure MacNaughton that "the idea of the organizers [of the *Gazette*] was to have a paper which would be devoted to the interests of the mining companies in the Copper Country." Members of mine management even sat on the board of directors of the *Gazette*. Later, MacNaughton told Shaw the local papers were "with us in this dirty fight from the very first. They have done everything in their power for us."

Foreign-language papers were more troublesome for MacNaughton and his peers. When they found they could not influence the policies of *Tyomies*—the Finnish Socialist paper—they began to help its competitors. As early as 1902, the *Gazette* began attempts to buy *Paivalehti*, a popular Finnish language paper with a circulation approaching that of the *Gazette*. When those attempts failed, MacNaughton formulated a ruse whereby he could gain control of the paper without his connection being seen—as some would certainly have attributed changes in editorial leanings to the *Gazette's* pro-management influence on any other paper it bought.

MacNaughton and other mine interests invested money into *Paivalehti* in 1904 through the local attorney, Oscar Larson. Larson was a Finn with no apparent ties to the mines, but who was also no friend to the Finns or the strikers. He was the one who prosecuted the Finnish Rockland strikers for the murders committed by the local mining deputies. The money Larson used to buy an interest in the paper came from MacNaughton and William Paine of the Copper Range Co. MacNaughton had run the plan by his Boston bosses saying, "No one knows nor would anyone know that the mining companies are interested in the paper ... We have a large number of Finlanders in our employ and this Daily is practically the only Daily they get. I am told that the paper aims to advise them along the proper lines regarding labor agitators and labor organizations, and think if we were to put any money into a newspaper it would result more advantageously to us by putting it in this way than having it known we were directly interested." When MacNaughton sought permission to invest $500 in the paper, one of his bosses in Boston named Alexander Agassiz wrote back authorizing him to invest $5,000.

Meanwhile, everyone seemed to weigh in on the question of the union. Even the local churches took sides. A local Methodist minister wrote an opinion piece for the *Miner's Bulletin* condemning the union. A Finnish pastor sided with the workers, saying they had the right to organize just as much as the investors in the mines.

At the time of the WFM vote, the union claimed 9,000 members, but the percentages varied widely from mine to mine. The official numbers given later showed perhaps only 7,085 members in July 1913. At the Calumet

& Hecla, union membership ran somewhere between only one-half and one-third of the workers underground. At some of the smaller mines, unionization efforts had reached nearly 100 percent. The Department of Labor concluded that this was caused by Calumet & Hecla's higher pay rate than the smaller mines and the fact that C&H employed nearly all the Cornish and Scottish workers in the district; for whatever reason, those nationalities did not seem open to unionization.

While the vote was taking place, a man named James A. Waddell arrived in the Keweenaw. He owned a company called Waddell-Mahon, which supplied private security forces, mainly to corporations that were experiencing labor disputes. In fact, Waddell bragged that he specialized in "strike breaking." He met with the Houghton County board of supervisors to see if they wanted to engage his services. The board consisted of eighteen officials ostensibly elected by the voters to handle the affairs of the county in an unbiased way. But the group was a who's who of the local mining economy.

MacNaughton sat on the board, along with A.D. Edwards, former chief clerk of the Atlantic Mining Co. Edward Hamar was general manager of Worcester Lumber, which supplied wood to several of the mines. A.G. Johnston also ran a lumber company. Rex Seeber was superintendent of the Winona Mining Co. Peter Hiltunen also worked for Worcester Lumber. A.L. Burgan was superintendent of Osceola Tamarack Stamp Mills, which processed copper. T. Hartmann was former superintendent of the Copper Range railroad and the brother of the superintendent of the Mohawk Mine. Charles Lawton was general manager of the Quincy Mining Co. Samuel Eddy owned a sawmill; his biggest customers were the mines. Edward Koepel was superintendent of the Copper Consolidated stamping mills. Charles Smith also worked for Calumet & Hecla, running their stamping mills. John Harris was superintendent of the Hancock Mining Co. Charles Mason dealt in coal and wood. His biggest clients were the mines. John Funkey sold hardware to the mines. Richard Hosking contracted brick and stone workers and masons to the mines. It appears that the only two members of the board who were not directly married to the mining industry were Richard Rourke Jr. and Patrick Sollman. They were a bartender and farmer, respectively. In matters pertaining to the mines, there were always sixteen votes for the mines, regardless of what the bartender or farmer thought was best for the county.

Although a strike was looming, the board decided not to hire Waddell at that time. MacNaughton said that any strike would be too short to require outside reinforcements. Waddell hoped he was wrong.

23

When the union ballots were counted, the WFM announced an overwhelming vote of "YES" on both questions. The membership wanted the Federation to negotiate on their behalf, and to call for a general strike if the mines would not agree to negotiate. It is noteworthy that there had been minor strikes in the Copper Country before, but none involving more than a single mine at a time. No one knew what to expect. Many miners left the region and sought work elsewhere in anticipation of the strike; many others left as soon as they heard the outcome of the vote. It was estimated that as many as 1,000 miners left as a result of the vote.

The five locals of the WFM drafted a letter to the mines explaining their demands, at the same time sending a copy to the WFM national headquarters in Denver. The executive board in Denver was not in session and asked if the locals could hold off on sending the letter. An exchange of telegrams did not solve the problem: The locals of the WFM were going to act whether or not the national WFM was on board. All the national board could do at that point was ask the locals not to take any further action until they could arrive in the Keweenaw and help coordinate. They could be there by the July 20, 1913.

The letter sent to each of the mines in the Keweenaw by the WFM read similarly to the one sent to the Calumet & Hecla:

> *Copper District Union*
> *Western Federation of Miners*
> *Box 217, Hancock Mich., July 14, 1913*
> *To the Calumet & Hecla, Tamarack, Ahmeek, Allouez, Centennial, Superior, Laurium, Isle Royale, and all other mining companies connected with and under the management of Calumet & Hecla; James MacNaughton, manager.*
> *GENTLEMEN: Your employees, organized into various unions of the Western Federation of Miners, have decided by referendum vote to ask that you meet their representatives in conference on some day during this month for the purpose of discussing the possibilities of shortening the working day, raising wages, and making some changes in the working conditions.*
> *The men working in your mines are dissatisfied with the wages, hours, and other conditions of employment. Realizing that as individuals they would not have sufficient strength to correct these evils or to lessen the burden placed upon them, they have organized into the local unions of the Western Federation of Miners, and*

through the local unions they have formed one compact body of the whole copper district, with an understanding and hope that from now on they may be enabled to sell their labor collectively with greater advantages for themselves as well as their employers.

While the men have decided that they must have greater remuneration for their services and that the working day must be shortened, it is not their or our desire that we should have a strike, with all the sufferings that it is bound to bring to them, to the employers, and to the general public. On the other hand, we earnestly hope that the questions that have arisen between us would be settled amicably, with fairness and justice to both sides. Should you have the same feeling, we believe that the friendly relations that have existed between you and your employees in the past will continue in the future.

However, should you follow the example given by some of the most stupid and unfair mine owners in the past, the men have instructed us by the same referendum vote to call a strike in all the mines owned and controlled by your company.

We hope you realize that labor has just as much right to organize as capital, and that at this age these two forces, labor and capital, while their interests are not identical, must get together and solve the problems that confront them.

If you agree to meet us our representatives will be ready for a conference on any day and at any place you may choose ... Your failure to answer this will be taken as proof that you are not willing to meet us and to have the matters settled peacefully.

Hoping to hear from you soon, we remain,
Respectfully, yours.
Dan Sullivan,
President Copper District Union of the
Western Federation of Miners
C.E. Hietala,
Secretary Copper District Union of the
Western Federation of Miners
Address all communications to C.E.
Hietala, box 217, Hancock, Mich.

Although the letter was not terribly diplomatic—calling mine owners who didn't negotiate "stupid and unfair"—it did lay out the most basic grievances: better hours, wages and working conditions. It also did not make any specific demands; it merely asked to meet with the owners to discuss these issues. The letter was sent to each of the mine owners in the district, registered and special delivery. The WFM might have first suspected a strike would be necessary when the letter mailed to the manager of the Quincy Mining Co. was returned unopened.

MacNaughton read the letter and forwarded it to his direct supervisor in Boston, Quincy Shaw. He complained that Sullivan and Hietala, the signatories of the letter, were not employees of the mines. Therefore, he considered it impossible to discuss "time or wage conditions" with them. They were not workers; it was none of their business. He also outlined the hard line that would become the strategy for the duration of the strike: "My present feeling is that I shall not acknowledge the letter in anyway whatever, for by writing a letter to the Secretary acknowledging the receipt of this one I would be in a measure recognizing the Union."

The union's organizing efforts would do more than merely allow the miners to bargain collectively. It would draw a great divide between the classes that would lead to a veritable civil war in the Copper Country. From the moment the WFM announced its presence in the Keweenaw, the residents were forced to choose a side: The miners and laborers were with the union. The management and the businesses that saw the mines as necessary for their success were with the mines. There was no middle ground. And, as is often the case with sides in a civil war, there were other characteristics unique to each side. The management side was English-speaking for the most part, and usually had more money. The miners were often speakers of other languages—many were born in other countries—and lived day to day on their weekly earnings from the mines. Although the strike did not cause the Italian Hall tragedy, the event probably would not have happened if there had been no strike for the months preceding the disaster.

Tensions Grow

"You leave those men alone or I will blow your brains out."
- MINE DEPUTY, POINTING A GUN AT STRIKERS -

The Strike

On July 18, 1913, MacNaughton received a brief telegram from Shaw: "Approve not acknowledging union letter." The WFM received no response to the letter from any of the mines. On July 22, the WFM called for a general strike. Because of the way the shifts at the mine were timed, many of the workers didn't go on strike immediately. Many struck on the morning of July 23; all were on strike by July 24.

The strike covered three counties: Houghton, Keweenaw and Ontonagon, although the bulk of the workers were in Houghton County, working for Calumet & Hecla or one of its subsidiaries. Mine employees numbered 14,278 through the three districts at the time of the strike, with 12,677 within Houghton County. Of the 14,278 workers in the range, 4,107 worked for Calumet & Hecla directly, and another 3,471 worked for mines like the Ahmeek and the Tamarack, which were subsidiaries of Calumet & Hecla Mining Co. All told, a little more than fifty-three percent of the workers in the Copper Country answered to Calumet & Hecla one way or another.

Trouble came to the Copper Country on the morning of July 23. Many of the Calumet & Hecla miners who were not members of the union decided to go to work that morning. On their way, they ran into large crowds of strikers who gathered near the mine entrances. Invariably, heated words were exchanged, tempers flared, and fists, rocks and bottles flew. As a result, at least five nonstriking workers were hospitalized. Although many of the injuries were not much more than cuts and bruises, both sides wondered what would happen if the situation escalated.

One of the mine operators refused to believe his workers would strike. While the official WFM vote was taking place, he had polled his workers to find out if they belonged to the WFM and if the WFM had permission to speak for them. When the workers overwhelmingly answered "no" to both questions, he took it as a sign that the WFM had no support. It didn't occur to him that a mine manager asking these questions to a man's face might get a different answer than the WFM would through its vote.

To add to the confusion, area firemen were having their annual tournament in Red Jacket, scheduled for July 23-25. As MacNaughton wrote to Boston: "In connection with this tournament there is a street carnival, all of which causes more or less excitement. I doubt if we shall be able to separate the sheep from the goats until early next week, but by that time we shall be able to tell who are real strikers and who are not." To MacNaughton, the area looked like it was in the throes of a holiday: "The day seems much like 4th of July or some other holiday, everybody is dressed up headed for Red Jacket to see the parade, and if it were not for the constant calls I am having on the telephone I would go there myself."

MacNaughton corresponded daily—sometimes more often—with his corporate brethren in Boston and kept them updated on the events at the mines. To communicate news, he often sent telegrams via Western Union. To make sure the messages weren't compromised or leaked, the messages—and the responses from Quincy Shaw—were often in code. Many of the telegrams survive and provide a fascinating insight into the thoughts of the men who ran the Copper Country.

"Subjugation on arson amen option," began his telegram of July 23, 1913. When Shaw received the message, he matched the words on the telegram to word columns the two had prepared. The sentence meant, "Strike on at all our mines." The rest—after translation—read: "In nearly every instance trammers refused to go to work and in most instances miners remained up. Two or three of the shafts at this mine are working but I have no doubt that by noon they will be closed down. Everything very quiet. We are beginning to swear in deputies to protect the property. Cannot yet ascertain whether strike has been called from Denver or not. No cause whatever for worry. Feel we have situation very well in hand and will keep you advised."

MacNaughton had received permission from Sheriff James Cruse—who answered to the board of supervisors MacNaughton sat on—to deputize his nonstriking workers. This meant workers loyal to MacNaughton were empowered to arrest those who were not. The deputies MacNaughton wrote of to Shaw were not the first sworn in. On the Sunday before the strike was called, more than 150 men were deputized in Painesdale, according to *The Daily Mining Gazette*. State law allowed for employees to be deputized if the employer was granted permission by the local sheriff. Each of the mines furnished identical affidavits to the sheriff, requesting a "General License ... to carry revolvers, pistols or pocket billies." Presumably, MacNaughton's local law firm of Rees, Robinson & Petermann had a secretary working overtime, typing the identical affidavits.

The deputized workers were then given cheap handguns. Calumet & Hecla reportedly issued guns by "the carload" to any and all deputies. The guns were cheap, but effective. The revolvers were .32 or .38 caliber, made by the firms of Harrington & Richardson and Iver Johnson, and people reported seeing a suitcase full of them, ready to be handed out to deputies like so much mining equipment. The guns became so ubiquitous in the Keweenaw that 70 years later, people were still finding them in closets, behind walls or beneath floorboards of homes. During one eighteen-year period from the mid-1950s to the early 1970s, the head of Calumet & Hecla security even made regular trips to a nearby lake where he threw in dismantled deputy guns that had been turned in by workers. The guns cost around $2 apiece at the time of the strike—a miner's day wages—but weren't considered accurate or reliable. The Calumet & Hecla security chief later said: "They were good for show. I don't think you could hit the barn with one." Still, even an inaccurate gun can draw attention to itself in a tense situation.

Interestingly, MacNaughton continued to state that he advocated keeping the deputies unarmed. In an interview that lavished "Big Jim" MacNaughton with praise, "The Czar of the Copper Country" told a reporter "he refused to permit [even] one of them to carry a gun." That story ran midway through September, more than a month after MacNaughton's attorneys had been printing up affidavits for the deputies to get their weapons permits.

A little later on July 23, events changed, and MacNaughton sent an update to Boston. "Two hundred men from the north end have just marched to Centennial shooting off firearms. Centennial is working with small force but

I have just given orders to close down. Every mine in the district is closed. About seventy-five percent of the men in Calumet branch working; No. 16 working but will undoubtedly have to close tonight. Have just had conference with heads of departments and have started swearing in deputies. Hope to have over five hundred deputies, possibly one thousand today."

As the day progressed and MacNaughton watched events unfold, he sent a third coded telegram to Shaw. "A mob of between four and five hundred is going from one engine house to the other demanding that the fires be drawn and that the men leave their posts. Thus far no material damage has been done. We are assembling and swearing in deputy sheriffs as fast as possible. Have about six hundred now and think we will have no difficulty in taking care of the situation."

MacNaughton also drafted letters that were typed and mailed to his boss in Boston; these letters would take longer to reach the East Coast so they were usually lengthier than the coded telegrams. Because they were posted in the U.S. mail, they were not encoded. On July 23, MacNaughton wrote a three-page letter to Shaw summarizing the day's events and the general situation in the Keweenaw. He said that the first he heard of the strike was in the form of gossip: "I was called up from the Ahmeek and told that delegations of men were going from house to house advising the day shift men who were then home to come out early this morning and meet the night shift men when they came up from underground, that a strike was to be called . . ." He further advised that there were many "strangers in town" who he felt were brought in by the union to bolster the strikers.

Although MacNaughton had managed to keep some of the men working, he noted that some of the properties were closed and that the situation did not look favorable for keeping the mines open in the immediate future. He did point out "we are swearing in deputies to protect the property." He hoped that by swearing in his own workers as deputies, the deputies would outnumber the strikers. "Practically all of our surface, shops, motive power and railroad forces will be deputized. They are all loyal and anxious to safeguard the interests of the Company."

Finally, he noted that he was taking steps to ship mining explosives out of town. Even though they were a necessary ingredient for mining, they were also an obvious catalyst for disaster. He told Shaw the deputized employees were being instructed to remain unarmed. "They will be permitted to carry clubs but we positively will refuse to have them act as deputies if they carry guns." It wasn't true, but once in a while MacNaughton told his superiors in Boston little white lies.

MacNaughton closed by pointing out that the calling of the strike was a relief in a way. "The suspense we have all been under for the past few months has been very trying and now that the strike has actually taken place we are feeling more or less relieved." Otherwise, he expected the strike to be over quickly and that the situation was under control.

That night, MacNaughton called a "council of war" with Sheriff Cruse at the Calumet & Hecla offices. He did not think highly of the sheriff, apparently because Cruse was slow to do his bidding. "The Sheriff means well, is willing to do anything we tell him, but lacks initiative and force." The two apparently fought over whose job it was to defend the private property of the mines. MacNaughton wanted Cruse to do it—or at least take responsibility for calling in outside reinforcements. "When the proposition was put up to the Sheriff that our local deputies would have to be withdrawn and were wholly unable to handle the situation, he threw up his hands and said that if we could not control the situation he certainly could not." MacNaughton and Cruse went at it until "Thursday morning," presumably until Cruse agreed to call Governor Woodbridge N. Ferris and ask for the National Guard to be sent. They tried phoning the governor, but found out he was in transit between Alpena and Big Rapids. At that point, Cruse sent the governor a telegram, requesting the troops MacNaughton wanted:

> *General strike has been called to-day in all the mines in Houghton County, backed by the Western Federation of Miners. Armed rioters have begun to destroy property and have threatened the lives of men who want to work. I am unable to handle the situation, because the territory to be covered is 28 miles long. The strike is on in 20 mines, with 15,000 idle men. I have taken every means in my power to control the outbreak, but I am convinced that the situation will become worse and will result in great destruction of property and possible loss of life unless I receive the aid of State troops. I will require about 2,000 men to cover the territory, and as Sheriff of Houghton County I ask that you call out troops to that number and detail them for service here at once.*
> *James A. Cruse*
> *Sheriff of Houghton County*

Many people were convinced Cruse had done nothing to prevent the "outbreak" as he had suggested to Ferris. Others suggested it was James Waddell of the private security company who was telling Cruse what to do. Congressman William J. MacDonald later told his colleagues, "The sheriff ... made not one, single effort to stop that violence. He immediately telegraphed for the troops, under the direction of Mr. Waddell ... who had charge of the sheriff's office." When questioned about his harsh criticism of Cruse, MacDonald did not back down. "The sheriff ... was acting under the direction and supervision of Mr. Waddell ... who was there for the purpose of breaking the strike and not for the purpose of enforcing the law."

Just as troubling for the congressmen investigating the events of 1913 were that Waddell was not even a citizen of Michigan, and he had been in town, "in charge" of strike breaking the day the strike was called. The calling for militia by the mines followed the precedent of the strike in the west: There, martial law had been declared when the mine owners had cried for help from the government. Later, the military had been used to harass the union and became a de facto force to do the bidding of the mines.

Cruse was not the only person in the Copper Country to send a panicked telegram to the governor. J. W. Black was a good friend of MacNaughton's and sent along a wire claiming that "Calumet was in the hands of a mob of five hundred men and that the presence of troops was 'absolutely necessary.'" Black was a local businessman whose name would appear from time to time during the strike, always aligned with MacNaughton's interests.

At 4:38 a.m., Ferris telegraphed back that he was ordering troops to the Copper Country. A little later, Ferris began to wonder exactly how serious the situation was up north. He sent another telegram: "Wire to-morrow morning, Friday, exact conditions of affairs in detail. Is situation as grave as first anticipated?" Perhaps a bit impatient, he sent another telegram an hour and thirteen minutes later that began, "What is the situation now?" It was clear that Ferris would send troops, although it looked like he might be questioning how necessary they were. The entire force at his disposal was sent: 2,354 enlisted men and 211 officers.

Although he had claimed he did not want his deputies armed, MacNaughton openly reversed himself the next day. In light of the "mob" and "rioting" he wrote: "If the Governor refuses to send troops it will become necessary and we will arm at least five hundred picked men." He then added—without explaining his source—"Strikers are undoubtedly being led by professional gun men brought into this country for this purpose."

The Houghton County Board of Supervisors met to discuss the unrest. MacNaughton reversed his official position about hiring an outside security force, notwithstanding the fact that troops were being sent by the state. The board voted to authorize Cruse to hire the strike breaker Waddell and some of his men for reinforcement. Waddell's men numbered only fifty-two, but their presence loomed larger than the small numbers suggest. These men were from New York and advertised that they could end strikes.

In Shaw's letter of July 24 to MacNaughton, he wondered if there might be "any possible advantage to see the heads of the other mining companies. None of them have telephoned me and I can see at present nothing to be gained. From what I gather, their course is in line with ours, though when any of them may weaken and flop over I am not prepared to say." Shaw may have been being coy about it, or maybe he didn't see what MacNaughton did. MacNaughton immediately had begun meeting with the other mine managers, to keep them from "flopping" on the issue.

There were twenty-one mines being struck, with Calumet & Hecla and its subsidiaries accounting for nine. The managers of the twenty-one mines met twice a week during the strike at the Houghton Club to discuss events and coordinate efforts. It was an interesting scenario: The miners were striking legally—after all, there were no laws against striking—but the mine owners were meeting illegally. Recent antitrust legislation, the Sherman Antitrust Act most notably, specifically outlawed combinations and agreements in restraint of trade, such as these meetings. MacNaughton and his fellow managers were well aware of the law. A few years earlier, Calumet & Hecla had considered buying up competing mines in the Keweenaw, but were threatened with legal action under the Sherman Act.

Some might wonder how the managers' meetings at the Houghton Club hurt trade or commerce enough to invoke the Sherman Act. It would have been possible during the strike that one of the smaller independent mines—for example the Lake Copper Co. with its 154 employees in Ontonagon County—could have chosen to recognize the WFM. If they had done so, they could have given their workers an eight-hour shift and a few smaller concessions and their mine could have been up and running in almost no time. The larger mines could not allow this to happen. It would be the first recognition of the WFM in the Copper Country and would inspire the workers at their mines to hold out for similar recognition. By meeting twice weekly in Houghton, MacNaughton—who had the most at stake from a mine manager's viewpoint—could keep an eye on and cajole the other managers into staying in line.

It took a few days for all the troops to arrive in the Copper Country, and then they merely threw up tents wherever they felt like it—on the Calumet commons, in churchyards, schoolyards and on almost every piece of the Earth's surface owned by Calumet & Hecla. Calm descended upon the region, and cooler heads began to consider the situation. Despite cries to the contrary, the strikers had "made no effort to damage any of the property of the mining companies" up to this time. The residents of the community began to get used to hearing "Taps" played at sundown each evening.

The next day, Shaw wrote back to MacNaughton to let him know the directors in Boston approved of his handling of the strike so far. He also mentioned that newspapers had hinted that the mines might remain open under the protection of the deputies. Shaw's coded two-word conclusion, HUM NUTMEG, translated simply: "Hope not." He believed the strike would be shorter if the mines remained completely closed.

Shaw also drafted a letter to MacNaughton giving more details on how the corporate bosses saw the strike. Most interestingly, he said: "Some of the papers this morning suggest that mines are planning to attempt work under protection of deputies. I hope that this is not true for, though my opinion is not worth much at this distance, I feel convinced that an absolute shut-down, with no effort on our part, is the only answer." Shaw also correctly anticipated one of the side effects of the strike: "The worst part of all this is that it is going to undoubtedly drive away a great many of our better men who don't want trouble ..."

The following day, MacNaughton's telegram began, "Everything quiet here today. Some rioting at South Range ... There is no destruction of property ... Think there is no more chance for rioting except between strikers and troops. Absolutely no cause for worry." The deputies were often flummoxed by their job: how to protect men who were being yelled at by strikers. Jack Chellew, a deputy at the Champion mine, pulled out a pistol and pointed it at strikers one day when he'd had enough of their yelling: "You leave those men alone or I will blow your brains out," the pro-mine *Gazette* quoted him as saying.

Although the telegrams often mentioned "riots and mobs," there was often nothing more than striking miners marching and demonstrating, peacefully but loudly, on the streets of Calumet. One of MacNaughton's coded telegrams described a demonstration he witnessed. "Procession of about eight hundred strikers from the north end have just passed the office. They were orderly."

Although the parades were peaceful for the most part, the news coverage often painted them as violent. As the strike progressed, the local newspapers became an accomplice of management, creating an atmosphere where people who were not in a position to actually see what was taking place in Calumet were led to believe that the strikers were out of control and dangerous.

The Parades

The strikers started parading regularly on the main streets of Calumet, in the morning and evening—timed with when workers would be heading to or from the mines if they were not honoring the strike. Often the demonstrations contained hundreds of people—striking miners along with their wives and children—and were usually peaceful until the deputies or Waddell men showed up. On July 26, a new face appeared at the front of the procession: A "tall, straight-backed woman, beaming confidence" went to the front of the crowd and raised a gigantic American flag. She was over six feet tall, and the newspapers said the flag was bigger than she was. The flag flew from a ten-foot pole. Her name was Annie Clemenc—her name appears with different spellings, as was common for the "foreign" names in the region—but everyone called her "Big Annie."

Annie was born in 1888 in the Calumet region. Her father was a miner and the family name was Klobuchar. She married a miner named Joseph Clemenc—most people pronounced the name "Clements." To many, she became the symbol of the strike. Her presence reminded everyone that it wasn't just strikers against big business—there were families involved in this. Although some thought it unusual for a woman in the early 1900s to get so prominently involved in something outside the home, Annie didn't mind the attention or criticism. In fact, she relished it.

Annie was not the only woman to become involved in the labor strife. Many women paraded and battled the mines alongside their husbands, fathers and sons. For example, fifteen women were among twenty picketers arrested in Calumet one day. Later, MacNaughton claimed he was shocked by their involvement, and even more shocked by the language they used.

On July 27, MacNaughton wrote a nine-page letter to Shaw detailing the events in the Copper Country from his point of view. He outlined how he had met with Sheriff Cruse the night the strike began and how he had worked to get him to call Governor Ferris for troops. He described the "great deal of political work" that had been necessary. The call to Ferris for troops had been made "through the citizens" as had the statements commending the governor for sending the troops. It was clear MacNaughton was taking credit for orchestrating the efforts. "Further, in order to put ourselves in the proper light before the people of the State it was necessary to give the right impression to the many newspaper correspondents both for the Associated Press and those of the State papers. All of this has taken time and great effort and all has had extremely good effect."

MacNaughton also pointed out that the strikers had committed a strategic error by letting the first day of the strike become violent. "If we had planned the whole affair before hand we could not have played into our own hands any better than the strikers did. The mob violence practiced by them put us in the best possible position. Outside of the ranks of the strikers themselves there is absolutely no sympathy for them anywhere, and now the feeling is general that the whole thing has been caused by imported leaders for selfish purposes."

The timing of the strike also appeared to be inopportune for the strikers: The state militia was planning its annual encampment at roughly the same time the strike was called. The notion that the troops could be sent to the Keweenaw Peninsula to patrol the strike region rather than practice their drills apparently played into Governor Ferris' willingness to deploy them as he did. MacNaughton admitted having a pipeline to the workings of the National Guard: He had met with General Pearley L. Abbey and the other mine managers the day before.

MacNaughton told Shaw he planned to work toward getting the Calumet & Hecla main site operating. Shaw initially had wanted to keep the mines closed to see which side starved first: The mines were in a much better position to survive a short strike than were the workers. However, if the strike was prolonged, it made more sense to management to see if they could get the mines operating, if even on a limited basis, and then gradually ramp up production without using union labor. If they succeeded, they might never have to deal with the unions.

MacNaughton knew he had more loyal workers at the C&H than any of the other mines, and he could count on many of them to ignore the strike and the strikers. He also hoped that keeping the C&H operating would be a moral victory for the mine operators. "If the Calumet and Hecla is in operation the strikers at the subsidiaries will lose hope."

MacNaughton relayed a bit of bad news to Shaw, though. The situation at other mines was not as good as it was at C&H, particularly to the north:

> *There, the strikers have had their own way and have met with no resistance. They have compelled the loyal employees to join their ranks; it is reported that even our shift bosses have joined the Union, this you understand is because they have been forced to do it and it is easier to join than to resist. Furthermore, these mines are in Keweenaw County; the Sheriff of that County belongs to the Union and his deputies are all Union men whose sympathies are wholly with the Union; he has positively refused to call on the Governor*

for troops and thus far the Governor has refused to interfere in Kewenaw (sic) County. As an illustration of the attitude of the Sheriff in Kweenaw: we made a formal demand on him yesterday through our local deputy at the Allouez [mine], to give us protection so we could load powder from the magazine in cars and ship it out of the district, we being afraid to leave this powder around. The Sheriff's reply was that he could not do anything until he had taken it up at the next meeting of the union which was to be held in the afternoon. This will give you an idea of how hopeless that situation is.

His only hope, he wrote, was to ask the governor to remove the offending sheriff from office. MacNaughton was not exaggerating when he described Keweenaw County's bias in the strike. The prosecuting attorney reportedly was a member of the union at one point and Sheriff John Hepting's deputies often sided openly with the strikers. The president of the village of Ahmeek went so far as to write a letter to the governor, asking if the troops could be removed from the town.

After a few more comments about the presence of troops, and how he had wished they wouldn't be necessary, MacNaughton wrote: "Rest assured that the sympathy of everybody outside of the ranks of the strikers is wholly with the Companies and that when this thing is once over with we will be relieved of the labor agitator." MacNaughton seemed to blame everything on Charles Moyer—the head of the union—and anyone MacNaughton ran up against was deemed either a member of the union or a Socialist.

Moyer was a worthy adversary for MacNaughton—at least, he was as stubborn as Big Jim. He had been jailed for his union activities out west, and had even brought his case before the Supreme Court of the United States. He lost, but he was not one to back down from a fight.

MacNaughton's correspondence often mentions his belief that the WFM had "imported gun men" to lead the "mobs." The C&H manager stopped staying at his home for fear of violence, and spent the night at different homes as often as possible. He traveled with an "ample" bodyguard and moved his family out of their home as well. Likewise, other officers of the C&H sent their families away while the strike was on. MacNaughton's fear was real; whether it was rooted in fact was another matter. He based his belief of the "imported gun men" on the fact that there were people in the parades "no one here can recognize" and for several days before the strike a law official had told him he'd seen "strangers ... on the streets whose appearance he did not like." It was a fascinating amount of faith to place in one's ability to recognize someone—in an area with a population in the range of 80,000 people.

The strikers and the WFM organizers complained loudly about the presence of troops. The troops appeared to be on the side of management; after all, they camped on mine property and were protecting the mine facilities. Governor Ferris gave an interview on July 28 where he insisted that the troops were not sent at the request of the mines: "The mine operators had nothing to do with calling the militia. The order was issued after the authorities informed me they were powerless to control the situation. I believe the troops are necessary at present to protect lives and property." Ferris either did not let on or did not know that Cruse had requested the troops at the behest of MacNaughton. He also said he had no intention of traveling to the Keweenaw and visiting the strike region at that time.

MacNaughton heard a troubling rumor on July 28 which had him scrambling: People were saying that the local businessmen in Red Jacket and Laurium were sending a petition to the governor demanding the withdrawal of the National Guard. After learning it was just a rumor, MacNaughton decided he should act anyway. He invited businessmen to a conference at C&H where he made one of the most famous statements of the strike. In a letter to Shaw he wrote: "I talked to them for about 20 minutes and told them we would never recognize the Western Federation and that grass would grow in the streets here before this mine or any of its subsidiaries would start up unless law and order was restored, and that nothing but complete annihilation of the Western Federation in this camp would satisfy us." The part about how "grass would grow in the streets" before C&H recognized the union was widely reported.

The same letter told Shaw how C&H has not "hired strike breakers or gun men or rowdies of any kind to help us out. Nor do I think we shall do so unless the troops be withdrawn before order is restored." He was being deceptive: Waddell's men had been hired by the Houghton County Board of Supervisors and had arrived in the Keweenaw on July 27.

Most of the troops were stationed around the Calumet area—in Houghton County—but some were eventually sent north to Keweenaw County. There were only two mines in Keweenaw: the Ahmeek and the Mohawk, which employed only 1,271 men. On July 29, Sheriff Hepting of Keweenaw County called the man in charge of the troops, General Abbey, and asked him to remove the troops from his county. He said he had no need for them and he hadn't requested them. The Ahmeek Mining Co., however, was owned by Calumet & Hecla, and later that day Hepting reversed himself. He wrote to

Abbey and asked for the troops to remain. He did this, he wrote, to protect the Mohawk Mining Co. He did not mention protecting the Ahmeek.

Hepting was not the lap dog MacNaughton wished; he had a reputation in the Copper Country for toughness—and for eccentricity. One day when Hepting returned home, his wife was said to have asked him about bullet holes she found in the back of their buggy.

"Well, they shot at me," he said, referring to a site of labor unrest he'd just visited.

"Did you shoot back?" she asked.

"No," he said. "They didn't hit me."

MacNaughton griped to his Boston bosses about Hepting, and how he wouldn't play along with the mine owners the way Sheriff Cruse did. Shaw wrote to him: "I am sorry to hear of the political situation with the sheriff and Keweenaw County."

On July 29, the president of the Quincy Mining Co. wrote to his general manager, C.L. Lawton, and expressed an interest in getting the various mines to "unite" in their actions. The parties got together that day: MacNaughton sent Shaw a letter—in code—that he met with Lawton and two other mine managers to coordinate their defenses.Lawton then claimed: "I understand that neither singly or together have any of our miners or employees presented any form of grievance or complaint, but have gone out on strike simply at the dictates and commands of an irresponsible labor union ..." No reference was made to the letter that Quincy had returned to its sender, unopened, which asked for a meeting to discuss miners' grievances.

The same day, Quincy Shaw wrote to MacNaughton and informed him of "endless calls" he was receiving from detective agencies, asking to be hired to break the strike in the Copper Country. "As you know, they are persistent devils," and some had told Shaw they had been hired by other mines in the area. Shaw wasn't sure if he should believe that, but he expressed concern about "Waddell, who handled (and badly, so people say) the Elevated strike." Shaw warned MacNaughton, "I have no doubt that he will call on you." Shaw apparently did not know MacNaughton and Waddell had already met. He ended the letter with an admonition: "But as for recognizing or dealing with the Western Federation, it is simply out of the question." Shaw wasn't the only one who thought little of the Waddell men. Governor Ferris wrote in a letter to Sheriff Cruse: "I don't like the presence of the Waddell men in the strike region. In my judgment, there is a prospect of serious trouble because of the importation of strike breakers or hired police."

While MacNaughton often told people the strike would be short, in private correspondence he conceded the strike might drag on for some time. On July 31 he wrote to Shaw, "this thing may be rather long drawn out." Later he noted that "we are getting the local Union leaders arrested; 12 or 13 of them are now in jail and more will follow shortly." He does not say what, if anything, the union leaders were jailed for. It's as if MacNaughton thought they belonged in jail simply because they were union leaders.

Attempted Resolution

On July 31, Western Federation of Miners officials met with Governor Ferris in lower Michigan and asked if he would help arrange a mediation of the dispute in the Keweenaw. Ferris thought the parties should at least meet, and agreed to help. Ferris thought the mine owners would be more conciliatory, based on correspondence he'd gotten from Quincy's management. He wrote a letter back to them on August 1: "It is to the interests of all parties concerned that this strike should end speedily ... Any prolongation of the strike will work serious injury to all parties concerned. I have done my level best to encourage a settlement that shall be abiding."

Although the threat of trouble and violence seemed to be a common theme throughout MacNaughton's correspondence, it somehow never seemed to explode. One incident came close. Near the end of July, seven striking miners were seen approaching the Red Jacket mine's shaft house. Worried they might be up to no good, National Guard troops stopped the men and took them into custody. While waiting for reinforcements—the miners apparently outnumbered the men—one of the strikers calmly pulled some dynamite from his pocket and held a lit cigarette near the fuse. The man, Joe Mihelchich, didn't try to light the fuse; he apparently wanted the men to know that he was armed—like they were—and that they should respect his position as an equal to be bargained with. Several of the guardsmen jumped on him. Mihelchich was huge—even by the standards of north woods miners—and several eyewitnesses described how he tossed the guardsmen around like toys. All the while he made sure not to drop his dynamite—and equally sure not to ignite it. Eventually, they overpowered him and one of the guards pulled the cigarette from his hand. The incident filled two sentences of MacNaughton's telegram of August 1. "Military guard last night arrested seven men approaching Red Jacket shaft house. When taken into mining captains [sic] office to be examined one of them attempted to explode three sticks of dynamite he had on his person. The dynamite was primed with fuse and cap." The next day's news was innocuous enough to be sent uncoded. It read: "Nothing new. Everything quiet."

Although MacNaughton had made much of how few of the C&H workers were members of the union—they were certainly a minority of the employees at the beginning of the strike—the strike had an unusual impact on that proportion. Many of Calumet & Hecla's nonstriking employees left the region because of the unrest. These absences shifted the balance toward the strikers. For instance, only 337 underground men struck at C&H, while another 450 "migrated." The net result was the strike cost C&H 887 of its underground workers, regardless of their union affiliation.

The WFM then appealed to the Department of Labor for help. The department had been created in March 1913, and one of its powers was to mediate labor disputes. It seemed to be the perfect solution. The Secretary of Labor designated John A. Moffitt to see what he could do to resolve the issues in the Copper Country. Moffitt first set off to Boston to talk with Calumet & Hecla's overseers. He also sent Walter B. Palmer to the Keweenaw to begin the investigation there. In Boston, Moffitt cajoled Shaw into a meeting, so long as the WFM was excluded from the talks. Moffitt then headed to Michigan to see if he could get the local managers to go along with the idea. Even though Shaw had agreed to the plan, MacNaughton refused to go along. He said he might be willing to meet with striking miners, but only if none of them were members of the WFM. It is unclear whether there actually were any striking non-WFM miners in the area. MacNaughton also insisted that he be given final approval of the two members the miners selected to represent them, and beyond that, he still saw nothing to discuss with them.

Ferris telegraphed General Abbey and asked him to notify both sides that the governor was also working toward getting the parties together. The WFM reacted positively to the news, but the mine owners rejected it as an impossibility. When MacNaughton was told of the offer, he huddled with his attorneys and spent the better part of an evening drafting a response that diplomatically rejected mediation. They hand delivered the response to General Abbey who—according to MacNaughton—agreed with the position taken by the mine managers.

MacNaughton used a local law firm, Rees, Robinson & Petermann, for most of his legal needs. He would give them enough work throughout the strike to keep them quite busy. MacNaughton told the other mine owners that they could have RR&P represent them. Although the lawyers pretended they were working for each mine independently, it became well known later that the owners and RR&P coordinated their efforts, with MacNaughton at the helm. For the next year, virtually every legal action taken on behalf of or in defense of the mines would be handled by an RR&P attorney.

Seeing the impasse, Ferris sent Wayne County Circuit Court Judge Alfred J. Murphy to the Copper Country to try and get the parties together. The appointment was mentioned in the papers, where MacNaughton first heard word of it.

MacNaughton decided to bring all his resources to bear on the question of keeping the militia in town. He wrote to Boston on August 10: "The Board of Supervisors will meet on Tuesday forenoon and I will have a resolution passed presenting the situation with regard to the troops and the possibility of our having to call on outside men in the event the troops are withdrawn, which resolution will be addressed to the Governor."

Once in the Keweenaw, Judge Murphy went straight to MacNaughton and introduced himself. He brought a letter of introduction from the governor. His mission, he told MacNaughton, was to "mediate if possible," but if that was unworkable, to "get at the facts on both sides of the controversy" and to advise the governor. Murphy wanted to meet with the mine management and the strikers, if possible. MacNaughton told him he would never attend such a meeting. It was only after Murphy promised that he would not even bring up the topic of the WFM that management agreed to meet with him. Once the meeting took place, Murphy "chastised them ... rather severely" for their obstinacy.

After that meeting, the mine owners had their lawyer draw up a letter explaining their position and MacNaughton delivered it personally to Murphy. Although MacNaughton refused to cooperate with Murphy, he did respect him. "From all I find out regarding Judge Murphy he is a most honorable man, clean cut, very serious minded and I imagine cold as a fish; at least his argument with me on Monday impressed me that way."

Be that as it may, MacNaughton hated the intrusion from Murphy—or anyone else. "If the Governor and the Labor Department in Washington and the U.S. Senate would keep their respective noses out of our affairs we would get along a good deal better."

Murphy left the region thinking the mine owners were being unreasonable. After he reported what he had seen, Ferris said: "I do not hesitate to say that the men have real grievances." He called the mine managers "arrogant and unfair." For his part, Murphy found that the men were entitled to organize, the managers were treating them in an "un-American" way, and if they were allowed to dictate membership in organizations, they could just as easily discriminate based upon race or religion, too.

Meanwhile, the WFM had offered to let the entire matter of the strike and all labor issues to be decided by a five-person mediation panel. Two members would be chosen by the managers, two would be chosen by the workers and would not be WFM members, and the fifth would be chosen by the Secretary of Labor. The WFM announced that if such a panel were convened, they would agree in advance to abide by its decision. The managers rejected the offer, saying that if they went along with it, they would be recognizing the WFM—even though the panel would contain no members of the WFM.

Under Military Rule

On August 3, Sheriffs Cruse and Hepting gave authority to General Abbey "to make arrests and to use such force as might be necessary to preserve order" in each county. The authorization allowed the troops to "prevent any violation or violations of the laws of this State," yet did not address how the troops would be qualified to make decisions regarding the law. Their actions of deputizing great numbers of untrained men indicated it was more important to get a large force of men on the streets under color of law, regardless of whether the force was properly trained. Cruse had also sworn in 430 deputies before the strike: Almost all were employees of the mines.

Within the first week of the strike, there were natural problems underground at the Calumet & Hecla. Most of the mines had a tendency to fill with water because of their great depths. The mines used gigantic pumps that were run often, if not constantly, to pump water out of the lower levels. Within five days, the C&H had water flooding its lower 300 feet. The nearby Tamarack Mine was taking on water so fast that rats were fleeing from its depths as if from a sinking ship. Witnesses said the subterranean rats were "too big for a cat to tackle" and were now roaming the surface, looking for food. Charlotte Kessler, a resident of Calumet, kept a diary during the strike and noted one day: "A plague of rats in Calumet."

In a letter to Shaw, MacNaughton had said that he would let all of the mines—save two—fill up with water before he agreed to negotiate with the WFM. Shaw wrote back on August 4 and asked if MacNaughton could rewrite the letter and remove that language, or at the very least, send another letter "clarifying" what he meant. "Your expression sounds a little brutal and indifferent to the interests of the other mines." MacNaughton did so a few days later, explaining that he had not meant any harm by the statement—since the mines could always be pumped out later.

On August 9, MacNaughton met with General Abbey about how long the militia would be in town. Abbey explained it was costly for the men to stay and withdrawals would begin within a few days. MacNaughton wrote to Boston that he would have to supplement the remaining militia with "local deputies" although they were not "very effective." He wrote that he asked the C&H attorney to draft a letter for Sheriff Cruse to send to the governor, saying that if the militia were withdrawn he—Cruse—would be compelled to hire outsiders to protect the area. MacNaughton does not explain why Cruse couldn't draft a letter on his own, or why he was so confident that Cruse would sign anything MacNaughton asked him to.

On August 12, Waddell presented his first bill to the Houghton County Board of Supervisors—among them James MacNaughton. For the work his men had done to date, he asked for and received $9,507. His men had been in the region since July 23. The board adopted a resolution which "highly commended" Sheriff Cruse for his action in hiring the Waddell men—even though it was really the board for whom they worked—an action they found necessary to "protect life and property."

On August 20, the WFM printed posters to discourage strike breakers from other states who might come to work in the stricken mines. The poster read:

Strike
Stay away from the copper mines of Michigan. Fifteen
thousand miners are striking for higher wages,
shorter hours, and better working conditions.
Don't be a scab.
Wages are low, the labor required excessive, hours long.
No real man will come to the copper district until a settlement is made.
Men hired for Michigan points are hired to scab.
Stay away.
By order of the Western Federation of Miners.

The first week of September saw the installation of "MacNaughton's Eye." The C&H set up a searchlight on top of a tower in the middle of their property in town. An employee of the mine would swing the light around and shine it on people who were walking the area at night. The Department of Labor later remarked how odd it was because "the strikers had shown no disposition to damage property." The Quincy mine erected a similar searchlight shortly after. The strikers resented the searchlights, which seemed more suited to a prison. A local newspaper marketed to miners ran a column called "Seen by the Searchlights."

MacNaughton kept track of the union's activities in every devious way he could. He tracked the finances of the WFM by getting confidential information of their banking activity "leaked" to him by friends within the local business community. Other mine managers in the area likewise leaned on their local bankers to feed them confidential information about the union's finances. MacNaughton and the others knew the WFM was on shaky financial ground, especially at the beginning of the strike. MacNaughton knew the WFM had only $8,000 on hand in mid-August, less than a tenth of what it would need to pay strike benefits.

Cruse increased the rate at which he was creating the new deputy sheriffs. By November, he'd deputized nearly 1,700. Governor Ferris became alarmed at the creation of this amateur law enforcement army. It appeared the sheriff's deputies could soon outnumber the National Guard. Ferris wired Cruse and reminded him that state law required each deputy to have "been a bona fide resident of the county in which the appointment is made of three months next preceding the time of appointment." It is unclear if Cruse changed his course of action after receiving the reminder. He did grant the deputies the right to carry firearms, which many had been doing since the strike began.

On August 4, MacNaughton had sent an optimistic note to Boston. He told Shaw that recent demonstrations by miners were smaller than before, and sentiment was changing in favor of the mines and their management. That same day, a large group of miners met at the Red Jacket town hall to discuss why they shouldn't merely return to work. The men in the crowd were mixed—some were staunch WFM members and some were just men who wanted to work. While the tide flowed back and forth between the two groups, someone ran and got Yanco Terzich, one of the WFM managers who was down the street at the union hall. Terzich jumped up in front of the crowd and reinvigorated most of the men into backing the union. The crowd dispersed but many of them met again later and chose a small committee to negotiate a return to work.

The next day, eighteen men from the Red Jacket hall went to see MacNaughton. Although they avowed no interest in the WFM, they said they would return to work if a few conditions were met. Then they listed all of the same demands the WFM had made, and added a few of their own. Among other things, they asked MacNaughton to hire underage boys to work underground in the mines—a practice common years earlier, but now illegal under Michigan state law. MacNaughton turned the men down and sent them on their way.

He wrote a letter to Shaw, explaining his surprise: they had made "all of the demands that are being made by the Western Federation of Miners with the single exception of recognition." To him, it was a sign "of how adroit the labor leaders were and my experience of the past 24 hours is an additional evidence of it. They have made even the non-Union men believe that they could get anything they asked for except recognition of the Union."

Meanwhile, in the shops of the Calumet & Hecla, nonstriking workers spent much of their time making wooden billy clubs the size of baseball bats. They gave these to the deputies and Waddell men for crowd control.

The recent optimistic telegram from MacNaughton drew a bit of a rebuke from Shaw. Recent stories in the Boston newspapers about the miners' strike had shown pictures of the manager and some of the mine facilities, along with the statement that MacNaughton earned $120,000 a year. Any favorable sentiment MacNaughton hoped for in the last telegram would certainly be tarnished when people compared this salary to the few dollars a day the miners earned risking their lives underground. Shaw thought MacNaughton ought to tell the *Mining Gazette* his salary was only about a third of that amount; if things went well, maybe the Associated Press would pick up on the story and repeat it. This would have been a lie; other contemporary reports placed his earnings at "perhaps $100,000 a year," a figure no one bothered to quibble with.

MacNaughton decided not to try and correct the "problem" with the salary statement; he wrote to Shaw that it was just one of many lies told about him and that he couldn't possibly try and correct them all. A few days later MacNaughton started to get unsolicited mail from around the country. A woman in St. Louis wrote him asking for $2 to buy medicine. A man in Cutler, Illinois, asked for enough money to buy a car. If MacNaughton sent the money, the man would have "profound respect" for him—but would not pay the money back.

Sheriff Cruse, worried that his hiring of private law enforcement rankled Ferris, wrote to the governor to explain the situation on August 10. He had deputized 600 men but still worried about his ability to protect the entire county from unrest. Although the Waddell men could not be deputized, they could "aid" the deputies and to act as night watchmen on the private property of the mines. He asked that the National Guard be left in place as long as possible.

On August 10, MacNaughton wired Shaw in code, and told him that a recent parade of workers contained 1,800 men. He said they came mostly from the "north" end—presumably Keweenaw County—and from the

Copper Range. As if he had second thoughts, MacNaughton also wrote a thirteen-page letter to Shaw in Boston. He told Shaw that more than 1,500 men were working at C&H in defiance of the strike. He did admit there was a problem getting more into the mines because so many men had left the region—often without picking up their final paychecks. "When this idleness was imposed on the men a great many took advantage of it to leave town. They did not want to be considered as strikers or in sympathy with the strike and they left here without notifying us or without taking their settlement. We have no means of ascertaining the number of these."

Interestingly, MacNaughton could not give precise figures for men who had left or who might have been willing to work, but he seemed to give precise figures when it came to the size of the union—always a low figure— or the number of men picketing—likewise always a declining number.

MacNaughton gave an interview that was printed in the *Detroit Free Press* and then reprinted in the *Hancock Evening Copper Journal* on August 11. There, he flat denied that the Calumet & Hecla officers had anything to do with the hiring of Waddell and said that he personally disliked Waddell. Some of the statements he made were factually true, but clearly aimed at misleading the readers of the paper. Waddell was not being paid by Calumet & Hecla, and Waddell's contract was not with the mine.

If MacNaughton was hoping to control the damage to the mine's public relations with the interview, further statements he made destroyed any chance of that. He argued that the strikers did not want to strike; they were merely misled by the WFM and were too stupid or ignorant to make decisions for themselves.

> *We have Croatians, Austrians, Hungarians, Italians from northern Italy, Poles, and other nationalities working for us, and they are industrious, loyal men; but they do not know our language or our customs, our laws, nor our ideals. They have been influenced by Western Federation of Miners' organizers and hired men who have been here in some cases for years. Constant dropping will wear a stone.*

He ended by promising that Calumet & Hecla would not evict any of the striking workers from homes owned by the mine. "We do this because we know that our men have been misled."

Governor Ferris was becoming increasingly upset with how the WFM was willing to talk with the managers, but the managers were unwilling to talk with the WFM. It made the managers look even worse that they refused to accept arbitration or mediation with a council that contained no WFM members. Ferris told people that "he would confer with the devil if the occasion arose but would not agree to accept the devil's views. 'I would at least accord him the privilege of a conference.'"

MacNaughton spent much of his time trying to organize a "back to work" petition drive. He had his supervisors try and get as many non-union men as possible to sign documents stating their desire to return to work. This move lent itself to the notion that many of the workers who were not showing up wanted to work, but every time MacNaughton wrote of the move, the news was less than optimistic.

MacNaughton had a long meeting with the board of supervisors of the county which "adopted a very strong set of resolutions, a copy of which was wired the Governor last night." These were the resolutions he had mentioned earlier that he would make sure were passed.

On August 13, Shaw wrote to MacNaughton and told him the financial condition of C&H was sound. At that time, C&H had more than $1 million in cash on hand, another $320,000 in receivables, over half a million in foreign exchange, and another $1 million in shipments of copper in the coming two months. In other words, C&H could afford to shut down for quite some time. Shaw asked MacNaughton's opinion on paying an upcoming dividend to shareholders. Shaw suggested they pay the usual large dividend—the only worry he had was that the strikers might try and use it to argue that the company made too much money off the backs of its workers.

While C&H was flush with cash, MacNaughton revealed to Shaw that he had inside information on the WFM. "We now have a very good line on their in side [sic] operations of the past; it's too long a story to write ..."

It didn't take long for MacNaughton to change his initial, positive view of Judge Murphy. MacNaughton and the rest of the mine managers met with him and continued their refusal to talk with the WFM. On August 14, MacNaughton wrote—in code—to Shaw, "Spent 4 hours with mine managers and Judge Murphy. The latter seems wholly against us." MacNaughton couldn't understand why Murphy kept pressing for the managers to meet with the union. MacNaughton told Shaw they had nothing to offer Murphy in regard to his question, and that he thought Murphy's presence was prolonging the strike.

First Blood

*"Nothing but complete annihilation
of the Western Federation in this camp will satisfy us."*

- JAMES MACNAUGHTON -

Murder on the Range

The amateur law enforcement in the Copper Country became the center of
a firestorm that they started. The town of Painesdale is south of Hancock
near a few of the smaller mines. Even so, Waddell men patrolled the area
in force. On the evening of August 14, strikers John Kalan and John Stimac
walked on a path they often took when heading home. They were returning
from Painesdale, where they had just checked on their strike benefits.
Kalan lived in Seeberville, on the outskirts of Painesdale.

An employee of the Copper Range Consolidated Mine named Humphrey
Quick, recently deputized and armed, told them to stop and turn back.
Quick spoke to the men for a few minutes; Kalan and Stimac ignored his
command and continued across the mine property. When they weren't on
strike, the man was a boss; now that they were striking, Kalan and Stimac
did not feel they had to take orders from him. Quick thought little of it:
The people in town had been using this route to walk home for quite some
time before the strike. Quick decided to take no further action.

49

A Waddell security man named Thomas Raleigh came over and asked Quick what had just transpired. After hearing the story, he insisted they arrest Kalan on a charge of "intimidation." A supervisor from the mine was nearby and asked the men what was going on. When they told him he said, "Go down and bring them [Kalan and Stimac] to me and I will speak with them." He did not ask for the men to be arrested; indeed, the mine manager had no legal authority to order anyone's arrest. Raleigh rounded up three more Waddell men and another deputy, and the six went off to get the two men. All the while, Quick wondered why Raleigh was making such a big deal over such a little incident.

The six men caught up with Kalan in the front yard of the boarding house where he lived, and one of them grabbed him by the shoulder, telling him, "I want you." *He did not tell Kalan he was under arrest.* Rather than go with Raleigh when he was grabbed, Kalan pulled away and called for his roommates to help him. The six men began beating him with billy clubs. Kalan's roommates grabbed him and helped him into the house.

Someone near the house threw a bowling pin toward the company men but it did not hit them. The pin merely brushed the brim of one man's hat. That man, Joshua Cooper, turned around and fired his gun at the nearest person to him who was not a deputy: Steve Putrich. Putrich was unarmed and standing in the doorway of the house. He had not thrown the bowling pin, but Cooper's bullet hit him in the abdomen.

The boardinghouse was home to seventeen people; fifteen were inside the home after the men ran inside. Among them were two women and four children. Frustrated at the escape of the men, the Waddell men and the deputies began firing their guns wildly at the house, through the windows and the back door. Before they were done, they were sticking their guns in through the windows and firing blindly—one man at each window of the house; rooms of the house filled with gun smoke so thick it was impossible to see.

The gunmen fired until they ran out of ammunition. The scene went quiet, because there were no guns inside the house. One witness later testified of the occupants: "They didn't have anything to shoot with except the spoons they had in their hands while they were eating."

One of the men inside the house—Diazig Tizan, who was also called Louis Tijan—was hit by a bullet and killed instantly. Steve Putrich's wound was fatal and he died the next day. A total of four men were shot, and a baby in the home was also injured by gunfire. Neighbors testified later that when the shooting stopped, the Waddell men gathered up stones and empty bottles and threw them into the yard to make it look like the men in the home had started the fracas. Before they did this, though, they searched the house with their guns drawn—and without a search warrant—hoping to find weapons.

It is important to review the Seeberville murders in conjunction with the events that led to the Italian Hall catastrophe. Even though the killings took place in the highly charged atmosphere of the strike, the coroner conducted an inquest that determined the shootings were murder and the prosecutor obtained an indictment and conviction afterward. The Seeberville killings act as a yardstick by which the actions of the coroner and the courts in Houghton County can be measured when investigating violent crimes in 1913. Presumably, whatever capability they showed in Seeberville should have been present when the largest mass murder in Michigan history took seventy-three lives a few months later—and just a few miles to the north.

Residents of the copper range were ignited with fury upon hearing of the shootings in Seeberville. Although there had been posturing and the threat of violence for some time, these were the first fatalities of the strike. Anthony Lucas, the prosecutor of the county, visited the shot-up boarding house and immediately deemed the shootings to be murders. He requested that Sheriff Cruse arrest all six of the shooters. Cruse refused and instead arrested Kalan. The men that Lucas wanted arrested for the shooting of Kalan became the star witnesses of the case against Kalan.

The day after the shooting, a few of the men involved in the shootings testified at a preliminary examination for the trial of Kalan. Kalan had been arrested on the charge that he had "intimidated" Deputy Quick. In the strange world of Sheriff Cruse, it made sense to arrest Kalan but not Raleigh, Cooper or the other gunmen. However, because the men did not yet know if they would be charged with Tizan's killing, they did not invoke the Fifth Amendment. As a result, the testimony at the trial of Kalan became the best record of what actually happened that day in Seeberville because the men admitted most of the key facts: They were not sent to arrest Kalan. They never told him he was being arrested. They were merely sent by a mine manager to get Kalan.

After the men testified, they went into hiding. According to Lucas, Cruse located a hideout for them that was just across the county line. Cruse had finally realized that the killings by deputized men reflected badly on him.

Prosecuting Attorney Lucas threatened Cruse that he would prevail upon a local judge or perhaps the governor if Cruse refused to arrest the men. Cruse had reason to take the threat seriously: Lucas was of Croatian descent—as were the residents of the boarding house. In fact, Lucas was the first person of Croatian descent licensed to practice law in the United States.

A lawyer for the men called the prosecutor and offered their surrender if the murder charges were dropped. The prosecutor refused and called an inquest. Amazingly, the six men showed up for the inquest, after which they were indicted for the murders. One of the Waddell men fled, leaving the other five behind to fight the charges.

The occupants of the home were Croatian and the neighbors were Italian and Finnish. The language differences in this "melting pot" were much more than a nuisance for law enforcement. They often signified a class difference between the laborers in the mines and the supervisors. Finns, Croatians and Italians were frequently given the more demanding physical labor in the mines, such as tramming, while Scots, Englishmen and Canadians were often given the foreman and supervisor positions. Although some claimed the English and Scots had more experience in mining from their homelands, it was usually more a matter of prejudice: If you spoke English—as did the owners of the mines—you were put in charge of someone. The mine owners and their representatives—the English speakers—often adopted the stance that those who could not speak English were faking and using their inability to speak English to their advantage. One of MacNaughton's attorneys went on record with such a claim before a congressional committee, claiming that an Italian-speaking witness who needed an interpreter actually could understand English when he wanted to, but was pretending not to understand English to gain sympathy.

On Sunday, August 17, 1913, there was a huge funeral for Diazig Tizan and Steve Putrich in Calumet. Thousands of strikers turned out for the affair and several leaders of the WFM spoke at the cemetery, denouncing the deputies and the men from Waddell-Mahon. The strike now had martyrs; it was common to see signs reminding workers to remember "our murdered brothers" anytime the workers rallied or paraded. Further, the murders shifted the tide of public sentiment from the mine owners to the downtrodden workers. Some say the killings gave the strikers the moral high ground and the encouragement to hold out longer.

MacNaughton sent a telegram to Shaw the day after the funeral. Interestingly, there were no telegrams in the archives where his papers are stored that mention the shooting. There are no telegrams or letters written by MacNaughton until August 18. This gap in coverage is caused either by MacNaughton not writing during that period—even though he usually sent one or two telegrams and letters each day to Boston—or by MacNaughton removing the correspondence from the collection sometime before the collection went to the archives. A more ominous gap occurs around Christmas 1913.

The telegram the day after the funeral describes it as a "very large demonstration. The killing of these men has given a serious setback to resumption of work."

The same day he wrote a letter to Shaw detailing the recent visit between the mine managers and Judge Murphy. Apparently Murphy did not like the written response put together by C&H's attorney. Murphy immediately wrote back to MacNaughton, telling him that their "attitude was indefensible." He asked for a meeting, which took place at Red Jacket. "I never had to listen to a greater scolding from anyone. He made a stump speech berating us for our conduct." The judge asked why the managers refused to meet with the WFM and why they had not responded to his simple question regarding the terms for re-employment. The managers asked if they could meet without the judge present to draft a response. The attorneys helped draft one and delivered it to Murphy. "When Judge Murphy read it he went up in the air," MacNaughton wrote later.

MacNaughton could not stand to be treated this way, especially by an outsider. He asked his attorney to set up a private meeting with the judge—man to man and off the record. The meeting was arranged, and the two met at a private residence. If MacNaughton's version of events is to be believed, he berated the judge in no uncertain terms for over three hours.

> *I can assure you that Judge Murphy now knows more about himself and my estimate of him than he ever did before ... I told him he had started this investigation by bursting into the back door and trying to work his way out through the front; that he was by training and disposition wholly unfitted for it, that he never could accomplish it; that he was egotistical to think he could effect such a meeting as he proposed or that he could mediate between respectable men and a crowd of thugs and murderers.*

It was apparently lost on MacNaughton that the only murders in the strike were committed by thugs and murderers he had hired, and that the dead were strikers.

MacNaughton also accused Murphy of misleading the governor in his reports. When the judge denied it, MacNaughton cited a letter the governor had written to Sheriff Cruse that suggested the managers refused to meet with the mine workers. It was true, of course, but the judge was probably surprised to find out how intimate MacNaughton was with Cruse.

Anthony Lucas made himself unpopular in some circles by insisting on a trial for the Waddell men and the deputies who had killed Tizan and Putrich. Despite overwhelming evidence against the deputies, mine owners and many local businessmen thought the men should not be tried; the strikers thought the defendants should be convicted of first-degree murder. Because Lucas was Croatian, many in the community respected him no more than the other "foreigners" in the area. One member of the community wrote to the governor:

> *The county Prosecuting Attorney Lucas, was born in a saloon, and raised right up in this same saloon from birth to manhood with 13 Austrian Rats, his brothers.*

Meanwhile, some men were trickling back to work in the mines. Even though the mines needed help, MacNaughton steadfastly refused to hire union men. "Today a man we call 'Slippery' Johns, one of the Executive Council of the Local Union, applied for work and offered to turn in his Union card; he was told to keep it as he might need it somewhere else and that he could not get work here."

MacNaughton let Shaw in on some of the espionage he was conducting in the Keweenaw. "I am keeping track of the financial condition of the Federation in the local banks; they have very little money, only about $8000.00 and are adding nothing to it." Since the mines were the banks' best customers, MacNaughton befriended many of the local bank managers. One of them, John Rice, would also play a prominent role in the organization MacNaughton would form to battle the unions. MacNaughton explained how the WFM could not possibly afford to pay its strikers anything substantial in the way of benefits, with so little cash on hand.

The good news MacNaughton passed along involved his living arrangements. He told Shaw on August 18 that he and his family had moved back into their house and were no longer worried for their safety.

Further, MacNaughton noted the arrival of "some new men" by railroad. The first two weeks of August had seen an influx of 169 more men than the same period a year earlier. MacNaughton seemed to think the tide was turning. He also noted an oddity: "Women acted as pickets for the first time today." Women had been picketing previously, but this was the first time MacNaughton admitted it to Shaw, or perhaps the first time he had noticed it.

On August 22, MacNaughton wrote to Shaw about how the talk with Murphy had the desired effect, claiming the judge told a friend that he was a "chump" for coming to the Keweenaw and getting involved in the strike. "It was a most complete back-down and a most ignominious crawl on his part." MacNaughton's attorneys told him "that my heart to heart talk with him last Sunday really got under his hide." Although MacNaughton thought he had persuaded Murphy to go home and leave the Copper Country as it was when he arrived, Murphy called General Abbey and advised him to start withdrawing troops. MacNaughton also told Shaw that he expected Murphy to not even bother issuing a formal report to the governor.

In the same letter, MacNaughton told Shaw that his sources inside the local banks informed him that the union was expecting an infusion of $25,000 that had not materialized yet. Meanwhile, the mine managers planned to meet again on August 24 to coordinate strategy.

On August 22, the Houghton County coroner's office convened an inquest into the death of Diazig Tizan. The coroner appointed a jury of local citizens—as allowed by law to ascertain the cause of death. The inquest lasted five days; four days in August were spent taking testimony, and then a fifth day in September. The last day was delayed so Tizan's body could be exhumed for an autopsy.

The inquest and the resulting transcripts were fascinating. More than twenty-six people testified, not counting the six men who would be accused of the murder. The coroner conducting the inquest was Charles Little, and he appointed six jurors to hear testimony. He then swore in two interpreters to translate the Finnish testimony, one to handle the Italian testimony, and two more to interpret Austrian and Croatian. The use of interpreters at this hearing is an important point because, oddly, after the Italian Hall tragedy, the coroner would not use any, even though the event was an even larger calamity than the Seeberville shootings.

From the beginning of the inquest, there were problems. The six men accused of the murder—even though they had been arrested—would not give their names to the authorities. Witnesses even claimed they did not know who the men were. One witness from the Champion mine said he knew two of the men—Edwin Polkinghorne and Thomas Raleigh—but he could not name the other four. This same man, a watchman for the mines who was present at the killings, also testified that the bowling pin that was thrown did not strike anyone. Later, the thrown bowling pin was erroneously reported to have hit one of the deputies in the head, instigating the attack. Most of the erroneous reports originated from the local newspaper coverage. Likewise, many newspapers reported that the strikers had been drunk during the incident, but Quick testified that "They might have had a glass or two of beer, but they were sober."

The survivors of the shooting spree testified through interpreters and told how the deputies tried to grab Kalan, how he ran into the house, and then how the deputies started shooting wildly into the house. When asked how many boarders he had in the house, the landlord, Joseph Putrich, said, "I had ten then, now I got eight." Joseph was the brother of the victim Steve Putrich.

When called, the deputies and Waddell men invoked their Fifth Amendment right not to testify and they refused to give their names to the jury. The coroner was forced to put Sheriff Cruse under oath and ask him to identify the men by name, even though they were standing right there. At one point, an attorney presented himself to the inquest and stated that he represented the men. Although it is common practice for an attorney to identify who he represents when he is in court, the attorney merely referred to them as "six men." Later, he gave their names, but only after extended argument between the coroner, the jurors and Lucas, who was present and conducting some of the examination. The other four defendants were Harry James, Joshua Cooper, Arthur Davis and William Groff.

The transcript of the five days of testimony was 170 pages. The evidence for indicting the deputies was overwhelming, and the testimony of the witnesses was extremely credible. While many of them were neighbors, they did not speak the same languages or even know each others' names. Several witnesses said that when the deputies ran out of ammunition they stopped firing, and then went out to the street where they emptied the spent cartridges from their guns and re-loaded them. When one of the men was dying, he turned to a roommate and asked that the money in his pockets be sent to his children. More than one witness told of how the deputies were crowding around the windows, trying to shoot into the house. When they couldn't get to a window, they fired blindly through the walls. Harry James admitted that he went with the other deputies to Kalan's house "just to see what the excitement was about," because no one had actually asked him to come along.

Amazingly, most observers missed the simple point: The Seeberville killers were not there to arrest anyone. *They were told to bring Kalan to the mine manager so the manager could "talk to him" about trespassing.*

The idea that they were on the Putrich property to make an arrest was a later invention, expanded upon by the anti-strike press. The day after the shooting—before the Seeberville killers knew they would be tried for the killings—they freely admitted their purpose in looking for Kalan and that they did not ever tell him he was under arrest. The argument that they were there to make an arrest is also contradicted by the fact that they did not have an arrest warrant with them. To arrest Kalan legally without a warrant would only have been possible if Kalan had committed a felony. The crime he was accused of—trespassing—was a misdemeanor. Again, the local media's treatment of the event was indicative of how far they would go to protect mining interests, regardless of the truth.

On August 25, MacNaughton made a secret trip to the mine at Wolverine to see the strike conditions for himself. There he met with the local union leader—a Hungarian named Jimmy Kelso—but did not tell the man who he was. After trying to decipher what the striker wanted, MacNaughton drew the conclusion he was "just a boy a little over 22 years of age, has anarchistic tendencies and is just a plain damn fool." From there, he went to Mohawk and met a dozen strikers, including three Cornishmen, and spoke with them for several hours. He concluded that these strikers were more reasonable and that they had legitimate grievances that were "local" and had nothing to do with MacNaughton or C&H. MacNaughton didn't bother heading further north to Ahmeek; there they were led by an "Irish bunch" that scared even him.

MacNaughton was wrong when he predicted Murphy would not issue a formal report when he returned to Lansing. There, he gave a report that MacNaughton referred to as "very radical against [the] Companies." As a result of this report, MacNaughton again expressed concern that the strike would be lengthened rather than shortened, and that the board should consider lowering any dividends it paid to shareholders to increase the cash on hand and enable the company to survive the strike.

Meanwhile, the strike breakers and deputies caused havoc on a shocking scale. Often, the Waddell men or the deputies arrested strikers on trumped-up charges. The treatment the strikers received while in custody was astounding for its gruesomeness. One organizer named Ben Goggia was arrested nine times during the strike. On one occasion his jailers beat him in his cell until a janitor walked by and yelled at the deputies to stop. A doctor arrived and was shocked by his condition, and later said that Goggia had been beaten only because he was a union organizer. On another occasion, a striker arrested for disturbing the peace was beaten so badly that he needed to be hospitalized; the charges were dismissed when the judge saw the man's condition and learned that the Waddell men had caused it.

Lucas testified before the governor in 1914 about some of the actions of the deputies and Waddell men. Once, Lucas came to the jail and found a recently arrested man in bandages. The deputy who arrested him admitted to beating the man because he resisted arrest. Why was he being arrested? He had called the deputy a scab. Lucas told Ferris that he found half a dozen cases like that one, where someone "made a face" at a deputy and was arrested. It was particularly bad during the first week of the strike.

Lucas wasn't the only person who saw how poorly the "law enforcement" was being handled by the Waddells and the amateur deputies. Congressman MacDonald said, "The sheriff and all his force have been neglecting the enforcement of law and have been directing their energies toward strike breaking." When asked how that might be in light of the large numbers arrested, he responded, "men were arrested in groups for yelling 'scab,' for coercion and intimidation [while] none of the felonies have been punished."

Court Intervention

One of the interesting facets of the Houghton County legal system during the strike was that the juries in the area were overwhelmingly favorable to striking defendants. This was despite the claims of the newspapers and the mine management that the union and its sympathizers had little support in the region. One prosecutor admitted: "Conditions were such that we found it almost impossible to get a conviction." By October 1, 1913, there were 181 arrests and only five guilty verdicts. The other cases had either been adjourned, dismissed, ended in acquittal or an occasional hung jury. The prosecutor's job—going against the grain of popular sentiment in the community—was perhaps the toughest in the county.

As a result of the Seeberville killings and the seemingly constant violence instigated by the deputies and the Waddell men, the WFM went to court and asked for an injunction against Sheriff Cruse and his employment of the Waddell-Mahon men. The WFM argued it was a violation of state law to employ men who were not residents of the state as either deputies—which Cruse insisted he was not doing—or as "aides" which Cruse admitted he was doing. It came down to a close interpretation of how different portions of the law should relate to each other, and since this situation had never come up before, it confounded the judge.

Judge O'Brien ruled on August 23 that Cruse could continue working with the Waddell-Mahon men as long as they weren't officially deputized.

He took his ruling as an opportunity to chastise the parties before him. He especially remembered his experience in Rockland, when he saw firsthand how deputies had held themselves above the law. "I shall expect the sheriff to keep his deputies and others in his employ within the bounds of their duties. They must not break up peaceful parades. The sheriff must assist neither the mining companies nor the strikers ... I regard it as a disgrace to civilization that no forum has been created for the settlement of these disputes, but as long as no such forum exists we as officers of the law must keep our hands off ... It ought to be the effort of both parties to this controversy to get together. We ought to have more Christianity."

The judge knew his admonishment was needed. After all, breaking up peaceful parades and siding with the mine owners was what the Waddell-Mahon men specialized in. They even bragged about it in their advertisements, calling themselves "an organization that specializes in labor disputes."

> *As an evidence of our ability as strike breakers, we invite your attention to the labor difficulties now ensuing along the copper range of the Upper Peninsula of Michigan between the Calumet & Hecla Copper Co., the Commonwealth Copper Co., the Quincy Copper Co., et al., and the Western Federation of Miners. We point with pardonable pride to the fact that this corporation has been selected by Sheriff James A. Cruse of Houghton County—the storm center of the strike—to aid him in maintaining the integrity of the law. We make this prediction at this time and if you will follow the story of the strike as it appears in the daily newspapers and particularly in the Boston News Bureau ... you will see that our production will be fulfilled daily. We are sure of defeating the Western Federation of Miners in this operation because we have met and defeated them before.*

Waddell-Mahon was not the only outside force brought in as hired muscle. Pinkerton furnished men to Calumet & Hecla. There were more than 112 such men in the region during the strike.

Interestingly enough, the strike-breaking Waddell-Mahon men were so blindly obedient to authority that they didn't even see they were being shortchanged by the owners of their company. Cruse and those who hired Waddell-Mahon men paid Waddell $5 a day plus expenses for their efforts. The men were paid $3 a day by Waddell. Waddell skimmed off $2 a day per man the entire time they were there. Some later pointed out that Waddell's men had more reason to unionize than did the striking miners.

Death's Door

Although calling in the National Guard had upset some of the strikers, the importing of "thugs" and "gunmen" as they were called by the strikers was even more incendiary, especially because many of the strikers knew of Waddell-Mahon's bloody scrapes with the WFM out west. The union's request that the governor intervene and order the Waddell-Mahon men from the region was to no avail. It is noteworthy that the two counties neighboring Houghton County specifically refused to hire the Waddell-Mahon men.

On August 23, MacNaughton wrote to Shaw and told of a parade involving 1,800 strikers. Although the number was impressive, MacNaughton was convinced they were "discontented and ... being held in line by threats on the part of leaders." On September 3, he admitted in a telegram to Shaw that there was "More picketing by strikers today than at any time." Even so, he reported fourteen men had come back to work the day before and thirty-five more had returned that day.

Despite the fact that they had murdered striking miners in Seeberville, the Waddell men submitted a bill to the Houghton County Board of Supervisors on September 9 for the work they had done in August. This bill ran to $19,045.77, and included $10,344.83 for salaries for the men and more than $1,300 for guns and ammunition. Presumably, some of that was the ammunition used to perforate the Putrich boardinghouse in Seeberville. The bill was paid.

On September 2, 1913, striking copper miners took to the streets again. The group numbered nearly two hundred and included many women and children from the neighborhood. When they reached the mine, they were turned away by the Michigan National Guard. They headed back to town, where they were confronted by fifteen recently deputized men. Insults were exchanged and the volume of the crowd rose. The deputies began firing wildly into the unarmed crowd, emptying their revolvers. A later investigation accounted for approximately ninety shots fired—but miraculously, they hit only one person and a few homes. When the firing stopped, the groups faced off through the haze of gun smoke. Realizing the deputies were now effectively unarmed—their guns empty—the crowd charged them. The fifteen turned and fled, rocks raining down on them as they ran, and scattered to the far corners of the town.

Injured that day was fourteen-year-old Margaret Fazekas, hit in the head by a deputy's bullet. Her friends and relatives were told to prepare for her funeral, as doctors had never seen a recovery from so severe a head wound. But, somehow she survived, and after several weeks she was deemed healthy enough to go home. MacNaughton mentioned the shooting in a letter to Shaw that began: "There is nothing particularly new to report." He then claimed a "mob" of five hundred, including women at the front, attacked a group of deputies who were trying to get to a mine. He reported that the deputies tried to withdraw and found themselves cornered and then pelted with rocks. He also said the mob was armed and shot at the deputies—although it was later proven that the group was unarmed. He argued the deputies then shot their guns into the air to "intimidate the mob and keep them back" and that someone in the mob shot Fazekas in the head. "Of course how she was shot and by whom will never be proven. The agitators will make a big fuss about this and in the event of the girl dying, which is altogether likely, the funeral will be the cause of an enormous demonstration." Fazekas recovered, but how could MacNaughton have believed that his armed deputies all fired into the air when they were facing an armed mob?

In the same letter he relays news that the governor had asked if MacNaughton would be willing to let a panel of three—presided over by Judge Murphy—hear the dispute and try to settle it. MacNaughton told General Abbey to convey his response: "I would not submit for a minute to having Judge Murphy connected with it, and that he, the General, might so state to the Governor for me. Judge Murphy's report places that individual where he can be flayed alive if we want to get after him." He accuses Murphy of "blatant Socialism" and tells Shaw that he considered hiring writers to "go after" the Judge and smear him publicly. Apparently, only the intervention of some of the other mine managers made him back down from this plan.

He also knew that a large infusion of cash the WFM was supposed to have received had not been deposited in their local account and—showing why MacNaughton was wise to code his own telegrams—the WFM had sent telegrams to various parts of the country "just last night" appealing for aid.

In a most revealing passage, MacNaughton writes:

> It may be that a legislative inquiry may be made at a later time in this strike matter and I would suggest that such of my personal letters to you as this be destroyed. I do not know what authority a congressional investigation might have but shall be careful not to have any records of this kind in this office and would suggest that you destroy letters such as these that I have written you.

The Department of Labor sent a man named John A. Moffitt to the

Keweenaw in September, and the newspapers reported that he would try settling the strike through a channel that did not involve MacNaughton. MacNaughton was so incensed upon reading about this in the paper, he vowed to Shaw that he would never allow Moffitt to attend any conference that MacNaughton was a part of.

On September 13, a group of strike supporters—led by Big Annie Clemenc—ran into a group of militia. The strikers wanted to parade through the suburb of Yellow Jacket, and the National Guard had been told to keep strikers out of that area. When the front lines met, words were exchanged and the situation escalated. A guard knocked a flag out of someone's hands and a horse allegedly trampled it. Big Annie stepped to the fore with her giant flag and flagstaff and put it between herself and the armed men on horseback. One of the National Guardsmen poked at her with a bayonet and she yelled at him: "Kill me! Run your bayonets and sabers through this flag! Kill me! But I won't move back! If this flag won't protect me, then I will die with it!"

After the crowd dispersed, many of the strikers reconvened at the union hall where they examined the tattered American flag. Moyer fired off a telegram to Governor Ferris, complaining of the National Guard's "outrage" and mistreatment of strike supporters and an American flag. As always, the involvement of an American flag brought scrutiny more quickly than the other claims. A military investigation was conducted the next day and although nothing official came from it, the captain who had been present at the flag altercation was relieved of duty ten days later and sent away with the next batch of militia.

Around this time, Big Annie took her first ride in an automobile. While picketing on the streets of Red Jacket, she got in a loud argument with a miner who wasn't honoring the strike. General Abbey happened to be nearby and came over to ask her to be quiet. When she refused, a car pulled alongside them and the General told her to get in. She was taken to "the dirty little Calumet jail," where she was charged with assault and battery and eventually released. She later retold the story of her first car ride to the *Miner's Bulletin*, which publicized the story widely.

The mine owners went to court seeking an injunction to stop the workers from picketing. To date, the bulk of the protests by the strikers involved marching the streets of Red Jacket in a show of unity and trying to discourage workers from going to or from the mines. Sometimes the discouragement included name-calling and yelling, but rarely did it involve violence. What violence occurred was almost always initiated by the deputies or Waddell men. Even so, the same Judge O'Brien who asked the parties to behave at a previous hearing issued an injunction that almost entirely foreclosed any form of protest by the union. Starting on September 20, they could not gather near the workplaces, homes or even the routes taken by workers to and fro. The injunction was a laundry list so comprehensive that it almost forbade the strikers from going outdoors. The union asked O'Brien to revise the order, and he did so on September 29. He let it be known that he was not officially siding with anyone in the matter: "This court will protect the right of every man who wants to work not to be interfered with by violence, intimidation or threats; this court will stretch out its arms to protect both sides in those rights."

MacNaughton wrote to Shaw that the injunction had been working. Now that O'Brien had reversed himself, MacNaughton wrote: "O'Brien's Socialistic tendencies have mastered him and he has gone into the hands of the enemy." The owners appealed O'Brien's action to the Michigan Supreme Court. MacNaughton always wanted it to appear that others were making the decisions, so the Baltic Mine was the named plaintiff in the action. Of course, the attorneys for Baltic were MacNaughton's lawyers, Rees, Robinson & Petermann. The Supreme Court reinstated the injunction—but it allowed for peaceful meetings and parades. The strikers were happy with the order. The court couldn't help itself when it noticed that the mine managers contradicted themselves when it suited them. On the one hand, a mine attorney had argued that the "backbone of the strike was about to be broken" when the injunction had been lifted. Later, the same attorney argued that the union was running amok in the Keweenaw and had control of virtually everything. "We find difficulty in reconciling this statement with the conditions" described in the affidavits of the mines, the Court wrote.

Among all the legal wrangling, the mines made a startling admission. There were only 4,000 men who wanted to work in the Keweenaw, willing to ignore the union. There were 14,500 miners in the region, leaving—according to management's number—more than 10,000 who were sympathetic with the WFM or who had left town. These numbers are similar to those cited by Peter Clark MacFarlane in "The Issues at Calumet," in 1914.

When critics of the mines pointed out the discrepancies in their math, allies of management created bizarre arguments to support their position. One was made by John W. Black in a letter to the governor, when he argued that many of the WFM members were not miners but "Finnish farmers." Presumably, Black wanted the governor to believe that farmers—who had no bosses to complain about—were paying union dues and risking their lives in picket lines to gain better working conditions for miners.

On September 12 and 13, MacNaughton wired Boston about strike conflicts: Twenty were arrested on September 12, including fifteen women. MacNaughton began to worry about how he looked, with everyone noting that he was the one who refused to meet and talk with anyone about the strike. On September 13, he told Shaw he had a plan to have the Copper Country Commercial Club make the "facts" of the case—as he saw them—public.

On September 15, Moffitt showed up at the C&H offices to meet MacNaughton. He was interested in mediating the dispute through the auspices of the Department of Labor, and MacNaughton reiterated that there was nothing to mediate. When Moffitt hinted he had the approval of Shaw to set up mediation, MacNaughton became angry. He wrote to Shaw that his impression of Moffitt was that he was "very crude." In later letters he sounded paranoid, writing that he suspected "Palmer [another man sent from the Department of Labor] was more friendly to the Western Federation of Miners than he was to us." He was suspicious of everyone from the Department of Labor. He thought they all had ties to unions, "although I have not taken the trouble to check up on it."

That same day, MacNaughton wrote to Shaw of his progress in getting the Copper Country Commercial Club to put out a favorable report on the position of the mine management. He claimed they had been "agitating" to get the facts out—maybe MacNaughton forgot that he had already told Shaw he would ask this group to write such a report—and they wanted to appoint a committee to investigate the strike. MacNaughton assured Shaw the committee would be friendly and that the report would certainly be something they would want to give to the press as soon as possible.

Imported Workers

The mines looked for ways to keep open and operating despite the strike. The Calumet & Hecla managed to operate on a limited basis with employees who were not striking. Other mines looked for labor elsewhere. Although Waddell-Mahon called itself a strike "breaker," the term was usually applied to replacement workers brought in from other regions who were not members of the union. The Quincy mine contacted the Austro-American Labor Agency in New York and asked if workers were available to come to the Keweenaw. Thus began one of the strangest chapters in the history of the strike.

On September 19, a train full of German-speaking men arrived at Hancock to be employed as miners at Quincy. Most of them had been promised good work at a rate of $2.50 for a nine-hour day, but there was more to their agreement than that. They had all agreed to contracts that made them pay the employment agency $24.50 for the cost of transporting them to the Keweenaw to be deducted from their wages over the first six months they worked in the mines. However, most of them could not read the English-language contracts and most of the contracts were not signed by the men.

The thirty-one Germans who arrived in Hancock were not accompanied by all the men who had boarded the train in New York: six had left the train when they found out that they had been deceived. They had been told there was no strike in the Copper Country and that they specifically were not being brought in as strike breakers. The thirty-one who did not escape the train ride were held captive for the duration of the trip and for a brief period of time when the train arrived in Hancock. During a Department of Labor investigation after the strike ended, Charles Lawton—manager of the Quincy—admitted the men were confined to the train until Waddell's men appeared with some troops to escort them to the mine. The men were not free to leave.

Many replacement workers were brought to the Copper Country after signing this document:

STATEMENT OF LABOR CONTRACT
IN ACCORDANCE WITH CHAPTER 700 OF THE LAWS OF 1910

Name of Employer	*Quincy Mining Co.*
Address of Employer	*32 Broadway, N.Y.*
Name of Employee	*Emil Rein*
Address of Employee	*152 Ridge*
Nature of work to be performed	*Untorirdiech in der Kupfer Mine*
Hours of labor	*9*
Wages offered	*$2.50 per tag*
Destination of persons employed	*Hancock, Mich.*
Terms of transportation	*$24.50 abezorgen, nach 6 monathe returniert*
Remarks	*Strike, 50 cents per month for doctor*

Later, the strike breakers told anyone who would listen that they did not know there was a strike in progress in the Keweenaw. The inclusion of the word "strike" in the contract was required by New York state law, but it was in English, a language none of them could read. Interestingly, the rate of pay, type of work and terms of transportation were all written in German.

Once the men had been escorted by armed guards to the Quincy mine—atop the hill that overlooks Hancock and Houghton—fourteen of them made a break. They escaped and sought refuge with the strikers. The fourteen managed to get to the Hancock headquarters of the WFM where they told their story again to WFM officials. When asked if they'd sign affidavits outlining their situation, twelve of them readily agreed.

> *We, the undersigned, depose and say that we have been hired by the Austro-American Agency, New York City, to work in the mines of the Quincy Mining Co., at Hancock, Mich., with the understanding that there is no strike on in the district. On September 19, 1913, at our arrival to Hancock, we were locked into a coach from 2 o'clock a.m. until quarter after 4 o'clock, and then we were taken to the Quincy mine location. On September 19, 1913, we seen [sic] by the thousands of strikers parading on the county road. Then we found out that we were hired under misrepresentation by the agency who shipped us here. And furthermore say that we were not held by the Western Federation of Miners at their headquarters at Kansankoti Hall, Hancock, Mich., against our will or any other way, and that we are not willing to work in the Quincy mine while the strike is on, and therefore we came to the Kansankoti Hall to get protection against the Quincy Mining Co., as we were in the belief that we would be forced to work in the mines under conditions against our will.*

The twelve signatories had first names such as Adolf, Karl, Emil and Josef. Their fears appeared to be well founded. Waddell sent armed men looking for the escaped Germans; when the Waddell men showed up at the Federation headquarters they caused a commotion. When they discovered the men had escaped, apparently with the help of the Federation, the Waddell men arrested one man at the headquarters for good measure and then left.

Despite the trouble with the fourteen wayward Germans, the mines were happy with the services of the out-of-state labor agencies. Quincy engaged the same agency—the Austro-American—and others in Chicago, to send up as many men as they could find. Another two dozen showed up on September 29, and their story bore a striking similarity to that of the Germans. Once in the copper range, armed troops got on the train before it arrived at Hancock to guard the men and assure they did not get off the train early. Once in Hancock, the men were marched up to the mine, again under armed guard. They began to wonder about the odd treatment, because they had specifically been told that there was no strike or labor unrest in the area. Once at the mines, they were little more than slave labor. They were confined to company housing under armed guard when not underground, and once underground, local supervisors beat them and yelled at them to work harder. When a worker complained, the supervisor merely hit him in the head and told him to get back to work. They described their condition with Quincy as being "prisoners." When they agitated too much, the mine photographed them and told them to get off the property—without paying them.

The bizarre stories of the imported strike breakers became commonly known in the region, as the mines imported 3,000 men to replace the strikers. Judging by the universal nature of the stories they told, they were almost all mistreated similarly, and many "escaped" the first chance they got. One group testified that they had been held at gunpoint on the train heading into the area, beginning at the Michigan-Wisconsin border. An article appeared in *The Daily Mining Gazette* stating, "The strike breakers imported by the Quincy during the past two weeks all quit work yesterday." It was common for such strike breakers to make their way to the WFM hall in Hancock, sign an affidavit about their experience, and then head out of town.

MacNaughton informed Shaw on October 25 that someone at the top of Quincy Hill shot at a train full of imported strike breakers. The soldiers on the train returned fire and amazingly, no one was injured. To the imported strike breakers, it must have looked like they were entering the Wild West.

Other workers were brought in after signing "employment slips" that were drafted in English. The forms used by C&H guaranteed a daily rate—for example, trammers received $2.75—and also refunded the train fare if the worker stayed for six months. One example of the employment slip in the Michigan Tech Archives & Copper Country Historical Collection bears a signature that is clearly traced over someone else's writing, leading an observer to conclude that the man who signed it could not write. One wonders if he could read.

In October, the militia and deputy sheriffs arrested men at the Allouez and Mohawk mines on the charge that they were violating the court order against interfering with workers at those sites. They arrested 209 men and struggled with the logistics of getting all of them to Houghton for processing. The authorities loaded up street car after street car with the men, sending them south, and a hearing was set for that afternoon. Again, Judge O'Brien had a courtroom full of strikers, miners and lawyers for both sides. The WFM lawyer argued that the charges should be dismissed, but O'Brien instead stated that he'd allow them all to be released without posting cash bonds—as long as they knew who had been arrested. It turns out that the deputies and sheriff had rounded up so many men that it was unclear who was being charged with what, and many of the men had no identification—and didn't speak English.

The judge—no doubt hoping he wouldn't have to deal with such a mass of humanity again—instructed the sheriff that in the future he could make arrests and merely give the defendant an order to appear in court. It would not be necessary to drag them all the way to Houghton each time they were accused of violating the order against picketing. He then told the strikers: "This court does not want to interfere with your liberty, but order and liberty should go hand in hand. The working class should respect this injunction. Do not interfere with men going to work. They have that right and the court will protect them in it. Respect the writ. I ask you to bear this in mind and tell the other strikers. Law and order come before even the solution of this industrial problem." Later, he added: "You are permitted to parade, but you must not interfere with men going to work." MacNaughton described O'Brien's statements as "semi-socialistic."

Meanwhile, the mines began eviction proceedings against strikers. Because almost all of the workers in the region lived on land or in homes rented from the mines, eviction was always a real worry. On October 14, the Champion mine became the first to begin proceedings against strikers. One of those notified was Joseph Putrich. *Champion was evicting the survivors from the Seeberville murder house.* Putrich found the money to get his rent caught up and forestalled the action. A court injunction was eventually entered forbidding evictions of some of the strikers.

The mines eventually made much of how they did not evict tenants wholesale during the strike—never mind the fact they legally weren't allowed to—but most of the strikers probably planned on paying the rent as soon as they went back to work. The miner who was evicted during the strike said, "I never say I don't pay. I say when I work [I] pay everything fair ... no more deputy, then I work like a man [and] I pay everything that I owe."

Violence escalated as the number of troops dwindled and the number of men going to work rose. Gunfire was often reported near cars or trains full of workers, and many cars arrived at the mines with bullet holes and cracked windows. The problem appeared to be worse in the north— where Sheriff Hepting patrolled. MacNaughton blamed him and the rest of law enforcement for the violence. "The Sheriff of Keweenaw County is a dummy, the Prosecuting Attorney a member of the union and one of the most vicious in the bunch."

Around this time, MacNaughton heard of a wild tale: A woman told a local newspaper reporter she had been hired by the WFM to blow up the newspaper's headquarters. MacNaughton was beside himself with excitement; if the story were true, he could get the entire WFM leadership thrown in jail on conspiracy charges. Each time the woman met with detectives, however, her stories became more convoluted. Although she produced no evidence to support her story, MacNaughton wired Shaw and told him to hire bodyguards; maybe the woman would go to Boston and blow up Shaw's home!

After trailing her and various WFM officers for a few days, even the police became convinced there was nothing to the woman's story. She knew members of the union, but never produced a bomb. MacNaughton was forced to explain the odd situation to Shaw.

> *Nothing new has developed in regard to the plan to blow either yourself or Dolf up with dynamite. The detective in charge thinks the girl told the truth, a perfectly straight story; he further thinks that the girl was originally mixed up in the plot as deeply as the other local Socialists but that she realized in blowing up the Gazette office her fellow [her contact in the WFM] would probably be killed and she could not bring herself to do that.*

Meanwhile, the head of the WFM, Charles Moyer, wrote a letter to Moffitt and the Department of Labor countering MacNaughton's repeated assertions that many men who were not union members were staying away from the mines out of fear for their safety. Moyer knew of "no men on strike who are not members of the local unions." He then reiterated his desire to have the owners of the mines meet with workers—even if it meant that the workers' representative was not a member of the WFM.

To bolster support for the WFM—and to let the general public of the Keweenaw know how reasonable the WFM was being—Moyer authorized the printing of flyers and had them placed up and down the copper range.

Death's Door

The "Notice to the Public" outlined the arbitration proposal, and promised that once management agreed to it, the strikers would return to work immediately. They would then agree to be bound by whatever the findings of the arbitration committee were. It seemed a reasonable offer—and a bold one. The WFM seemed confident the arbitration would go their way. It must have infuriated MacNaughton. It was a dare he could not take.

The Copper Country Commercial Club issued its report on October 8 and—to no one's surprise—it sided completely with mine management. Ostensibly, the "Strike Investigation" was presented as an open letter and report to the governor on the situation. It read like a propaganda piece drafted by MacNaughton himself. "For upwards of seven weeks a condition of affairs has existed and today exists in the copper country which is nullifying every effort and every purpose of this organization." The purpose of their organization included promotion of the "welfare of all of the people of this community." The CCCC claimed it was time that they rose up to demand that "violence, rioting and bloodshed must cease in this community." The problem was that the CCCC claimed these things were brought to the area by the WFM, but the only murders to date were committed by Waddell-Mahon men, hired by the Houghton County Board of Supervisors, and the dead were members of the WFM. The report contained some falsehoods as well; it claimed that the Copper Country had been "free from strike troubles" before the arrival of the WFM. There had been strikes before; they were just never as widespread as this one.

And in a display of how circular propaganda can be, the report stated that the amount of violence and lawlessness in the Keweenaw was evidenced by the sheriff's appeal for state troops. "These facts are substantiated by the action of the sheriff of Houghton County in appealing to the governor of the state for the aid of state troops in restoring peace and stamping out lawlessness, which appeal was sent in during the night of July twenty-third." They left out how MacNaughton had to lean on the sheriff for the better part of the evening before Cruse relented and called for troops. The report was signed by twelve members of the Copper Country Commercial Club, including A.F. Heidkamp. Heidkamp was the manager of Bosch brewing, a local brewery that was experiencing labor problems with its recently unionized workforce. J.W. Black, the man who sent the telegram to Governor Ferris echoing MacNaughton's alarm at the riotous mob in Calumet the first day of the strike, also signed. Another signatory was J.P. Petermann, attorney for Calumet & Hecla.

The twelve signatories included local businessmen, Joseph Selden,

Frederick Guck, W.R. Thompson, Thomas Armstrong and John Dee. Also signing were five men who belonged to the Miscowaubik Club with MacNaughton: Henry Baer, James Fisher, Homer Guck, J.P. Petermann and Edward Ulseth. The C&H ordered 12,000 copies of the report to distribute to its shareholders and to anyone else they could think of, and Shaw even lobbied for newspaper reporters and writers to use the report as a basis for "objective" stories. On one occasion, he promised to buy 500 subscriptions to a magazine called *The Gateway* as long as it published a favorable article based on the report. Shaw wrote to MacNaughton and asked him for names and addresses of people who might want one of the subscriptions sent to them. When Moffitt again asked MacNaughton if he was willing to negotiate an end to the strike, MacNaughton declined, but sent along a dozen of the Copper Country Commercial Club reports for Moffitt to study.

On October 16, Quincy Shaw wrote to MacNaughton and said he wished that Moyer and the other WFM leaders could be shipped off to Isle Royale—an island in the middle of Lake Superior, closer to Canada than it is to the U.S.—and left there for the rest of their lives.

Further Relief Efforts

In November 1913, the WFM announced it would open commissaries in Calumet and other locations. The stores would be stocked by the WFM and strikers would be paid benefits in the form of coupons redeemable at the union stores. The stock for the store openings was said to have filled thirty railroad cars. The opening of the union stores, however, caused an unusual backlash in the community. Local store owners who'd been asked by strikers to extend credit and give discounts were now facing competition. At this point, observers believed that "established storekeepers" joined the mine managers in a "war of destruction" against the WFM.

While hired help was coming in to help the mine owners, labor leaders from around the country came to the area to support the strikers. For the most part, they were volunteers. One such leader was Ella Reeve Bloor, a self-proclaimed Socialist leader who'd spent the years before the copper strike helping out with labor strikes in New York. One strike was against General Electric, and it too began in 1913. There were also quite a large number of workers on strike there, numbering 15,000. One difference in that strike, according to Bloor, is that Schenectady's mayor was an avowed Socialist who deputized the striking workers. When replacement workers showed up—Bloor called them "scabs"—the deputized strikers told them to leave and when they refused, they were arrested.

This reversal of roles probably played a big part in the General Electric strike being settled favorably for the strikers, who returned to work late in the fall of 1913. The workers there told Bloor of the situation in Calumet, and they raised a fund for the women and children of the copper strikers. Bloor agreed to deliver the money to the Keweenaw personally and to help with the strike as needed. Bloor wrote an autobiography years later, and although some of her recollections prove accurate, much of it is peppered with exaggerations. For one thing, she claimed that the workers went on strike because "the wages of the workers were unbelievably low, under a dollar a day." She also claimed that 1,700 Waddell-Mahon men were hired—she was off by more than a factor of ten.

MacNaughton was fuming at the way the recently arrested strikers were being treated by the Houghton County court system and wrote to Shaw about it. O'Brien had let them all go without posting bail and then ruled that he would try their cases by affidavit—rather than call any witnesses to testify live, they would submit sworn statements which the judge would consider before making his ruling. MacNaughton thought this was unfair; while the mine management would be limited to the truth and actual witnesses, the strikers would merely fabricate false affidavits and the situation would turn into a "fiasco."

In the same letter, MacNaughton claims he met with O'Brien and a few others who asked about ways to end the strike. The judge told him the union "said they were whipped." They would withdraw from the region and call off the strike if the workers would be taken back. MacNaughton refused any such offer because he wanted to retain the right to refuse employment to the most problematic union members. And had the union really admitted to O'Brien they were "whipped"? MacNaughton was prone to exaggeration so there is no way of gauging the accuracy of that statement. Or if it had been said, was O'Brien repeating it literally or had O'Brien said that as a way to open negotiations? Some historians take the statement from MacNaughton as gospel, without noting that MacNaughton told Shaw that O'Brien had told him that the union had told O'Brien. In mid-November, MacNaughton claimed that O'Brien visited him again, saying: "there was a great deal of dissatisfaction in the ranks of the strikers; that the officers were having a hard time holding them together." If they had been "whipped" previously, this would not have been news.

MacNaughton tells Shaw of another amazing admission, supposedly made to him by the president of the company that published the Finnish paper *Tyomies*. MacNaughton claimed they met at a bank in Hancock at the request of the president, and after discussing the strike, the bank president "admitted that he didn't see what the men were striking for." MacNaughton then called the man "the leader among the Socialist Finns," and "just an ordinary, common mutt."

MacNaughton also told Shaw of a "miscarriage of justice" before Judge O'Brien in a case against some Croatian strikers. He told Shaw that "the judge is a Socialist," the prosecutor "belongs to their union" and the defendants "required an interpreter" as if speaking a foreign language was a handicap. MacNaughton complained that the judge allowed "Oppman the Hungarian Jew, paid organizer for the Union, as interpreter. It is needless to say the defendants were promptly found not guilty."

Meanwhile, even the forces of nature appeared to be conspiring against MacNaughton. Usually, the Copper Country has harsh winters; when the peninsula is buried in snow the locals measure it in feet, not inches. MacNaughton and the other managers assumed the workers would be inspired to return to work when the winter turned mean and their homes became cold and snowbound. However, the coming winter of 1913-1914 did not arrive in force. Some communities had received less than a foot of snow by Christmas, and much of the ground was not even covered—a most unusual circumstance for the region.

On December 6, Judge O'Brien re-issued the injunction against picketing, after being ordered by the Michigan Supreme Court to do so. This time, the injunction was not as broad as before. O'Brien also took the occasion to rule on the cases of the picketers who had been arrested for violating the previous injunction. He found them all guilty—MacNaughton was wrong in thinking the "trial by affidavits" meant instant findings of not guilty—but then suspended all of their sentences. He lectured the convicted men, telling them he would not be so nice if he had the same defendants in his courtroom in the future. The local press went ballistic, berating O'Brien as a traitor to the community.

The mine owners were stunned. Within twenty-four hours, however, they would have their new rallying cry. Logicians and philosophers argue that when one event is closely followed by another, it is a fallacy to claim that the second event was caused by the first merely because of the timing and order of the events. Therefore, what happened on the night of December 6 was not necessarily caused by what had happened earlier on December 6. At least, according to logicians and philosophers.

Bloody December

"Foreign Agitators Must be Driven from District at Once"
- *DAILY MINING GAZETTE* HEADLINE -

The Second Round of Boardinghouse Murders

On the night of December 6, Painesdale would once again be rocked by deadly gunfire. Harry and Arthur Jane—two Cornishmen who'd left the area when the strike was called—returned upon hearing that the mines were back in operation. They moved into a boardinghouse filled with other Cornishmen. The house was run by Thomas and Julia Dally. In many respects, the Dally house was like the Putrich house—company-owned and originally designed for single families. But the Putrich house was filled with Croatian-speaking strikers. The Dally house was filled with English-speaking non-union men.

The first night the Jane brothers were in Painesdale, someone fired several rifle shots into the home. It was a few minutes before 2 a.m. Sleeping inside the home was a young man named Kenneth Nicholson who wrote an account of the shooting years later: "It seemed as though all of the windows in the house were breaking, at once! We could hear continuous volleys of rifle shots! We could hear the bullets ripping through the wooden house, and splinters were flying everywhere." His father yelled for him to lie down. Bullets narrowly missed him, going over and under his bed.

Nicholson's sister Mary was hit by two bullets. Bullets also went through her pillow as well as another sister's pillow without hitting her. Thomas Dally was hit in the head, while his wife sat in bed next to him, unscathed. One bullet hit one of the Jane brothers in the head, and traveled further, hitting the other Jane brother, also in the head. Both were killed instantly. Dally died a few hours later.

Nicholson's mother attended to his sister; she was a nurse and she managed to extract the bullet from her daughter's shoulder. Meanwhile, Nicholson's father ran a mile to the nearest phone at Siller's Hotel. He called the mine doctor who hitched up a horse and buggy, picked up the father, and hurried to the boardinghouse. It was too late for the Jane brothers—or Dally: "There, in an unforgettable scene, using the flickering glow of a kerosene lamp, he dressed my sister Mary's wounds."

When the sun rose over Painesdale, the sheriff searched a nearby hillside and found shells from a 30-30 rifle scattered by a fallen tree. Judging from the placement of the shells, he determined there were at least thirty-two shots fired by two men who had used the fallen tree to brace their rifles. Cruse called Lucas—the prosecutor—to the scene. When Lucas got there, he was surprised to see a familiar face: Raleigh, one of the defendants in the Seeberville killings, was assisting Cruse at the scene. When Lucas asked Cruse about it, he shrugged and said that until he was convicted, he was still a deputy. It turned out that the Seeberville defendants had all been bailed out of jail—with substantial bail amounts— by the superintendent of the local mine. Later, Lucas wrote:

> From my personal observation and investigation that morning, I became suspicious that the imported guards had a hand in this atrocious killing. They had a motive and all of those who were on duty at or near this boarding house carried high-powered rifles, whose shells were of the same caliber as those picked up in the snow; and not one of the eight or nine guards who were on duty near this boarding house went out to see who did this shooting or what was being shot at. Three of them were, at the time, in the guard headquarters across from the house that was shot up.

Lucas was convinced the shootings had been done by deputies or Waddell men who wanted to turn the tide of public sentiment back to the mines. In particular, it bothered Lucas how intimately Raleigh was involved with the case and its investigation—while he was awaiting trial for murder. Later, witnesses that Lucas considered credible told him deputies had admitted they had done it. The problem was Lucas could not get the grand jury to indict. It was also ominous how these killings took place the night after O'Brien suspended the sentences of the convicted strikers.

Careful observers noticed how the local (pro-management) newspapers handled the Dally-Jane murder case. The Dally boardinghouse was described as a warm home, where Julia Dally was "like a mother to the young men who came here from England." Before they died, the brothers had "spent a merry evening in the Dally home, singing and talking together of the people in Cornwall." The papers even somehow knew that the Jane brothers would have attended church the next morning if they had not been gunned down by foreigners.

The Citizens Alliance
Right around this time, a group calling itself the Citizens Alliance formed. The group was modeled after a similar group that had been involved in the copper mine strikes out west and claimed to be comprised of regular citizens and businessmen who merely wanted the strike to end. They claimed to be nonpartisan, but in reality they were a tool of the mines. In fact, to join the Alliance, a member had to sign a pledge:

> *I believe that the presence of the Western Federation of Miners is a menace to the future welfare and prosperity of this district, and that therefore in the interest of Law, Order and Peace, the Western Federation of Miners must go.*

The group was first mentioned by MacNaughton in correspondence in November when he told Shaw "a movement was started to form a Citizens' Alliance." He does not say who started the movement or how he heard about it, but within two weeks he wrote that it had 7,500 members and almost ninety-five percent of his loyal employees were members. More importantly, "Each man who belongs to the Citizens' Alliance will wear a button. This will tend to give more assurance to the men who are now out but who fear to return to work; it will also tend to put a lot of men on record who have avoided going on record thus far." MacNaughton said the local papers had not reported on the Alliance yet, because they "have been asked to keep quiet about it." Local WFM officers became aware of the formation of a Citizens Alliance as early as November 12.

By December, the Alliance was publishing its own newspaper, *Truth*. The December 2 issue claimed a membership of 8,675 and reminded readers, "You Promised 'To Wear at All Times WHERE IT CAN BE SEEN' the Button Indicating Your Membership." The buttons were round and white, with the words "Citizens Alliance" in tall red letters. The paper was filled with anti-union rants—often in all capital letters—such as:

> *DO YOU THINK YOU ARE WISE, DO YOU THINK YOU ARE BEING HONEST WITH YOURSELF WHEN YOU PERMIT YOUR OWN CHILDREN TO SUFFER IN ORDER TO PLEASE MEN LIKE MAHONEY AND MOYER?*

None of the diatribes were signed; there was no reference to anyone at the paper, nor an address given where they might be reached. The only possible hint of ownership—and it wasn't all that revealing—was the line beneath the title: "Published by authority of the Citizens Alliance to tell the truth about the Western Federation." The printing costs were paid by Calumet & Hecla, at the direction of MacNaughton.

Truth was countered by the *Miners' Bulletin*. Compare the hysterical writing of *Truth* with that found in the *Miners' Bulletin*. On December 2, the *Miner's Bulletin* wrote:

> *The really dangerous feature of the situation in the Calumet District is not that the miners are shockingly underpaid, though their wages certainly are not adequate, nor that the conditions in the mines are extremely dangerous or unsanitary, though they ought to be improved in both respects. What should give us concern is the undoubted fact that Houghton County, Michigan, in the heart of what purports to be the purest democracy on earth, is being governed by an oligarchy.*

To make sure the debate stayed as ugly as possible, MacNaughton helped *Truth* get the rights to publish the "confession" of Harry Orchard. Orchard had confessed to a potpourri of crimes—including murder—that he said he'd committed at the direction of the WFM. Orchard was controversial to say the least, and his "confession" was owned by *McClure's* magazine. MacNaughton asked Shaw to approach *McClure's* and seek permission to print the "confession" in *Truth*. Shaw received permission and the lurid tale was published.

Strangely, Orchard's testimony had been used by Colorado prosecutors trying to convict Bill Haywood and other union organizers of a variety of crimes. Orchard confessed that he had bombed numerous sites—to have single-handedly committed virtually every unsolved crime attributed to the unions—and killed people, all at the direction of the unions. Despite Orchard's nice manner of speaking and wonderful attention to detail, the jury did not believe him. Haywood was not convicted.

The Daily Mining Gazette—in case anyone wondered whose side they were on—ran this headline on December 8: "Foreign agitators must be driven from district at once." Presumably, this was in response to the Dally-Jane murders, but if that was really the case, perhaps the headline should have mentioned finding the killers first. The implication was that the union members were all "foreign"—from out of state. But the members of the WFM locals were for the most part citizens of the Copper Country; the few outsiders were Moyer and the other national leaders who had come in to help the locals.

Of course, there was an uglier side to the "foreign agitators" pronouncement: It gave sanction to the English-speaking members of the community—mine management, the Citizens Alliance and others—to point at anyone they disliked and treat them as second-class citizens. And for those who might wonder about the *Gazette's* allegiance, the paper's president, William G. Rice, was an admitted leader of the Citizens Alliance.

On December 9, the *Gazette* reported on upcoming Citizens Alliance rallies and publicized a threat to the union: "Full details have not been worked out, that is as to speakers and plan of action to follow the meetings. In a broad way the purpose, it is understood, is to notify the Western Federation of Miners, Agitators, that they have twenty-four hours in which to leave the district; if they do not act upon this notice they will be sent out of the district in the manner that suggests itself as most convenient and effective. This is the purpose of the Citizens Alliance of Houghton and Keweenaw counties."

On December 10 huge rallies were held in Houghton and Calumet, ostensibly put together by the Citizens Alliance to show their support for the mines and to protest the recent Dally-Jane murders. The mines gave their employees the afternoon off with pay and sent them to the rallies. The two big events were orchestrated by the local law firm of Rees, Robinson & Petermann, which rented halls, hired entertainment and chartered the workers' transportation. All of these bills were passed on to the mines, which paid them. No such orchestration of public outcry occurred when Diazig Tizan and Steve Putrich were murdered by MacNaughton's allies.

MacNaughton coyly sidestepped the issue of who created the Citizens Alliance. "It has no officers, no executive committee, no one knows who started it, and the more mystery surrounds it, the greater terror it is to the Western Federation officials." Yet later in the letter he admitted that he was behind a drive to solicit signatures for the organization. The local papers played along. Reports claimed 40,000 people marched in Calumet and another 10,000 in Houghton, all in support of the Citizens Alliance.

In an unusual telegram, MacNaughton wired Shaw his outrage over the Dally-Jane killings. Although mostly uncoded, its last sentence was in code:

> *As a result of the killing of three innocent men while asleep at two o'clock yesterday morning in Painesdale a mass meeting was held in Houghton a special train chartered for Calumet and a mass meeting held in armory in afternoon. Object of meeting to protest against the action of County officials in not enforcing law and a general protest against the existence in this community of the foreign agitators. A set of resolutions was adopted providing for the closing down of all industries on Wednesday afternoon and for the holding of mass meetings at various points throughout the County. The public is thoroughly aroused and* ticking lugs liveliness the bate of the embarrass of wade imperiousness ticking copartner. *[this looks like the beginning of the end of Western Federation of Miners in this country.]*

The local newspapers were so vehement in their condemnation of the WFM in the wake of the Dally-Jane murders that MacNaughton asked Shaw to write the editor of the *Gazette* "a letter congratulating him on his efforts." There had been no evidence to date pointing toward the WFM for the killings. The mine management needed martyrs to counter the ones the WFM had gained at Seeberville.

The December 10 Citizens Alliance rally at the Amphidrome in Houghton was a frightening affair. The chairman of the meeting was John A. Doelle, who whipped the mob into a riotous frenzy with charges against the WFM of the most vile nature:

> *Why is it that in a community that was free for years from robbery, is not free at present? Why is it possible that innocent young women are being followed and chloroformed in order that they may be robbed of their virtue?*

After loud cheering and more crazy allegations, Doelle was followed by Reverend J.R. Rankin, who was no less militant in his stand on the WFM:

> *My sentiments since the beginning of this labor trouble, and I expressed them to some of the leading men in this town, are that the agitators of this trouble should be deported; driven out of the county, for I claim today that they were the cause of all this trouble and crime that has been committed.*

The Reverend was interrupted in his ranting by applause and "cries of Hear, Hear." Later in the same speech, while rhapsodizing on the American flag, Rankin said of the WFM members:

> *That kind of a man has no right to the protection that that flag affords. That man has no right to live in a country where that flag floats.*

He was interrupted by thunderous applause.

At this point, the Citizens Alliance became a roving mob, a mobile riot, out of control. The Citizens Alliance openly "raided" the headquarters of the union and other places members were known to frequent. They trashed the buildings and took anything they deemed helpful to the union. At South Range—not far from Painesdale and Seeberville—they instigated a battle at the WFM headquarters and then rounded up union members, threatening them if they did not leave town. They also claimed they had "confiscated" guns and ammunition; they announced this to try and scare the rest of the populace with the notion that the union was armed and dangerous. One reason the "raids" were unopposed by the law was that there were deputies and Waddell men among the Alliance members conducting the raids.

Another Alliance agitator was A.E. Petermann, attorney for Calumet & Hecla, and the agent by which MacNaughton controlled and funded the Alliance. Petermann would be rewarded for these activities later by taking over the presidency of C&H. At one rally Petermann exhorted his mob to "clean up this county and clean it up quick." He referred to the union members and organizers as "poisonous slime." Another frequent Alliance speaker was Petermann's law partner, Allen Rees. The activities of the Alliance were so openly taken that Petermann's speeches were reprinted in *Truth* and the *Calumet News*—the latter being an outlet that would have toned down or ignored the story if they found it disparaging of the mines.

A common theme of the Alliance rallies was that a state of lawlessness had taken over the Copper Country. It was ironic: The rallies themselves resulted in lawlessness on a scale previously unseen in the region. Because it was sponsored by the mines and the businessmen, none of the instigators such as Doelle, Rankin, Petermann or Rees were ever prosecuted for inciting the riots. In fact, they were hailed as heroes by the local pro-management press.

Assuming that justice worked for everyone, the WFM went to court and sought an injunction prohibiting the Citizens Alliance from molesting them. Because the Citizens Alliance leadership never revealed itself, the WFM attorneys named the organization as a whole, and then listed prominent members. Among them were Samuel Eddy and Edward Hamar, who sat on the board of supervisors with MacNaughton, and the president of the *Gazette*, William Rice. Also, John Rice, bank president; Fernando Petermann and J.P. Petermann, merchants; John W. Black; Fred Bawden, president of the village of Houghton, Michael Messner Jr.; and John Manderfield, a farmer.

In what was seen as a shocking move by the newspapers and the other pro-mine organizations, Judge O'Brien issued a restraining order on December 10. Rees, Robinson & Petermann ran to court and complained loudly. O'Brien gave them a copy of the twelve-page injunction and told them to abide by it. The injunction named only the ten most prominent members of the Citizens Alliance, but applied to the whole group. The WFM organizers were so concerned with the threats of kidnapping and deportation that they sought—and were granted—language from the court that the Alliance members:

ABSOLUTELY AND ENTIRELY DESIST AND REFRAIN From in any manner interfering with, molesting or disturbing Charles H. Moyer, John C. Lowney, Yanko Tersich, Ben Goggia, Mor Oppman, Peter Jedda, William J. Rickard or by way of threats, personal violence, intimidation or by any means whatsoever, calculated or intended to compel Charles H. Moyer [et al.] to leave this District against their will.

All of which WE STRICTLY COMMAND YOU TO OBSERVE until the further order of this court in the premises.

Presumably, Moyer could rest easy, knowing he would not be forcefully ejected from the region.

The Citizens Alliance Grand Jury

The Houghton County Clerk convened a twenty-person grand jury to investigate the Dally-Jane murders and other strike-related crimes, and immediately the WFM and the strikers became worried. Grand juries are supposed to be impartial panels of members of the community who can issue subpoenas, take testimony and issue indictments against those who should be tried for crimes. This grand jury included at least nine members of the Citizens Alliance—some counted as many as a dozen. County officials quietly complained that evidence implicating Waddell men was excluded by the jury; one of the jurors refused to return an indictment against a Waddell man named by witnesses, saying: "That will not do, because that will affect the strike." Afterward, Governor Ferris interviewed people familiar with the grand jury to see if any of the claims were true about its bias; Judge O'Brien confirmed that there were "at least nine" members who were in the Citizens Alliance and none were members of the WFM.

The members of the grand jury and their occupations were:

A.F. Heidkamp, foreman of the jury, general manager of Bosch Brewing
Michael Messner Jr., contractor
P.C. Audet, carpentry boss at Quincy Mining Co.
Edgar Bye, MacNaughton's chauffeur
M.H. Cunningham, foreman at stamping mill
Thomas Dunstan, foreman at C&H stamping mill
W.H. Dee, president of a cigar company

Xavier Gillet, retired jeweler
Charles H. Lang, accountant
W.H. Faucett, real estate and insurance broker
Edward Leach, merchant
F.H. Lewis, hotel keeper
John McCarthy, clerk and justice of the peace
Henry Parks, farmer
George Pfeiffer, merchant
F.C. Schubert, engineer for Hancock Mining Co.
James W. Shields, superintendent of the Quincy Mining Co.
John Smith, engineer for Portage Coal Co.
Patrick Sollman, farmer
George Williams, agent for Copper Range Railroad

This grand jury should go down in history as being one of the most twisted and misguided legal entities to sit in such a position. It did the bidding of the mines and attacked the strikers—regardless of whose side the law was on. MacNaughton acknowledged to Shaw that members of the Alliance were on the grand jury, but pretended not to understand why there might be anything untoward about their presence. Although grand juries are supposed to conduct their business in secret, only revealing their findings by issuing indictments, it was not hard for MacNaughton to know the inside workings of this grand jury; his chauffeur was one of the Citizens Alliance members sitting on it. Even better for MacNaughton, mining interests dominated the jury. Besides MacNaughton's chauffeur, there were two employees of Quincy, along with employees of the C&H and Hancock copper mines. The Copper Range railroad made its money from the mines, as did the Portage Coal Co., and the man who worked for the unnamed stamping mill. Faucett and Shields were also members of the exclusive Miscowaubik Club with MacNaughton.

The manager from Bosch had reason to be biased against the strikers. The Bosch brewery was recently unionized and the workers there had gone on strike as well. In fact, the brewer was one of the signatories on the "Strike Investigation" by the Copper Country Commercial Club. Patrick Sollman—the farmer—was the same farmer who sat on the Houghton County Board of Supervisors and authorized the hiring of the Waddell-Mahon men. It is easy to see why it would be impossible to get this grand jury to hand down any indictments that reflected poorly on deputies,

Waddell-Mahon men, or the mines. Judge O'Brien oversaw some of the grand jury activities, but he could not control who was called to sit on it. That was the job of the county clerk. This goes a long way in explaining how—in a county with a population of 90,000—MacNaughton found so many of his friends and allies in the pool from which the jury was drawn.

MacNaughton told Shaw: "We hope shortly to get indictments for all officers, organizers and agitators of Western Federation of Miners for conspiracy." Of course, each of the members of the grand jury who were Alliance members had previously signed the pledge reading:

> *I believe that the presence of the Western Federation of Miners is a menace to the future welfare and prosperity of this district, and that therefore in the interest of Law, Order and Peace, the Western Federation of Miners must go.*

Sadly, Judge O'Brien could not bring himself to disqualify Alliance members for cause. He later said that he questioned the men about their ability to be fair and unbiased, and when they answered appropriately, he felt he had to let them serve. Nowadays, none of the Alliance members could have sat on the grand jury after signing the pledge these men signed.

The last surviving letter MacNaughton wrote before Christmas included an observation regarding the strike situation: "From all indications there is a great deal of discontent in the ranks of the strikers. Notwithstanding this discontent the leaders are holding them together very well and but few of them are returning to work." MacNaughton and Shaw's correspondence—now surviving in the archives at Michigan Technological University—suddenly has gaps; none of their letters or telegrams from December 18 through December 24, 1913, survives. One wonders if MacNaughton's previous admonition to Shaw that incriminating correspondence be destroyed was the cause.

It is unclear when, but Calumet & Hecla managed to plant a spy within the ranks of the WFM locals. "Operative No. 1" reported to C&H on the daily activities of the union, as if taking minutes at each meeting.

DECEMBER 21, 1913.
Clyde Taylor and Witmer were speakers at Italian Hall. Keep up heart until after Christmas ... Victory will shine in your face. Must hold meetings all through the district instead of parades.

On Christmas Eve, *The Daily Mining Gazette* ran an article about some recent gift-giving in the sheriff's office. Sheriff Cruse was given a "handsome and costly" gold watch by the deputies who earned their keep watching over the striking workers. The watch was a "solid gold case Hamilton." It was "plain to be seen that 'the big fellow' was quite overcome" by the gift. Along with the watch, the deputies gave him a diamond scarf pin, a gold Shriner's pin for his coat, a gold-handled, diamond-studded knife and a sterling silver smoking set for his desk.

Meanwhile, MacNaughton's attorneys went to court and answered the injunction granted to the WFM. Rees, Robinson & Petermann filed an official appearance with the court, stating that they would represent the Citizens Alliance in disputing the injunction. The *Calumet News* noted the appearance of the attorneys on its Christmas Eve front page, and also wrote that WFM representatives had called the Citizens Alliance "plug uglies and gun men in the employ of the mining companies." Likewise, *The Daily Mining Gazette* ran a story on the appearance of attorneys for the Citizens Alliance, and ran the same "plug ugly" quote.

Although the injunction addressed only ten members of the Alliance by name, the attorneys who appeared on behalf of the Alliance claimed to act on behalf of 20,000 others. Without listing them all, the attorneys presented the court with a list of prominent citizens who were members of the Alliance, although it is unclear if these members had sought the publicity that came with the pronouncement. According to the Alliance attorneys, they represented more than eighty members who were not named in the injunction, including a reverend, a priest, several pastors and the president of the local university.

Also on the list of Citizens Alliance members were at least seven members of the Copper Country Commercial Club, including six who had signed the report sent to the governor—Selden, Fisher, Ulseth, Black, Frederick Guck, Petermann and George L. Price. Black was the same man who'd sent the telegram the first night of the strike, telling the governor that Calumet had been taken over by a rioting mob. And Bawden, Fisher, Guck, Petermann, Rice and Ulseth were members of the exclusive Miscowaubik Club with MacNaughton.

Death's Door

*"I would suggest that you destroy
letters such as these that I have written you."*

- JAMES MACNAUGHTON TO QUINCY SHAW -

Christmas Eve

Once off the train at the Calumet Depot, Ella Bloor, a Socialist leader who volunteered to come to Calumet, made her way to the WFM hall where 800 women were meeting. Annie Clemenc answered the door. Annie was a "big fine looking Slav girl, about 24 or 25 years old." Bloor's description of Annie as "big" is misleading; she was also called "tall Annie" as she stood six feet two inches tall.

Annie questioned Bloor and asked if she had a union card. Bloor produced a Mine Worker's Union card and a Socialist Party card for good measure. According to Bloor, when Annie saw the Socialist card, "her face lighted up and she said, 'I have one of those, too.'" Bloor said Annie was wearing a "Socialist Party" button when she answered the door.

One of the questions Annie Clemenc raised at the meeting was about a Christmas entertainment for the strikers' children. She said the children must not be deprived of their Christmas because of the strike,

and she was trying to collect enough money for Christmas presents.
Next day she went to the nearby towns of Houghton and Hancock and
collected fifty-eight dollars for the strikers' children—a brave thing to
do with the agents of the mine owners watching every move. With
the money, Annie bought mittens, stockings, toys and candy.

It should be noted that Bloor's accounts of her time in Calumet must
be tempered by a healthy dose of skepticism. Many of her stories are
exaggerated or embellished. For instance, she wrote that Big Annie
carried a huge Socialist "red" flag when leading the strikers. Hers is the
only account that didn't see it as an American flag. Likewise, she is not
mentioned by anyone in any of the testimony taken nor does her name
occur in connection with the telling of the Italian Hall tragedy by anyone
who was there, even though many describe who was on stage—where Ella
later claimed she had been.

The *Calumet News* looked with optimism on the upcoming holiday. "NO
CHEERLESS FIRESIDES IN CALUMET ON CHRISTMAS," it headlined a story
about the relief efforts. "In spite of the strike and a condition of special
poverty requiring heroic measures of relief, I do not believe there will be
a single cheerless fireside in Calumet tomorrow. I know of no instance of
need where some material relief has not been extended," the paper quoted
an officer of the Calumet Associated Charities as saying. A Salvation Army
worker weighed in similarly: "The situation has been a trying one, but I
believe it has been successfully met. The Salvation Army has supplied all
requests for assistance received from worthy poor." The charities told the
paper they'd spent more than $3,000 alleviating the needs of the poor in
Calumet as Christmas approached.

Deeper in the Christmas Eve edition of the *Calumet News*, among local
items few people would have noticed, was the headline: "NEW SCHOOL
DOORS PLACED." The news brief explained that the doors in the nearby
Hancock High School had been "repaired so that they will swing outward."
Once this change was made, Hancock High became only the second
building in Hancock that complied "with the city fire ordinance which
requires that all doors should swing outward."

The Women's Auxiliary of the WFM had arranged for the Italian Hall
to host their Christmas Eve party for the children of striking miners.
The Italian Hall had a troubled history. When it was being built, the half-
completed structure was blown down in a windstorm. Then, in 1907, the
building burned to the ground after a New Year's Eve party. The blaze

broke out after partygoers had left the building, so there were no injuries. It took the better part of a year for the Hall to be rebuilt, this time out of brick and stone. The two-story building was capped with a facade reading, "Societa Mutua Beneficenza Italiana"—the Italian Mutual Benefit Society. Everyone called it the Italian Hall. The lower floor housed a saloon owned by Dominic Vairo and an Atlantic & Pacific Tea Co. store. To enter the hall upstairs, visitors went through a stone archway and doorway on the far left side of the front of the building. There, a vestibule led to a staircase to the upper floor hall. According to newspaper accounts in 1908, the stairway was "wide and easy" to travel, and the main hall had eighteen-foot ceilings. The newspaper account claimed that all the doors to the building opened "outward." Five years later, few would ever agree on which way the doors to the Hall opened.

The party took place in the second floor of the building, above the saloon and the Atlantic & Pacific grocery store. At two o'clock children began arriving, in groups and with friends, often accompanied by a mother or the mother of a friend. At first, all anyone needed to enter the Italian Hall was some form of identification showing an affiliation with the WFM. Elin Lesh watched the door and checked to make sure that only children of strikers got in; she even turned away a few children who were not related to WFM members.

By three o'clock—Calumet & Hecla time, a half hour faster than the rest of the world—Lesh went inside the main hall to help with the festivities on stage. She asked some of the men standing in the vestibule at the top of the stairs to watch and make sure only union members and their families were admitted into the hall. Once she left the area, however, the rule was not enforced. That afternoon there were almost always people standing in the area at the top of the stairs. The landing was in front of a ticket window and there were swinging doors to the right side of the landing that led to the main hall.

Inside, there were rows of theater seats facing a twenty-foot-wide stage. Toward the back of the hall, tables and chairs had been brought in to accommodate more guests. As the afternoon progressed, hundreds of people entered the hall. On stage, there were two scantily decorated trees and a piano. At one point, a young ballerina danced on stage for entertainment. They played the piano and sang Christmas carols in English, Finnish and other languages. Many, if not most, of the audience only spoke English as a second language. Important stage announcements were repeated in English and Finnish.

A play had been planned, but the number of children in the hall became large and the crowd was restless. The decision was made to start handing out presents early. The plans called for another party for the adults to follow the children's program. A woman on stage announced that children could come up on stage and get their gifts. Many children ran straight to the stage. Others stood in line to the right side of the stage and went up the stairs of the stage in turn. The children received presents and candy; the gifts might be the only ones they would receive that Christmas.

The children were then sent off stage to the left side of the room, where they went down some steps to a narrow hallway that ran parallel to the main room. Some children sneaked through the line more than once until a woman on stage noticed; she asked a Finn to watch the doors to make sure the children left the stage area once they'd gotten their candy. Although no one had taken a headcount at the door, some estimated there were as many as 700 people in the hall, with perhaps 500 or 600 children.

Some children left the hall after getting their presents, but most stayed to see what else was on the schedule. Some families visited with friends and neighbors. Groups formed based on common language; a few Italians discussed the news at the top of the stairs. A group of Finns sat in chairs on the landing, likewise outside the main room. The noise level inside was remarkable. Women on stage could not hear each other speak; they worried their announcements could not be heard more than a few feet from the stage. Some of the men on the landing had gone there to get out of the noise. Others stood on chairs to look for their children in the crowd.

Anna Lustig was ten feet from the hall door when she saw a man burst in and yell, "Fire, fire!" Although the man frightened her and set off a stampede toward the door, Lustig noted that the man was wearing a Citizens Alliance pin. Lustig frantically looked around for her five children and realized that one had been swept up in the rush to the doors.

John Burcar, a twelve-year-old, stood nearby and was facing the door when the man stepped in and yelled, "Fire." Burcar had just come from the stage where he'd gotten his Christmas gifts and was coming down the hallway toward the landing at the top of the stairs. When the man yelled "Fire," Burcar was only two feet away from him Burcar noted that the man was wearing a hat pulled low over his eyes and had a mustache. He saw a Citizens Alliance pin on the man's breast pocket. Burcar stayed near the wall as the man fled down the stairs, followed by a mass of people from within the hall. When the landing cleared, Burcar made his way to the back of the hall and climbed down a fire escape.

Mary Koskella was a little further inside the hall than Lustig had been, and she clearly saw the man come in. He yelled "Fire" and then ran out. Those around her began repeating the cry, in English and other languages, and pushing toward the stairs. She noticed that the man had a hat pulled down toward his eyes and he had a white pin on his coat, although she could not read what it said. She did not join the swarm toward the stairs and survived, along with her children.

Hilda Forester was searching for her children when she headed toward the stairs to see if they had stepped out of the hall. There, she saw the man step into the hall and yell, "Fire." The man wore a dark coat and a cap pulled down toward his eyes. A Citizens Alliance pin was on his coat. Thinking that her children were already out of the hall, Forester ran after the man as he headed down the stairs. Although the man escaped the crush, Forester did not. She was pinned against the wall by the mass of bodies and lost consciousness from the weight bearing down on her. She regained consciousness inside the hall, seated in a chair. She had no idea who placed her there or how long she'd been unconscious. Her children survived.

Ted Taipalus was ten years old, attending the event with his father and five siblings. He sat in the theater seats with his brothers when they heard the cry of "Fire." Although his brother Ed refused to run—he said he wouldn't leave his seat unless he saw smoke or a fire—Ted and Bill, who was twelve at the time, scrambled for the stairs. They nearly made it out of the building, but got bogged down by those who had fallen and were struggling on the stairs. Ted and Bill were pinned together near the bottom of the stairs but were near the top of the pile of bodies. They could breathe, but those around them were screaming and dying. Ted began to holler, but Bill assured him it wasn't necessary and calmed him down. The two held onto each other until the pile was untangled. He would find out later that evening that his two sisters had died on the stairs.

Mary Lanto was carrying her eighteen-month-old child around the hall and was standing near the stage when the panic began. She did not hear anyone cry "Fire," and had no idea why everyone began rushing for the stairs. She placed her baby on the stage and tried her best to stay out of the current of bodies flowing toward the door. The noise level was incredible. During the stampede, Lanto saw Theresa Sizer step from the stage onto a desk and wave her arms at the crowd. Lanto could not make out what Sizer was saying but interpreted the frantic motions as gestures for people to flee the hall. Even so, Lanto pressed against the stage hoping she could find a safe way out of the building with her baby. She and her baby survived.

Not far from Lanto, seven-year-old Henry Snabb stood with his cousin near the stage. They had already received their gifts when the panic started. Henry had no idea what to make of it: He heard people crying "Fire" but thought the woman on stage was yelling that there was no fire. Henry and his cousin started running toward the stairs when Henry's father caught them both and held them back. They soon realized how close they came to dying. They stood and watched as the rescue efforts brought injured and dead back into the hall. It was a memory that would stay with Snabb for decades.

Paul Jakkola was among the Finns who stayed outside the doors to the hall at the top of the stairs during the party. He saw the man come up the stairs and step through the doors into the main hall. He'd stood only two feet from Jakkola who could have reached out and touched him. Jakkola noticed that the man was wearing a cap pulled down over his forehead, had a mustache and a Citizens Alliance pin on his dark coat. Jakkola saw the man shout "Fire" and then run back down the stairs. Jakkola followed the man and stepped into Vairo's saloon to see if there was a fire downstairs. Jakkola didn't see where the man went after he ran out into the street.

Charles Olsen was looking for his wife and children in the crowd and stepped up onto a chair for a better view. As he scanned the hall, he looked toward the door just as a man stepped through the doors, yelled "Fire" and ran back out of the hall. The man wore a cap and a dark coat with a white button, which Olsen believed to be a Citizens Alliance pin.

Peter Lanto was another Finn who stood outside the main hall at the top of the stairs. Lanto spoke little English and could not make out anything being said inside the hall because of the noise level and because of the mix of languages being spoken. When the rush of people came though the landing, Lanto was pushed backward down the stairs.

Walter Lahti was thirteen years old and went to the party with his mother, brother and three sisters. Walter was the oldest of the five children; their father was a miner who'd gone to Canada to find work because the union strike benefits weren't enough for the family to survive. Walter and his brother volunteered to go up on stage and get presents for the sisters so their mother could take them home rather than have all of them stand in line. As it got near time for the two to go up on stage, the commotion broke out behind them. Walter didn't hear what anyone said but he saw his younger brother bolting into the crowd. Walter ran after him and headed down the stairs. Partway down, he got caught but managed to keep his arms in front of his body as the mass of people pressed in on him. Stuck, he could breathe, but he had no idea where his brother had gone. Next to him was another young boy who calmed him down by telling him to ignore the yelling and screaming going on around them. Walter thought the floor in the staircase had given way because his feet were not resting on anything: he was being suspended by those around him.

After an hour and a half, Walter was freed and brought back into the hall. Ghastly images confronted him. People were being brought into the hall and laid on the floor or placed in chairs. Some were dead, some were injured. Many of the dead had their eyes open, and Walter could not tell which were which. He ran to the back of the hall and climbed down a fire escape. He was in such a hurry that he leapt from the bottom of the escape and slammed into the ground. Dazed from the fall and what he had just seen, he sat on the ground for five minutes before heading around the building to go home. There, he ran into his younger brother, who had apparently headed into the crowd and then turned around before reaching the stairs. He went down the fire escape instead. Walter's brother had been outside the entire time, waiting for word on Walter!

The pileup on the stairs caused a mass of confusion in the street as well. Others saw deputies pushing people away from the doors to the Italian Hall. Although they may have meant to keep people from going in and adding to the confusion, their actions fueled the anger and hatred that had been brewing all year. A man named Jalmer Olsen watched from the street as the deputies roughed up a Finn who was trying to get into the Hall. They stood between the man and the doors and when he persisted, one of the deputies grabbed him by the neck and dragged him away. Olsen followed and saw the deputy shove the Finn and say: "If you come I will have you thrown in jail." After a few minutes, the two of them walked back toward the Hall. When the deputies saw the Finn return they began beating him with their clubs. Olsen and the Finn ran off into the night. Olsen later returned with the others from the neighborhood and watched as the stairs were cleared of bodies.

Peter Lanto, the Finn who had been pushed down the stairs with the rush of the crowd, made it to the bottom without being injured. He remained to help untangle the bodies and help survivors from the stairwell.

A crowd began to gather on the street in front of the doors to the Italian Hall. Rumors swirled. Within the hall, some people yelled that it was the work of scabs and that "the deputies are coming." Peter Petchetino stepped outside moments before the commotion and had no idea why people suddenly began fleeing the building. He headed back toward the front entrance when he was confronted by two men who barred his way into the building. Petchetino even knew the men by name; one was a deputy for the mines. Frantically pleading to see about his wife and children, the men told him he had to wait outside; one of them had a billy club.

Anna Lustig's husband came to the entrance of the Hall and was pushed back by deputies. "I have a wife and five children up here," he told them as he tried to push his way through. Two deputies began beating him with their clubs when he continued arguing with them. "I want to know if my boys are dead," he cried.

Many had seen the man who cried "Fire," and more than half a dozen said he wore an Alliance button. Those in the street when the calamity occurred had seen deputies in pushing and shoving matches with people on the streets. Had they been trying to hold rescuers back? Did they somehow cause the bottleneck that had killed so many people? To bystanders who had just arrived, listening to the conflicting stories in so many languages, punctuated by screaming and sobbing of the grief-stricken, anything seemed possible.

A Finnish man named William Nara who ran a photo studio nearby visited the Italian Hall and the fire hall, and photographed what he saw. His photographs became some of the best-known images of the tragedy. Later, more than two dozen of them were printed onto cards to be viewed in stereoscopic viewers, which allowed them to be seen in seemingly three dimensions. The stereo cards bore captions in English and Finnish, and a stamp indicating that they were printed in a union shop. Collectors of stereo format photographs of the era point out that union labels were "nearly unheard of" during this era. Nara may have been pro-union, perhaps hoping that his photos would gather sympathy for the strikers. In fairness, it must be noted that the Copper Country Commercial Club—a prominent anti-union organization—had handbills printed by union printers as well in 1913. It may be that the printers in the area were unionized, or that the CCCC didn't view the printers' union as a problem since they weren't causing trouble at the time.

One of Nara's photos is of the Italian Hall on Christmas Day; in it, the flag on the roof is at half-staff. Others in the set include a close-up of the front doors of the Hall, entitled "The disastrous stairway." In it, the doors at the entrance of the Hall are clearly visible, and from the angle it was taken, it appears that the doors open inward. Other views show dead children laid out in the fire hall and the open graves where they would be buried. He even photographed the inside of the hall, showing overturned tables and chairs. Consumers who bought the full set wound up with a virtual documentary of the event; decades later, people in the Keweenaw hold onto these photos.

As night fell on Calumet, it seemed everyone was near the Italian Hall. Survivors staggered home or were taken to the hospital. The dead were first laid out inside the Hall and then were later taken to a temporary morgue at the fire hall a block away. Among the gathering crowd, the mayor and police were present, as were members of mine management and union officials. The *Calumet News* rushed to get a special edition out that evening. William Fisher, the county coroner, decided to convene an inquest, which required a jury of six members to help him sort out the disaster. Six members of the local community were chosen and they gathered at the fire hall to view the bodies. They were sworn as members of the jury that night, although they would not begin working on the matter for a few days.

Strangely, another fire alarm was called into the Red Jacket fire station just 45 minutes after the call had been made for the Italian Hall. A "chimney fire" was reported at the "McNaughton" house in Hecla. The log book for the fire department is still kept at the Village Hall in Calumet, and tells the story of Christmas Eve 1913, briefly, in longhand script. The name was misspelled, but the notation below read, "Hecla Superintendent." The entire run took the department only a half-hour, the same length of time they show for making runs on false alarms, meaning there was little or nothing for them to do when they got to MacNaughton's house.

The entry for the run to the Italian Hall read:

> *Fire alarm Dec. 24/13. Box 45 for Italian Hall. Disaster. No Fire. Xmas festival for children of the W.F. of miners. Fire call and a stampead [sic] following down stairway. All piling on top one another at foot of stairs. 73 lives were crushed out. Mostly children about 10 grown persons.*

For the first few days after the tragedy, the names and number of those killed in the Italian Hall changed daily. On the day after Christmas, the *Calumet News* published its "REVISED LIST OF DEAD."

1. *Ala, Herman, aged 50*
2. *Aho, Lempi, aged 8*
3. *Aaltonen, Wilma, aged 7*
4. *Aaltonen, Mrs. Oscar, aged 30*
5. *Aaltonen, Silvia, aged 4*
6. *Bronzo, Mrs., aged 28*

7. Bueff, Ilka, aged 4

8. Butala, Jos., aged 8

9. Burcar, Victoria, aged 12

10. Gregorich, Kate, aged 10

11. Isola, Mrs. Henry, aged 35

12. Jesit, Mrs. Barbara, aged 35

13. Jesit, (baby)

14. Jackoletti, Jennie, aged 6

15. Kemppi, John, aged 4

16. Klarich, Christiana, aged 5

17. Klarich, Mary (no age given)

18. Klarich, Kate (no age given)

19. Kotajarvi, Annie, aged 4

20. Kotajarvi, Amy, aged 3

21. Kalunki, (girl), aged 6

22. Kalunki, (girl), aged 4

23. Karkela, John, aged 7

24. Kalunki, Mrs. Peter, aged 35

25. Lustig, Jacob, aged 5

26. Lanri, John, aged 4

27. Lesar, Ralph, aged 5

28. Lesar, Mamie, aged 11

29. Lindstrom, Arthur, aged 12

30. Luomi, Lydia, aged 5

31. Lantto, Mrs. Peter, aged 35

32. Manley, (child), aged 4

33. Manley, (child), aged 12

34. Manley, Mrs. Herman, aged 35

35. Mihelchich, Agnes, aged 4

36. Mihelchich, Paul, aged 5

37. Murto, Matt, aged 6

38. Montonen, Edrum, aged 5

39. Montonen, Albert, aged 3

40. Millykangas, (boy), aged 5

41. Millykangas, (boy), aged 3

42. Niemala, Abram, aged 40

43. Nauer, Samma, aged 5

44. Niemela, Mrs., aged 35

45. Peteri, Mrs. Kate, aged 32

46. Piira, William, aged 5

47. Papsh, Antone, aged 52

48. Papsh, (girl), aged 20

49. Ristell, Ellen, aged 5

50. Renoldi, Miss, aged 13

51. Satio, Aliti, aged 6

52. Staduhar, Frances, aged 10

53. Smuk, Mamie, aged 7

54. Swikovietch, Nick, aged 40

55. Tueppo, Mrs., aged 42

56. Tueppo, Mamie, aged 4

57. Wuolukka, Helja, aged 42

58. Westola, J.P., aged 48

59. Taipalus, Elena, aged 6

60. Taipalus, Sandra, aged 5

61. Tallbach, Juto, aged 4

62. Jokipi, Uno, aged 16

63. Heikkinen, John. Aged 9

64. Heikkinen, (boy) aged 5

65. Heikkinen, (boy) aged 7

66. Krunie, Mary, aged 12

67. Kotajarvi, Mrs. Matt, (no age given)

68. Takola, Henry, (no age given)

69. Saari, Yalmer, aged 5

70. Lantto, (girl), (no age given)

71. Isola, Philemena, (baby)

72. _____, (girl), aged 14, died Christmas morning at home in Tamarack Junior, name not learned.

Although "revised," the list contained errors. For example, only two Mihelchich children were listed when other papers reported that three had died.

As might be expected from such a horrific event, there were injured along with the dead. Three were reported taken to the Calumet & Hecla hospital: Irene Ala, Mellie Tolvi and Lempi Kenttala. The three were aged seven, eight and nine, and were suffering from bruises and "nervous shock" from the experience. Waino Saari, a seven-year-old whose nine-year-old brother had died in the event, was taken to a hospital in Laurium, and an unidentified victim was said to have been taken to the hospital at Tamarack.

One little girl was laid out among the dead and taken to the temporary morgue at the Red Jacket Village Hall. A half-hour later, someone noticed her hand move slightly. She was resuscitated and taken to a nearby hospital.

Ted Taipalus attended the event with his father and siblings. When the cry of "Fire" was raised, he and his brother ran to the stairs and got caught up in the crush:

> *We held on to each other, side by side. The pressure was getting greater and it was hard to breathe. We kept wiggling until our heads were close to the ceiling. The moaning and groaning and screaming were awful. I even joined in on the hollering until Bill shook his head for me to stop. I don't know how long we were in that situation; I know I had a hard time breathing … suddenly I felt the pressure lessening and I felt a hand on my feet pulling me up. I had to slide backwards over people, one on top of another. Bill was still with me. We stuck together like pants and shirt.*

Taipalus got out of the building by a ladder in the back and made his way home, not realizing that anyone had died. Later that evening his father came home and broke the news that two of his sisters had been killed. It was the first time Taipalus had ever seen his father cry.

Dominic Vairo had climbed a ladder and entered the upper floor of the Hall after realizing there was a problem above his saloon. He spent several hours helping the rescue workers upstairs. Later, when he returned to his saloon downstairs, he found that his till had been emptied and much of the saloon's stock of liquor had been stolen. His infant son had been grabbed by a grief-stricken woman who insisted the child was hers. Mrs. Vairo finally convinced the woman that the month-old child lived in the building, and that her child must be somewhere else.

Slanted Reporting

"While people were lying dead all over the hall, she is reported to have said the man who gave the cry wore a Citizens' Alliance button."

- *THE DAILY MINING GAZETTE*, REPORTING ON BIG ANNIE -

The day after the tragedy, the *Calumet News* reported that "ARRESTS ARE EXPECTED:"

> *Ten detectives and a number of special operatives of outside agencies are conducting an investigation into the cause of the disaster, which it is asserted, may lead to arrests at any moment.*

The *News* does not say who the "outside agencies" were—Waddell-Mahon?—but then tells of how men in the saloon at the bottom of the stairs "clamored for liquor" and continued "yelling hilariously" while women and children were dying in the stairwell. "None of the men made any effort to assist in the rescue." These kinds of statements, which were not attributed to any particular witness or person, wove throughout the newspaper's coverage. Vairo's saloon was known as a hangout for union sympathizers, so the papers considered them fair game.

Later, *The Daily Mining Gazette* identified the detectives working on the case as the Burns and Asher Agency, one of the strikebreaking agencies hired by the mines. Not surprisingly, the Burns and Asher men never found any suspects, and they never publicly reported any accomplishments. This statement was probably written by the *Gazette* to convince readers that the mines were somehow helping in the aftermath of the tragedy.

The *Calumet News* also used the disaster to sing the praises of the Citizens Alliance and the Waddell security guards. Although some Waddells and Alliance members were present in the street after the tragedy and helped with rescue efforts, the paper made them out to be the saviors of the day:

> *Deputies, mounted police and members of the Citizens' Alliance worked hand in hand and by their untiring efforts, possibly hundreds were saved … The heroism of Captain Manley, head of the Waddell Mahon force in Calumet resulted in the saving of many lives, though he came within an ace of having his life crushed out. Through a mob of people, he surged up the fire escape and pushed his way into the struggling crowd to the stairway where he assisted in moving the dead and injured. He was so severely hurt that his life was in danger until a late hour.*

Despite being "severely hurt" he apparently did not go to the hospital. At least, the reports of those who *were* at the hospital did not mention him.

Meanwhile, condolence messages poured into the region from around the country. The governor of Michigan received a telegram from the governor of Wisconsin the day after the tragedy. Likewise, the mayor of Detroit telegraphed his sympathies and extended $1,000 in assistance. Although the offer was made in the name of the city, he said the money could be drawn "on me, care of Wayne County Home Savings bank."

The WFM members met on Christmas Day; their activities were recorded by MacNaughton's spy. According to the spy, Moyer was criticized by members for being too quiet about the tragedy. Moyer brushed off his critics and stated that the union would take care of the grieving and dead from Italian Hall. "We, the entire labor union of the United States, are going to look after them all." That same day, Moyer visited an undertaker's parlor and fainted at the sight of the dead and grieving.

The community surrounding Red Jacket was overcome with sympathy and grief, in one of the region's first unifying moments since early summer. The Citizens Alliance even gathered money and said they would provide it to any family in need as a result of the tragedy. Moyer and the WFM said they would not accept money from outsiders or the Alliance. Moyer promised the strikers that the WFM would take care of them; he was quoted: "the Western Federation of Miners will bury its own dead." He also urged "state and national executives to bring about an immediate investigation into the cause of the disaster." His refusal to accept Alliance money was understandable considering the stories swirling that the man who cried "Fire" wore an Alliance button.

Quincy Shaw heard of the tragedy sometime the night of Christmas Eve, and wired a message to MacNaughton.

> *I feel sure that even without this message you will do everything in Co's power to give assistance to the victims and their families in the frightful accident. See some way through the local papers. Will you convey my sympathy to the men and women to whom the loss is a personal one, and to the whole community who have to face such a dreadful tragedy?*

MacNaughton immediately had the telegram retyped, minus the sentence "See some way through the local papers" and gave a copy to the local papers. The *Daily Mining Gazette* ran the edited version on its front page, right below a similar condolence message from the governor.

The *Calumet News* and other media outlets associated with the mines seized the opportunity to attack Moyer and turn the event into one that would rally the community against the WFM. On December 26, the *Calumet News* told of how the Alliance's aid had been rejected even though many were in need. "Cases of poverty—families in absolute need of aid—were found to be numerous." Again, they did not cite examples or names of people who "found" these things. The attacks would get worse. They served two purposes: They roused the citizenry against the WFM and they deflected attention from trying to solve the murders at Italian Hall.

On Christmas Day, just one day after the tragedy, *The Daily Mining Gazette* ran the following ad:

$1000 Reward
ONE THOUSAND DOLLARS
($1000) REWARD,
EACH,

will be paid by the County of Houghton for information leading to the conviction of any or all person implicated in the murder of John Dally,

Arthur Jane and Harry Jane at Painesdale, Michigan, on December
6ᵗʰ, A.D. 1913.
SIGNED,
HOUGHTON COUNTY,
By James A. Cruse, Sheriff

Why—just twenty-four hours after the largest mass murder in Michigan—would the sheriff offer such a large reward for information on the murder of three men when no such reward was or ever would be offered for the person who killed seventy-three at Italian Hall?

This was the same edition of the paper that announced the tragedy in the Houghton-Hancock region. The headline: "80 PERISH CHRISTMAS EVE TRAGEDY AT CALUMET; FALSE CRY OF 'FIRE' THE CAUSE." The *Gazette* told of how the "Shout from unknown man brings panic," and estimated eighty dead. According to the *Gazette*, deputies stood at the top of the stairs and stopped the stampede of people into the stairwell—sheer fantasy, considering deputies were non-striking miners and no witnesses would place them inside the Hall until after the tragedy.

Interestingly, Sheriff Cruse also ran his ad in the Finnish language *Amerikan Suometar*. He announced a $1,000 *PALKINTO* for information in the Dally-Jane murders. The text is in Finnish, of course, and one wonders who drafted it for Cruse. In Finnish, "Palkinto" means "Prize," whereas "Palkita" would have been the more appropriate "Reward."

The propaganda efforts of the *Daily Mining Gazette* came to the fore on its front-page coverage of the disaster on Christmas Day. Below the "80 PERISH … " headline, it ran a story on Charles Moyer's actions the night before. The story said Moyer had wired the president, the governor and others, asking for an investigation into the tragedy. According to the paper, he suggested the tragedy was not caused by union members. The *Gazette* ran a sensational headline on the story that was wildly incendiary:

While Copper Country Mourns for Its Dead,
Moyer Tries to Make Capital of Disaster.
USES CHILDREN'S DEATHS TO BENEFIT HIS STRIKE.

The *Gazette* noted that Moyer told people there were witnesses prepared to testify that the man who cried "Fire" was wearing an Alliance pin. The *Gazette* dismissed this notion as preposterous and said—in another sub-headline—that "Moyer's Attitude [is] Shocking." The *Gazette* claimed: "This attempt on the part of the strike leader to make capital out of the terrible calamity generally was resented throughout the district last night." This statement made no sense. How could people in the region even know of Moyer's actions before they were described in the paper? The paper had not conducted any polls; it was merely running with the version of the story the mine managers wanted it to print.

The most amazing part of the paper's coverage of the events from less than twenty-four hours earlier is how it anticipated one of the major issues, and knew which way to start contorting the facts to protect mine management. "It is generally known that no members of the Citizen's Alliance or any others that were not identified members of the Western Federation of Miners or their families and carried their cards could possibly gain admittance to any of the meetings in the hall." It was generally known? By whom? If that was the general belief, it was false as will be shown shortly. However, that the *Gazette* knew to trot out this defense on the first day following the calamity is telling.

The Finnish-language newspaper *Tyomies* published an extra edition on Christmas Day, recounting the events at the Italian Hall. The paper said its story was based on the first phone call to Hancock with the news. "As customary, there are several kinds of rumors and stories in circulation about this disaster and without doubt they are exaggerated and some entirely without foundation." Having gotten the disclaimer out of the way, *Tyomies* went on to say that people were accusing deputies of preventing escape and rescue, and that they had beaten people with clubs at the doors to the Hall. Some reported the fire whistle blowing before the panic; could it have been a false alarm, deliberately raised to instigate panic?

The Detroit News ran coverage of the tragedy on Christmas Day. It was a more balanced story, headlined: "COPPER COUNTRY OFFICERS SEEK MAN WHO CRIED 'FIRE'; 80 DEAD—Little Children of Miners are Trampled to Death and Suffocated in Wild Panic." The paper did not attack Moyer like the English-language papers of the Keweenaw did. Along with the main story, the reporter wrote a sidebar about coming across Joe Mihelchich outside the Italian Hall. "Strength of Giant Is as Water as He Looks on His Dead."

> *On his knees in the snow, stroking with trembling hands the dead faces of his three children, crushed to death in the panic at Italian Hall, Joe Mihelchich shook and coughed and sobbed, a broken man.*
> *Through the minds of those who saw the grief-wrecked spectacle ran another scene of five months ago. When the strike was still young,*

the story of Joe Mihelchich, powerful of build, wielding a thunderbolt of death, determined for a principle to blow himself and 200 others to eternity.

Two hundred Jackson troops under Capt. Blackman held the Red Jacket mine shaft house. Outside the shelter, in the twilight, hundreds of strikers shouted defiance and curses until the mob cry grew in menace and the nerves of the soldiers strained to the breaking point. There was a sudden rally, the strikers were dispersed and Joe Mihelchich, ringleader, was brought captive to the shaft house.

Herculean of torso, face pale with the pallor of years underground, Joe stood sullen. While his captors were calling civil authorities over the phone he reached for paper and tobacco and rolled a cigarette, so the military men said. He asked a soldier for a match and it was given him. Keenly alert, he awaited his chance, struck fire, and with a sudden movement, snatched from his pocket two sticks of dynamite bound together, detonated and short-time fused. Two of the soldiers were on him before he could put the match to fuse. He threw them off with ease, but a half dozen more were on him. The mad giant threw them about like manikins. The fire was extinguished in the palm of a corporal.

It was this man, strong and desperate, whose muscles refused to bear him up as he mourned, dumb with agony, over the bodies of his three children.

The tragedy was front-page news across the nation. Understandably, details varied from story to story; many said there were eighty dead. One story that gained traction in the first day after was of a "bearded man" with alcohol on his breath who cried "Fire." Later, this would turn into a man with a mustache. Some papers listed the names of those killed, but early reports identified only fifty or so. There were also reports that seventy-four bodies were at the fire hall and that as many as six more were carried away by relatives. There would never be agreement on the number of dead from the tragedy.

The *New York Times* reported "an intoxicated man staggered to the door of the little hall and shouted 'Fire!' " It also reported that there were 700 in the hall and that eighty died, and fifty-six were children. "More than seventy-five dead have been accounted for ..." and the *New York Times* said seventy-four bodies were recovered from the building but another dozen had been carried away. They even had the name of a witness: a "Mrs. Caesar" who claimed to have grabbed hold of the man who cried

"Fire", but that he got away after he started the panic. She claimed she could identify him if she saw him again.

The following day, *Tyomies* put out another extra edition covering the Italian Hall disaster. *Tyomies* was a major newspaper in the Keweenaw at this time. Its circulation had topped the 10,000 mark in 1911, and it was known in the Finnish community for being aligned with workers' interests. In its December 26 story, *Tyomies* reported that a man wearing a Citizens Alliance pin had run up the stairs to the hall, cried "Fire! Fire!" and then made his escape. *Tyomies* said it had interviewed five eyewitnesses. After the man had made his escape, the witnesses said, deputies stood at the bottom of the stairs, obstructing the escape of the people inside the Hall, and laughed as the tragedy unfolded. One man told the paper that a mining captain—presumably not on strike, and not on the side of the strikers—had told him "something horrible" was going to happen Christmas Eve. According to the *Calumet News*, *Tyomies* had written: "From all we have seen, we learn that it was a put up job by the Citizens' Alliance."

The troubled history of Italian Hall was detailed in the *Calumet News* the day after Christmas. The Italian Benevolent Society of Calumet was the oldest such organization in the area, and their meeting place had been plagued with troubles, according to the story. When a local contractor named John Wilmus first set out to build a wooden structure for the society, a "terrific wind storm demolished it." It had to be completely rebuilt the following year. Then, six years before the tragedy that took seventy-three lives, the Hall had burned to the ground. On New Year's Eve 1907, the building succumbed to flames during one of the worst winter storms the area had ever seen. When spring arrived, the Italian Hall was quickly rebuilt, this time in stone. The new stone building was dedicated on October 10, 1908.

Many people of Calumet gathered to adopt a resolution regarding the tragedy. Their resolution was published in the *Calumet News* the day after Christmas, just forty-eight hours after the disaster.

> *On the day, which throughout all Christendom is set aside as a day of rejoicing over the birth of the Savior, Calumet, stricken to the heart by an almost unbelievable catastrophe, stands mourning by the side of its dead.*
>
> *All bitterness and ill feeling that has existed in this community during the past months is wiped away by one great, common affliction. Today the people of Calumet can only see their neighbors,*

their brothers, their sisters, and their little children staggering under an almost unbearable burden of distress and grief.

It is not for us today to try to ascertain the cause, nor to speculate as to how it might have been prevented. With feeble mortal minds we grope about in vain, we try to penetrate the veil which hides the logic and the reason for the acts of God, and from the hearts of our people the cry goes out today, Why must this overwhelming blow at this time strike a community and a people who have already suffered so much? And there is no answer. We can only bow our heads and know that somewhere, sometime and in His own good way, He Himself will give the answer.

And so today we have gathered here to devise some means of alleviating the suffering of our people. With the kindliest feeling for those who offer it, we ask no outside help. These are our own people and this is our sacred privilege to care for our dead and comfort the living.

Therefore, in order that the purpose of the meeting may be carried out in an orderly way and that the heartfelt sympathy of not only this community but of the entire state and nation may be conveyed to each one of the afflicted, it is

Resolved, That the chairman of this meeting and the presidents of Red Jacket and Laurium appoint a committee of twelve as a relief committee;

That such committee meet at once and choose a chairman, a secretary and treasurer;

That such committee be instructed to take charge of the work of receiving contributions and extending to the sufferers all comfort and assistance in their hour of distress;

That such committee may at any time call for all such assistance as it may need in its work and,

That by this meeting, representing the people of Calumet, such committee is bidden Godspeed on its errand of mercy.

Immediately after the mass meeting adjourned, a committee was put together as called for by the resolution. They also agreed to assemble a committee of women to help with the relief work. It was said that these committees "will do their utmost to console those in each home which is stricken by death."

Prosecuting Attorney Lucas began an informal investigation, and was soon overwhelmed by the number of witnesses and their varying accounts of what had happened. Although he had not had a chance to sort through all the witnesses available to him, he issued a statement on December 26:

> *In view of the many conflicting statements that have been made with regard to the origin and cause of the Italian Hall disaster, I wish to state to the public at this time that I have personally interviewed a great number of witnesses who claim to have been in the hall at the time the trouble started and others who came to the scene of the disaster within a half a minute or so afterward. The result of my investigation is that no person deliberately entered the hall and cried "Fire" for the purpose of causing a panic.*
>
> *The person or persons who did cry "Fire" in the hall, on the evidence gathered so far had some ground for believing that there was a fire in the hall. One of the occupants of the flat in the rear of the Italian Hall made an affidavit to the effect that she and her servants had both seen a little boy carried down the rear fire escape with the top of his cap on fire and shoulder and chest covered with ashes.*
>
> *I assure the public that a thorough investigation of this matter is being made and the blame will be placed where it belongs. I will do everything in my power to see that the matter is given a thorough and searching investigation, and any person who knows anything concerning it should notify my office.*

On December 26, the coroner spent the better part of the day filling out death certificates for the dead. Most of the documents gave the cause of death as "Killed Dec. 24, 1913, at Calumet, Mich. in a jam caused by a false cry of Fire by someone, at present unknown." Some contained variations on the "jam," and forty-three contained no description for a cause of death. There were seventy-three death certificates filed by the coroner in the case, each giving the age and other information on the deceased, as well as where they would be buried. All seventy-three certificates gave Lakeview Cemetery as their final resting place.

The *Calumet News* began its efforts to clear the Citizens Alliance of culpability on December 27. According to the *News*, affidavits had been gathered that disproved the charge that someone wearing an Alliance button had first raised the call. The *News* wrote that affidavits had been secured by prosecutor Lucas and others; witnesses were willing to testify that the cry of "Fire" came from within the hall. That statement alone was flawed, for it presupposes that a man wearing a Citizens Alliance button couldn't have gotten into the Italian Hall. Nonetheless, one witness—Theresa Sizer—was quoted as saying that the man definitely did not wear a button. It is unclear if the reporter writing the story was basing it on affidavits that he had seen or if this was all hearsay. It is an important point, though: Mrs. Sizer would later testify that she did not notice if the man had a button on and, more importantly, no one at the inquest would ask her if she had signed an affidavit.

It is possible that the *Calumet News* was mistaken about the existence or contents of affidavits as they described. Lucas mentions one affidavit, but he never produced it at the inquest later. A few affidavits were taken, though. In the archives at Michigan Technological University in Houghton are at least three: Mrs. Mary Chopp, Bridget Brown and Jenevive Sandretto each signed one-page statements. Chopp was near the stage when the cry of "Fire" went up from the audience; she did not see who said it first. Brown was near the stage when she first heard the cry of "Fire" but did not see who said it. Sandretto was on the stairs heading out of the building when the commotion started; she did not hear a cry of "Fire," nor did she go back into the hall afterward. Two of these affidavits, however, were signed on December 29, the first day of the inquest—several days after the story in the *Calumet News*. Only one is dated in such a way that it may have existed at the time the *Calumet News* wrote its story. Brown's was dated December 27, and she claimed that a child fainted moments before the call of "Fire" went up. She did not see who cried "Fire," nor did she testify at any of the hearings. Strangely, none of the three were called to testify. None of these witnesses saw the boy whose cap was on fire. That witness, presumably Mrs. Meyers, did testify, but she was never asked if she had signed an affidavit for the prosecutor.

According to the *Calumet News*, a "mass" of such affidavits would be made public at the inquest when it was convened. The *News* opined that the story about the man wearing a Citizens Alliance button was "traced to Annie Clemenc, the woman who became notorious through her connection with violence during the strike. In the presence of physicians and newspapermen, while people were lying dead all over the hall, she is reported to have said the man who gave the cry wore a Citizens' Alliance button." The newspaper does not quote her—it quotes someone else as quoting her. Unfortunately, the statement attributed to Big Annie became part of unalterable legend. For example, one author wrote in 1984, "Annie told a *Mining Gazette* reporter that a man wearing a Citizens' Alliance button had come in the main doors and cried, 'Fire!' "

The *Gazette* does not mention Annie in its first day of coverage of the tragedy, on December 25. It did not publish the following day and it wasn't until December 27 that the *Gazette* claimed: "Mrs. Clemenc, on Christmas Eve, told the *Gazette* reporter at Calumet that she saw a man rush into the door and cry 'Fire' and that he wore a Citizens' Alliance button." A few days later, the *Gazette* wrote: "On the night of the panic she made and repeated and spread the statement that the alarm of fire was given by a man who wore a Citizens' Alliance button." Of course, if the unofficial spokesperson of the WFM had made such an important charge in the wake of the tragedy, it wouldn't have taken the *Gazette* a few days to remember that she had made such a claim. It is also noteworthy that each time the story is told—attributed to Annie—it gets more detailed and more gruesome.

Later, Annie would testify that she never saw the man who cried "Fire," but that she had heard the cry. The *Gazette* knew the mining interests hated Big Annie, so attributing the claim to her may have seemed a good thing to do. According to the *Gazette*: "She made it in the hall with people dying all around her."

The Daily Mining Gazette launched into its best efforts to smear the WFM and to deflect attention from the Citizens Alliance. According to the *Gazette*, because of the WFM's refusal to accept outside aid, "children are dying of starvation" in Calumet. They do not give the names of any children who had actually died, nor do they explain why a child would die of starvation within forty-eight hours of the tragedy.

Amazingly, that seventy or more people died in the Italian Hall was not the only tragedy of Christmas Eve 1913, according to the *Gazette*. The paper was more upset by charges linking the tragedy to the Citizens Alliance. "That any set of men could have the temerity to bring such a charge against the leading citizens in one of the most enlightened and God-fearing communities in the country is one of the worst horrors of the disaster." Of course, the bigger question must be asked: The Citizens Alliance was the nameless, faceless organization with no leaders that supposedly sprang up from the grass roots all on its own. Who exactly was so mortified by the accusation? Perhaps the paper knew who was behind the Alliance.

The *Gazette* continued to hammer on the point of whether a Citizens Alliance member could have gotten into the Hall. Calling the notion "ridiculous" and "illogical," the paper repeated the falsehood that entry to the Hall required showing a WFM membership card. It also claimed that

Dominic Vairo from the saloon below vouched for those turned away, as if many people were initially turned away by a doorkeeper.

The *Gazette* also boldly announced as "fact" that "it was proven by the investigations of Prosecuting Attorney Lucas that the Moyer charge that the disaster in the Italian Hall was caused by the Citizens' Alliance was a base untruth." As noted previously, Lucas had suggested he was leaning that way, but had also indicated he was carrying on his investigation and sought information from any witnesses to the event.

Meanwhile, Sheriff Cruse must have read the *Tyomies* articles—or someone Finnish told him about them—and he requested a local justice of the peace named Eichern to issue warrants for the arrest of the reporters and editors of *Tyomies*, on the charges of publishing material to incite a riot. Most troubling, he claimed, was that the article had accused Cruse's deputies of "murder." Actually, the article had said something to the effect that deputies at the doors to the Hall "prevented the egress" of people from the Hall, contributing to the disaster. Although many had made that charge, Cruse thought it wise to shut down the paper.

Cruse's men appeared at the *Tyomies* office on Saturday, December 27 and arrested four men they found there; they returned the following day and arrested another. In all, the justice issued twenty warrants for employees of *Tyomies* or others "interested in the publication of the *Tyomies*."

At their arraignments, the men could not post $1,000 bond each and were jailed. For the time being, *Tyomies* was out of business. Another Socialist publisher from Milwaukee offered to continue printing the paper, but *Tyomies* passed on the offer. As for the fifteen who weren't arrested, many of them lived outside the state of Michigan, and it appeared that the issuance of the warrants merely served to keep them from returning to the area. When the story appeared in the *Calumet News* on December 29, it was anticipated that a few more arrests would be made, although the subjects of the other warrants were not identified.

No one seems to have pointed out that the Citizens Alliance had actually incited riots at its rallies through incendiary speeches by Doelle, Rankin, Petermann and Rees, and no one had been charged despite the obvious connection between the rallies and the violence that immediately followed. Yet, when *Tyomies* published reports that did not instruct anyone to break the law, they were arrested for inciting violence that was never called for nor instigated. The Keweenaw had become a bizarre place, if one wanted to guess which laws might be enforced.

Interestingly, the *Gazette* found itself at a loss for words trying to explain why an entire newspaper—albeit a competitor—was shut down for publishing a story based on statements of witnesses who repeated what had been said many times before in the community. Rather than publish the statements that were the basis of the arrests, the *Gazette* wrote:

> *The copy of the translation of the article contains so many statements of such a cruelly shocking nature and so inflammatory in their details that its republication at this time would seem inadvisable.*

It was a great solution; the *Gazette* could claim it was protecting the community by not reprinting the material. The *Gazette* listed the men arrested: Servias Nuomivorri, Arthur Vuorela, Matt Kokko and John Alanne. Although Nuomivorri was the editor, Vuorela was only the man who ran the printing press, and Kokko and Alanne were the secretary and the bookkeeper. Of the four men, three of them had no control over the editorial content or policy of the paper. Their court appearances were scheduled for January 3.

The *Gazette* also did not mention how the *Calumet News* had published equally incendiary—albeit anti-union—lies immediately after the tragedy. It was the *News* that had written that men in Vairo's saloon "clamored for liquor" and were "yelling hilariously" while the people in the stairwell were dying. "None of the men made any effort to assist in the rescue," the *News* had falsely stated.

One problem exists in knowing exactly what *Tyomies* reported: It was published in Finnish and copies are rare today. Archives that have *Tyomies* on microfilm do not have a copy of the issue in question. All that exists are the translations made by people at the time, which most likely have varying degrees of accuracy. One translation of the article was sent by Citizens Alliance leader J.W. Black to Governor Ferris. According to Black's translation, the headline read "Eighty Dead"—instead of "83 Murdered." Then, deputies "thrust across the open door some obstacle (which our informer could not see) and waving their hands, laughing and jeering, prevented the children and others from coming out of the hall." It is noteworthy that the *Tyomies* article did not say the doors were held shut, as has been claimed by many writers since, but that the deputies blocked the egress with the doors open. This portion of the story was not true, but that is not the point. The various stories attributed to *Tyomies* were wildly different, and often untrue.

Later, the same translation read: "There was no fire anywhere and this fire alarm and the remarkable conduct of the deputies at the hall door was then, someones, or somebodys invention to disturb the celebrations of those 'undesirables,' possibly 'unintentionally.' " Writing that the result—seventy-three dead—was perhaps unexpected by the person or persons who cried "Fire" makes *Tyomies* a little less militant than it has often been made out to be.

One version of the *Tyomies* articles is presented as stating a headline of "83 MURDERED." Underneath, "Christmas Celebration of Strikers Children of Calumet made into a Crime sacrifice for Capital." The story placed blame on the Alliance and stated that gunmen blocked "the passage of the panic stricken people." According to their sources, more than twenty gunmen gathered in Vairo's saloon with the intent to cause the massacre. One ran into the hall and cried "Fire" while another called in a false alarm of fire to the Red Jacket fire station. The *Tyomies* article reached its zenith with the charge that a deputy picked up a child, twisted the child's neck until it snapped, and threw the dead youngster under the feet of the panicking crowd. As crazy as it seemed, *Tyomies* pointed out that its sources were prepared to testify to what they had told the paper and—more importantly—"As usual about this holocaust many different rumors and stories are current, which no doubt are magnified and perhaps altogether untrue."

Tyomies raised another interesting point: In the weeks preceding the Italian Hall tragedy, the blowing of the fire whistle had been used to call together the Citizens Alliance. When the Citizens Alliance rioted and plundered the South Range headquarters of the WFM, their actions had been preceded by the fire alarm. According to *Tyomies*, it had been widely publicized that the fire alarm could mean either a fire or that the Citizens Alliance was declaring some sort of emergency need to gather its members. In light of the past actions of the Alliance, could the blowing of the fire whistle in Calumet on Christmas Eve have caused WFM members to believe that they were about to be attacked by the Alliance? *Tyomies* posed this possible explanation for the sheer panic that appeared in the hall that evening:

> *But the first question that came into the mind of this writer was: Why and Who gave the fire alarm at No. 45, which means that there is a fire in that district where the Italian Hall stands—though there was no fire anywhere?*
>
> *Then I recalled vividly the night of the 11th of December when*

the fire alarms were given in Houghton and Hancock—though there was no fire anywhere—calling together the members of the Citizens Alliance who seized the rifles from the Houghton Armory and started, possessed by a senseless fury, for their nightly marauding expedition to South Range.

But what caused this uncommon terror which compelled people to thrust themselves and others straight into the mouth of death? We are told someone called "Fire!" but no fire was to be seen, not even smoke.

"Continuous blows of whistle mean that Citizens Alliance members should come together at Armory." This signal system was published in the papers. Children have read it. " ... now those bad men are coming here." They had heard about the double murder of Seeberville, the treble murder of Painesdale, about the attack into the dwelling and office of the Secretary of the Union in South Range ... fearful thoughts filled the minds of the people ... away, away from here, they come, deputies, gunmen ... they shoot ... they kill ... and panic-stricken they rushed to the door—out?—home?—safety?—to death.

There is no question that the fire whistle was blown to gather deputies and other anti-union forces before the Alliance riot in South Range. Further, both the *Calumet News* and *The Daily Mining Gazette* informed their readers that the Red Jacket fire whistle would also be used to gather Alliance forces in an emergency. The use of the fire whistle to gather the anti-union forces was so widely publicized, it was mentioned on the front page of the *Chicago Daily Tribune*. The fire whistle had been blown the night of the Italian Hall tragedy, but there was little evidence that anyone within the Hall had heard it before the panic began. If it had been blown as part of a greater conspiracy, it would have been ineffective, and played no part in the calamity.

A simpler, less sinister explanation is available for the blowing of the fire whistle. With people running from the Hall yelling "Fire," someone on the street merely called in a fire alarm. In such a situation, it would not be necessary to assume that someone wouldn't call in the alarm under the circumstances, even without evidence of a fire being visible.

Twisted Justice

"It is not charity we want; it is justice."
- E.A. MCNALLY, WFM ATTORNEY -

Moyer's Kidnapping

Charles H. Moyer, president of the WFM, had been outspoken about the Italian Hall tragedy and who he thought was behind it. He said witnesses were prepared to testify that someone wearing a Citizens Alliance pin had raised the cry of "Fire" at the Italian Hall. Moyer—like *Tyomies*—was repeating what he'd been told by eyewitnesses. The Citizens Alliance wanted to deflect attention away from accusations that they had caused the tragedy and focus instead on their offers of financial help. Moyer suggested any money offered by the Alliance was done from an unclean conscience. Members of the Citizens Alliance met and discussed what should be done about Moyer.

The Citizens Alliance felt that it could take drastic measures against Moyer, especially with the local papers castigating him constantly. Moyer and Charles Tanner, another WFM official, were staying at the Scott Hotel in Hancock, south of Calumet. On December 26, Sheriff Cruse stopped in to see him along with a group of men—Citizens Alliance members—that included

A.E. Petermann, the attorney for C&H and the fiery speaker from the Alliance rallies. Also present were M.A. Thometz, John H. Rice, Joseph Wills and Frank Schumacher, all well-known Alliance members, and James T. Fisher, who was both an Alliance member and signatory of the Copper Country Commercial Club report. The party later claimed they merely wanted to discuss Moyer's refusal to accept charity from the Citizens Alliance. Later, one of the members even typed up a memorandum of the discussion—most likely toning down what was actually said—and listing the members of the party who visited Moyer in his room. The memo neglected to mention that the party had been escorted to the room by Sheriff Cruse.

Moyer reiterated to the men that the WFM would "take care of its own unfortunates." They demanded that he publicly renounce any statements that blamed the Citizens Alliance for the Italian Hall tragedy. He refused. After a brief discussion in which Moyer made it clear he would not change his mind, they threatened him. "He was then asked by a member of the Committee if he fully realized the feeling that existed here in the copper country toward [him] and was asked if he was willing to assume the responsibility for anything that might occur within the next day or two because of the attitude he had taken." Then, the men left. It was a bizarre request to make of Moyer: The Alliance wanted him to renounce statements he had made which were true. He *had* been told by witnesses that the man who cried "Fire" had worn an Alliance pin—these witnesses would later so testify under oath on more than one occasion. Further, the Citizens Alliance members were clearly violating Judge O'Brien's order of December 10, which prohibited them from using "any means whatsoever" of threats or intimidation aimed at getting Moyer to leave the area against his will.

They had "barely left the room" when a "mob" of twenty men appeared at Moyer's door. Later, Moyer said the mob arrived within four minutes of Cruse's departure. It was about 8:35 p.m. The mob entered Moyer's room and began beating him and Charles Tanner. Someone slugged Moyer in the back of the head with a handgun, which discharged. The bullet lodged in Moyer's left shoulder. The mob then dragged Moyer, bleeding from the head and shoulder, more than a mile to the train station in Houghton. Along the way, the riotous crowd crossed the Houghton-Hancock bridge, where several members yelled that they should throw him over the side. Someone else had a noose and suggested they hang Moyer.

There was an even larger mob at the train station. The Citizens Alliance members had blown the fire whistles in Houghton. Moyer's kidnappers placed him onto a train bound for Chicago. Two members of the mob boarded the train with him to make sure he did not try to get off before it left the Copper Country. The two men were identified later in the newspapers: Deputy Sheriff Hensley and Deputy McKeever. The two were so open about their participation they even paid for the tickets of Moyer and Tanner! Hensley and McKeever wore their deputy badges and Citizens Alliance buttons the whole time. They ordered the porter not to allow Moyer to send any telegrams until after they'd gotten off the train, which they did at Channing, Michigan, not far from the Wisconsin border. Before they left, Hensley told officials on the train to send any bills incurred by Moyer and Tanner, including medical bills for the gunshot wound, to Sheriff Cruse.

The men who attacked Moyer were not only breaking the law—kidnapping, assault—but were also violating Judge O'Brien's injunction of December 10. The men told Moyer to "leave the country forever." At the first opportunity, Moyer wired his story back to his union and got word out to the press about being attacked. The *Calumet News*—ever friendly to the mine owners—called the story "Not Substantiated" and said Sheriff Cruse believed "Moyer's sudden departure at this time was a frame-up on the part of Moyer to excite the sympathy of the outside world." According to the *News*, the manager of the hotel went so far as to say that when Moyer left the hotel, "he was all right."

Not to be outdone, the *Gazette* claimed Moyer's assertions were so unbelievable that they were being "ridiculed." The truth of the matter—according to them—was that Moyer had skipped out on his hotel bill. Apparently, the *Gazette* thought Moyer—after being shot and beaten—should have stopped at the front desk and settled up with the hotel keeper before being dragged a mile and a half to the depot.

News coverage by *The Daily Mining Gazette* and the *Calumet News* in 1913 was so flawed it cannot be relied upon for factual coverage of any of the day's events. At best, their coverage showed the mood of the day to some extent, but also what the mine managers thought and feared. That they published outright lies—saying Moyer wasn't shot, for example—shows how unreliable they are as a source of facts. The newspapers refused to call Moyer's kidnapping anything other than a "deportation," as if his forced exodus from the Copper Country was lawful.

In an amazing act of propaganda, the *Calumet News* declared two days later in a headline: "MOYER WAS NOT SHOT IN HOTEL." It based its assertion on an interview it said it conducted with William Bellke, the proprietor of the hotel. Bellke was quoted as saying:

> *If Mr. Moyer was shot while a guest in this hotel it is news to me and any of the employees about the building. I was standing near the doorway about the time that Moyer stated he was shot. If a shot was fired, I was in a position where I would surely see and hear it, and as the doors on the different floors of the hotel were open, any guests in the hotel at the time would also have heard the report of a revolver. After Moyer left I entered his room and the only disorder which would show a scuffle had taken place was an overturned chair.*

The *Calumet News* didn't question the statement, or even compare it to the one that he'd made two days earlier that Moyer was "all right" when he left the hotel. In fact, they appeared to endorse it with their headline even though the statement is highly suspect on its face. Which door was Bellke standing near? Moyer's? For him to have seen the shot, he would have to have been inside the room or looking through an open door. He merely states he was near "the doorway." Even if he was near the doorway of Moyer's room, it does not mean much if the door was closed.

Bellke was probably nowhere near the attack, if he was even in the hotel that night. If he had been near the event, he would have known that Moyer had been shot. Everyone who saw Moyer in the next forty-eight hours witnessed him bleeding from the gunshot wound and beating. It would have been extremely foolish for Bellke to argue such an untenable position if he were there and knew Moyer had been shot: Whether a person has been shot or not is not something subject to much debate. Most likely, someone approached Bellke and asked if he'd be kind enough to cast some aspersions on Moyer; as a local businessman, Bellke could hardly have resisted. It was an indicator of the times that Bellke would make such a bold and false statement and the *Calumet News* would run it as a headline, as if it were true.

As if offended that the *Calumet News* was having all the fun attacking Moyer, the *Gazette* reached new lows on December 28: It began a story on Moyer, identifying him as "Charles H. Moyer, the inhuman monster of the strike in the copper country."

To continue the smear of Moyer, Sheriff Cruse likewise denied that Moyer had been shot. "Cruse Denies Moyer Charge" headlined a story where Cruse "indignantly denied" Moyer's recent assertions. "He has been unable to date to clear up the mystery of Moyer's unexpected departure Friday night. He found there was no disturbance in the Scott Hotel at the time Moyer is supposed to have been taken from there."

The various fictionalized versions of what happened to Moyer were distributed by the pro-mine magazines and newspapers: Some of them were fabulously inventive. Elbert Hubbard, who published his own magazine and was known for his folksy and whimsical take on things, was so pro-mine that he wrote in May 1914 that the Citizens Alliance was merely talking to Moyer when they found the need to disarm him. He had not one, but two guns on his person which he violently refused to give up. In the struggle, he accidentally shot himself in the back. Of course, it was all untrue.

The *Calumet News* failed to raise the two most obvious questions relating to the statements of Bellke and Cruse. Wouldn't Bellke be inclined to deny that one of his guests was beaten and shot by a gang of men who barged into the guest's room? Wouldn't Cruse be inclined to deny that a gang of men passed by him in the hallway of the Scott Hotel, beat and shot the man Cruse had just visited, and dragged the man for a mile through the streets while Cruse offered no assistance? Even if Cruse failed to see any of the incident—which is only possible if he was the most incompetent sheriff who ever lived—it happened on his watch, while he was in the neighborhood. The questions didn't seem important enough for the *Calumet News* to ask.

Although Cruse was not in the party that beat and shot Moyer, it is highly likely Cruse knew who was. After all, Cruse's group of more than a dozen men was in Moyer's room moments before the second group arrived. Cruse's suggestion that he did not see the group of more than twenty men entering the hotel—and did not hear the gunshot or see the subsequent melee—is absurd. Bellke's statement is just as unbelievable.

The train carrying Moyer made a brief stop in Milwaukee, and reporters flocked to Moyer's car to get his story. Reporters noted his "pillow and bed linen were soiled with blood from wounds in his scalp and back." When he arrived in Chicago, Moyer spoke with the press in greater detail. He made the shocking allegation that MacNaughton had been at the train station in Houghton. MacNaughton denied the allegation and told the paper he had an airtight alibi: He had been visiting fellow Miscowaubik Club member Henry Brett that evening. Around the time of the assault on Moyer, the two were walking over to the club for a talk with some unnamed gentlemen. The paper did not challenge MacNaughton on his alibi.

The most amazing part of Moyer's story is that he said the shooting was probably accidental! "I do not think that anyone shot me deliberately. I think that the gun used in hitting me on the head was discharged during the action." Moyer's statement was perhaps the biggest show of self-restraint on the part of any person or organization during the entire strike. The fact that he had been beaten by a mob and shot could easily have been used for propaganda purposes—and no doubt Moyer would get some mileage from the story—but to attribute the shooting to an accident could only be seen as a statement of honesty. It also calls into sharp contrast the statements made by Cruse that the entire situation was invented by Moyer for sympathy; if Moyer wanted sympathy, he certainly wouldn't blunt the impact of the story by saying the shooting was an accident.

When Moyer spoke with reporters a few days later, he presented them with a signed statement that bore two signatures. One was a Dr. Story's who confirmed he treated Moyer for the lacerations on his scalp and a gunshot wound. The other signature was of a deputy sheriff from Chicago who vouched for the injuries to Moyer. Even with the mounting evidence that Moyer had been shot and run out of town, the *Calumet News* continued treating the story as if what had happened were unclear.

On December 27 MacNaughton wired Shaw. His coded telegram said Moyer was "put on board [a] train last night ... They were accompanied by a couple of others who will see to it that they reach destination." His intimate knowledge of what the kidnappers planned to do with Moyer, and his facetious use of the word "put" shows MacNaughton knew much more about the incident than he was letting on. This telegram is significant for another reason. It is the first correspondence written by MacNaughton that survived to be archived years later. Letters from the eight-day period preceding this—encompassing the Italian Hall tragedy and the funerals— somehow disappeared.

On December 29, Shaw sent MacNaughton a telegram asking about the Moyer affair, as he had read about it in the newspapers. He wanted to know "how much of this is a frame up to gain sympathy?" MacNaughton immediately wrote back and told Shaw he had issued a statement to the Associated Press denying that he had been present at the attack on Moyer. He did not answer Shaw's question.

The WFM posted handbills shortly after Christmas recounting the events of the past few days and calling for the union to gather. One poster promoted a mass meeting to be held on New Year's Day, where speakers would address recent events:

> *Chas. H. Moyer, president of the Western Federation of Miners, was shot and forcibly deported from Calumet, Mich., Friday night,*

December 26th by the Waddell-Mahon gunmen and members of the rich anarchists of Houghton county known as the Citizens' Alliance. This same gang of law breakers are responsible for the awful calamity on Christmas Eve when 85 human beings mostly children were smothered to death in a panic caused by the action of a man who wore the badge of the Citizens' Alliance. This man yelled "fire" through the door of the hall where the children and parents were about to celebrate Christmas Eve ... The truth about this terrible catastrophe and the suffering of the miners in their fight against the starvation wages of the copper barons of Michigan for the past five months will be told.

The Funerals

The funerals for more than seventy people created logistical nightmares for the community. Most of the dead were to be buried at the Lakeview Cemetery, west of town, one of the few pieces of land not owned by C&H in the county. To bury that many required an enormous amount of digging. A hundred miners, accustomed to spending days hammering a few feet through rock, found themselves in the cemetery digging trenches for caskets. The day before the main funerals, the workers marched from Red Jacket to the cemetery, with picks and shovels over their shoulders. On December 27, four victims were buried. Most of the dead would be buried on December 28.

The number of dead also taxed the supply of caskets. Local funeral homes appealed to neighboring communities for extra caskets that could be spared on short notice, particularly smaller ones for children. Shortly before the funerals, a delivery was made on a sleigh "stacked with coffins."

Six churches were chosen for simultaneous funerals, with rites in various languages and religions. Three churches were Finnish, and the others were Italian, Croatian and Slovenian. Seventy of the dead were to be remembered on Sunday, December 28.

A committee had been set up by the striking miners to coordinate the funerals. The dead were taken to the churches for the services. To handle the large numbers, the services were held in groups. The service for the Taipalus children included a row of twelve coffins at the front of the church. From the churches, the coffins were brought out and placed into hearses, most of which were horse drawn. The children's coffins, which would comprise the bulk of the procession, were to be carried on the shoulders of men from the community. The papers anticipated that it might be the largest such procession ever seen in the region. From the six churches, the individual processions would flow into one mass procession, which would then head out to Lakeview Cemetery. Some of the coffins were carried three miles to the cemetery.

As with the other confusion surrounding this tragedy, the details of the funerals are similarly muddled. The papers said six churches would have funerals for seventy dead, but they reported later that only four ceremonies were held for fifty-nine victims. Still, six churches held services—either funeral services or memorial services—and the ensuing procession was awe-inspiring. From the individual services at the churches, the hearses and other vehicles slowly traveled to where the various processions joined on Pine Street. Annie Clemenc led the way—as she so often did—carrying her huge flag, now draped with crepe. Behind her were fourteen hearses—every one available in the community—followed by three undertaker wagons and then a lone truck carrying three coffins. Some of the hearses were actually sleighs and some were wheeled. These vehicles carried the older victims; one was flanked by eight women as pallbearers for their fallen Women's Auxiliary comrade.

There was little snow on the ground. While the funeral progressed, a very light snow began to dust Calumet. Many of the stoic miners and townspeople managed their composure as the procession rolled slowly by. Church bells in Red Jacket and the nearby communities tolled in the distance. After the vehicles headed out of town, many in the crowd were overcome by what followed. Forty-four children's white caskets, covered with flowers, each carried by a group of four miners, filled the streets. Although many of the coffins were small, the weight of the task appeared crushing. Grown men, some who pushed trams for hours without complaint, collapsed in grief and handed the coffins to those next to them. Tears streamed down the faces of many strike-hardened miners. The silence along the roadway was punctuated by sobbing and crying. Some couldn't handle the image before them and struggled home before the procession was finished.

A contingent of singers followed the coffins: Fifty men chanted hymns in a style that had been brought over from the Cornwall mining districts, including "Rock of Ages" and "Nearer My God to Thee." Following the singers were miners from the local mines as well as many who had come in by special coach from the iron mines elsewhere in Michigan. They were followed by a band and then others in the community who wanted to walk to the cemetery. The procession was so long that it had reached the cemetery gates two miles out of town before the last members had joined in. The road between Calumet and the Lakeview Cemetery was lined with mourners the entire distance.

Once at the cemetery, the spectators saw trenches that had been dug for the coffins. Although the graves would be marked individually, it would have been too difficult to dig all of the graves separately. On the Catholic side of the cemetery there were three trenches for twenty-five caskets. On the Protestant side there were two trenches for twenty-eight coffins. The remaining dead were buried in individual graves. At graveside, people addressed the mourners in several languages. Eulogies were delivered in Finnish, Austrian, English and Croatian. The comments were brief. The attorney for the strikers, E.A. McNally, addressed the issue of charity they had turned away from various outsiders and from the mines. "It is not charity we want; it is justice."

Much was made of the fact that Clarence Darrow, the famed labor attorney, had not come to Calumet for the funerals. It was well known that the WFM had invited him and asked him to deliver a eulogy. However, Darrow was frightened after hearing what had happened to Moyer. In a message sent to the local union members just hours before the funeral, Darrow expressed fear that he might be kidnapped and run out of town by the Citizens Alliance if he came to town at that time.

As unthinkable as it might seem, some wondered if there might be more violence the day of the funeral. Five hundred fellow miners—iron workers from the nearby iron fields of Negaunee and Ishpeming were not on strike—chartered a special train and arrived for the funeral. Ella Bloor claimed later they had come to the Copper Country "ready to protect their fellow workers."

One spectator, Mrs. W.H. McGrath of Houghton, fell while attending the funeral. She fractured her left arm.

The Gaumont film company sent a man to Calumet to film the funeral and procession. The company filmed many news events and rented the films out to "moving picture houses" and anticipated the film of the huge funeral would be well received. They sent a man named William Hair to town with filming equipment and he captured as much of the day's events as he could, moving his cumbersome cameras from place to place. The lighting the day of the funeral was less than ideal for the ancient movie camera, especially as the day progressed and the sun set over Lake Superior. At the end of the day, Hair left the film canisters in his room and went to dinner. Someone broke into his room at the Michigan Hotel in

Calumet and stole the film; the canisters were later found in the middle of the street, but the film was missing. Most people suspected the Citizens Alliance and mine management as the most likely culprits. Everyone knew how incendiary the film of the funeral would be; it could only serve to help the cause of the strikers.

Later, the film turned up and Hair said he had emptied the film canisters, anticipating foul play. He had safely hidden the film in the WFM office safe and managed to get it back to Gaumont for distribution. The film was shown in theaters across the country along with other presentations on the tragedy, promoted by pro-union forces. Some included slides of photographs taken in the Red Jacket fire hall, showing rows of dead children laid out for identification.

The Coroner's Inquest

William F. Fisher, coroner for Houghton County, called an inquest and impaneled a jury of "good and lawful men" to help him sift through the testimony of witnesses. One problem was that Fisher was not a doctor and had no medical training; it was not uncommon at that time for a coroner to have no medical background. Previously, Fisher had been elected justice of the peace; similarly, he held that post with no legal training. Again, it was not an uncommon situation. The jury members were chosen and sworn in on the night of the tragedy, although they would not conduct hearings for a few days. On the panel were Jacob Talso, Dan Yauch, Jacob Pessonen, Bert Barnham, George T. Talbot and Matt Chopp.

They met for three days—December 29-31—in the Red Jacket town hall and also occasionally convened in the Italian Hall itself. Although their stated mission was to inquire into the manner of death for those who perished on Christmas Eve at the Italian Hall, it is clear from reading the transcript of their proceedings that they had an ulterior motive. In fact, the coroner had already noted causes of death on most of the death certificates that he had filed the day after Christmas. As the inquest unfolded, however, the local media—primarily the pro-management papers—reported on the investigation in such a way as to make it look as if the inquest absolved many of the initial suspects. Of course, no one had named individuals by name, but many had suggested a member of the Citizens Alliance had raised the cry of "Fire," while others suspected Waddell-Mahon men of being involved.

Fortunately, the inquest was recorded by a court reporter who wrote down the dialogue between the jury and the witnesses, and later typed it up. In 2004, Lawrence J. Molloy transcribed and published a copy of the transcript: "Italian Hall: The Witnesses Speak."

Although the inquest would last three days, the *Calumet News* was confident enough of the outcome to publish a headline—on the afternoon of the inquest's first day—declaring, "MAN WHO CALLED 'FIRE' DID NOT WEAR ALLIANCE BUTTON, INQUEST SHOWS." The text of the article is as skewed as the headline, and people not present at the inquest would get a completely different view of what was actually being discovered—or not—than people who were there. For example, the paper wrote of the first witness, John Sandretto:

> *He testified that he came from Wolverine and went to the Italian Hall to escort his son home. He and Batisto Rastello entered the saloon beneath the hall and remained there for a period of fifteen minutes. While seated at a table he heard the stamping of feet and the overturning of chairs. He ran to the entrance to the hall leading to the stairs and beheld a mass of humanity at his feet and extending nearly to the top of the stairs. All about him were crying and yelling. Above the moaning and groaning, he heard the cry of "fire." At his feet a little boy was pleading to pull him from the mass.*

Sandretto's testimony was not so clear—nor as articulate—as the paper suggested. How he actually testified:

> *I had a partner there, one of my friends, up from Wolverine. I went down from Wolverine in a funeral, in a parade, and then I was over here in the street we come back; all the parade come back. I went in the Italian Hall look for my baby, my boy; I had a boy up there. I was tired and dry and was in the saloon for about fifteen minutes with my friend Batisto Rastello. Then we was there, take a glass of beer sat down by the table and I hear upstairs big noise, running of children, something like that. I was going up to see for my baby.*
> **Q: How did you try to go up?**
> *A: The saloon door leading upstairs. Then I opened the door and I see the stairs full of people coming down; chuck full from the bottom up to the top. I was surprised and asked him "What you got the people over here?" All kids crying and then I hear a voice. I can't tell where it came from, outside or upstairs, because it was a big voice, say –*
> **Q: What did the big voice say?**

125

> *A: I hear "FIRE." I say "Where is the fire? What trouble you got upstairs?" Then I come back, one fellow took me by the shoulder and said "Get Back."*

Interestingly, Sandretto did not testify to some of the things the *Calumet News* says he did. He did not have a little boy at his feet pleading for help. He did not hear the "stamping of feet" and the "overturning of chairs"—unless the words "big noise" can be translated into those two phrases. This sort of mistranslation—from what each witness actually said to what the paper wanted them to have said—was consistent throughout the inquest.

This, of course, leads to the headline exonerating the Citizens Alliance on the first day of a three-day hearing. The second witness of the day was Mrs. Theresa Kaisor. Her name is variously given as "Sizer" and "Caesar"—most likely because "Kaiser" is German for "Caesar" and to those who only heard the name, it might be spelled "Sizer." The disparate spellings of names is an issue that permeates every aspect of the Italian Hall tragedy.

How did Kaisor testify regarding the Citizens Alliance pin others claimed they saw? She said she saw a man who cried "Fire;" she went to him and asked him to be quiet as there was no fire.

> **Q: What kind of a looking man was he?**
> *A: He was a little about the medium height. He had a dark mustache and his suit was more of a dark color.*
> **Q: Did he have an overcoat on?**
> *A: I do not know.*
> **Q: Did he have a "Citizen's Alliance" button on?**
> *A: I do not know.*
> **Q: Did you see one?**
> *A: I did not see any. I do not know if he had any because I did not notice.*
> **Q: You did not tell anybody you saw a "Citizen's Alliance" button on?**
> *A: No I did not. I only passed the remark that I did not notice anything on him.*

Simply put, Kaisor did not notice if the man was wearing a button, and considering the circumstances, her testimony was credible.

The next two witnesses were Mr. and Mrs. Charles Meyers who ran the Atlantic & Pacific store on one side of the lower floor of Italian Hall. They were in the store when the commotion occurred and neither could testify as to what the man looked like who cried "Fire." Mrs. Meyers did, however, give one of the crazier versions of the tragedy: She claimed she saw a little boy carried from the Hall whose "cap" was on fire. No one bothered to ask her why someone would carry a boy out of the building without first removing his burning cap.

Likewise, the next three witnesses were downstairs at the time in question: Florence Moore was in the kitchen with Mrs. Meyers (and also said she saw the boy with the flammable cap, although she said she only saw "sparks" coming from it), and Dominic Vairo was the proprietor of the saloon on the ground floor that bore his name. Vairo's partner also testified. None of them was asked about the presence of a Citizens Alliance pin, presumably because none of them was in the Hall when the cry of "Fire" was made.

Big Annie testified next. They asked her if she saw anyone wearing a pin and she said that she had not. She testified that she had not seen the man who cried "Fire;" she only heard him. The newspaper accused her of being "one of the women who was first to sound the cry that the man who cried fire wore an Alliance button." Yet, the coroner's jury did not ask her if she had made any such statement previously. This is the kind of oversight that casts the entire work of the inquest into doubt: Witnesses in court proceedings are often asked about statements they have made in the past. The newspapers had been reporting that Big Annie had said the man wore an Alliance pin; shouldn't they have asked her if she'd made such a statement? And if so, why had her story changed?

Several others who did not see the man who cried "Fire" testified and were not asked about the Citizens Alliance. Then Mary Coscalla testified that she saw the man.

> **Q: Did you see any button on him?**
> *A: Yes I saw a button on him but I don't know what it was. I cant [sic] tell you what button it was. It was a white button but I can't swear to what it was.*
> **Q: How could you see from where you were?**
> *A: I did because it was a big white button. My little girl told me, "What did that man come in and holler 'Fire'? He had one of those white buttons on."*

Later, she testified:

> *A: I cant [sic] tell you what button it was, if it was one of the "Citizens Alliance" buttons or not. I cant [sic] swear on that. It might have been something else. It was a white button but cant swear what button it was, he was not near enough to read it.*

Everyone knew that the Citizens Alliance buttons were white. They did not bother to call Mary's daughter to testify, even though her mother said that she had seen the pin as well. To try and bolster the argument that there were no Citizens Alliance buttons being worn in the Hall, the *Calumet News* cites John Fretz, who testified that he was there that day. One problem with his testimony is that it is unclear where he was standing.

Q: How many people were in the hall that afternoon?
A: I don't know. I was outside in the hall.

Although he was not there in any official capacity—wherever he was standing—he was questioned about a pin.

Q: Did you see anybody come up there with a Citizens Alliance button?
A: Lots come up but did not notice anybody with a button.

From the testimony above, the *Calumet News* determined that "Inquest Shows Untruth of the Rumors Following Disaster" in that the man who cried "Fire" "DID NOT WEAR AN ALLIANCE PIN." This, from one witness who said she did not know, another who said she was not in a position to see, and from a man who said he did not notice. The finding would not appear as clear as the headlines suggested, in light of the witness (and the daughter who was not called to testify) who did see a white pin—similar to a Citizens Alliance button—but could not make out what it said. To be fair, the paper should have said the jury was still out—which they were, and would be for at least two more days.

It is necessary to review the news coverage by the national newspapers to see how contorted the local coverage was. The *Chicago Record Herald's* headline read the complete opposite: "SWEAR SHOUTER OF 'FIRE' WORE ANTI-UNION MARK." There, the reporter began coverage with the sentence: "Two of a score of witnesses testified before a coroner's jury today that the man who caused the Christmas Eve disaster wore a white button like the badge of the Citizens' Alliance."

The next day, the inquest reconvened and even went over to Italian Hall for some testimony. Again, reading the *Calumet News* coverage of the inquest gives a completely different view of what actually transpired in the hearings. The headline summarizing day two of testimony read: "TALKED WITH UNION MEN BEFORE GIVING TESTIMONY—Two Witnesses at Inquest Into Italian Hall Disaster Make This Admission." Perhaps the *Calumet News* was concerned its readers might have been unconvinced by the headlines the day before that the Citizens Alliance was not involved. This day, they claimed "MAJORITY SAW NO BUTTON" under the headline claiming that the union was trying to influence testimony. One of the first paragraphs read:

> *The preponderance of the testimony introduced today showed, like that of yesterday that the cry of "fire" came from some person who was in the hall throughout the Christmas entertainment and who did not wear an Alliance pin.*

This statement was far from the truth. The first witness was a twelve-year-old girl named Annie Rader. She described the man wearing a grayish suit waving his hands at the beginning of the panic, but she could not hear what he said. The *Calumet News*, inexplicably says she called his suit "gray or green." She called it "grayish." As for a Citizens Alliance button, "I did not notice any if he had one."

John Auno testified he was near the top of the stairs when the cry of "Fire" was heard and as he rushed out of the Hall he was knocked unconscious. He did not see anyone go into the Hall wearing a Citizens Alliance pin while he was at the top of the stairs. The paper reported this, but left out that Auno had only stood at that spot for five minutes before the rush.

The next witness, John Antila had just arrived when the panic occurred. In the minute or so he was in the building, the inquest jurors thought he might have been looking for a Citizens Alliance pin.

Q: Did you see anybody going in there with a "Citizens Alliance" button on?
A: I did not notice. I did not take time to notice.

The papers thought it odd that Antila had spent the few minutes inside the building struggling for his life, rather than looking at the accessories worn by the men in the crowd.

Often, the papers exaggerated testimony of witnesses. Mrs. Joe Mihelchich, who lost three children in the disaster, was asked about the man she saw crying "Fire." She described him: He was dressed in black, but she only glanced at him briefly before she began to look for her children. Still, they asked her:

Q: Did you notice if this man had a button on of any kind?
A: I did not see him quick enough to see.

This statement was translated by the *Calumet News* into "She saw no fire and no one in the hall who wore a white button." It was true that she had seen no fire. They also added that she said he "wore whiskers," which is nowhere in the transcript.

The strangest testimony of the day was given by a woman who is listed as Mrs. Emmer Ratz in the transcript. Mrs. Ratz was apparently Hungarian, and her English was not strong enough for her to stumble through questions-and-answers in English as the jury had done with the previous witnesses. Another woman slated to testify that day, Theresa Czabo, acted as an interpreter for her. Through her interpreter, she claimed that three gunshots were fired into the building moments before the cry of "Fire" went up. She was in the barroom of the Hall, she said. The inquest then moved over to the Italian Hall and investigated to see if there was any evidence of gunshots; there was none.

Ratz appears to be the only witness to use an interpreter, perhaps because she was fortunate enough to have someone present—another witness—who was bilingual when she was called to testify. Ratz's testimony is also remarkable for how well it reads: If the reader did not know it was through an interpreter, one would have thought she spoke perfect English. Strangely, there is no mention of an interpreter in the transcript; that fact is found only in the newspaper coverage of the inquest. It is worth noting that the papers are believable when they report facts that are either innocuous, or do not appear harmful to their pro-mine position.

Theresa Czabo testified next. She was adamant that she saw a man wearing a dark coat who yelled "Fire," wearing an Alliance pin. He also wore a hat, she testified. Similar testimony came from the next witness, Mrs. Anna Lustig. She was insistent that she had seen a Citizens Alliance button on the man.

What about the headline that suggested witness coaching by "Federation Officers?" Anna Lustig was recalled: her entire testimony follows:

Q: Did you tell the officers of the Union?
A: Yes sir.
Q: Where were you when you told them?
A: They came to my home.
Q: Who came to your home?
A: Oppman and McNally.
Q: You gave them the same story as you gave here?
A: Yes sir.

Although the papers insinuated that the testimony was tainted by her having told the story previously, there is no evidence—at least from this exchange—that Mrs. Lustig altered her testimony based on contact with the WFM. There is nothing in the law suggesting the testimony of a witness becomes unbelievable merely because they have told the testimony to someone before they were called as a witness.

The paper also wrote that the next witness, Hilda Forster, "admitted she had conversed with Attorney McNally and Mor Oppman before being called to the stand." The paper does not state what they conversed about, or why that was made into a headline and not the fact that Mrs. Forster identified the man who cried "Fire" similarly to many of the other witnesses.

Q: When did you talk to Oppman?
A: This morning.
Q: What did Oppman say to you?
A: I got to tell the truth. I told him the same story as I told you.
Q: Was Oppman down your house?
A: No sir, he was not. He was up here (Italian Hall).

The *Calumet News* wrote that the next witness, John Jokopii, testified that he saw "no one with an Alliance pin and heard no one cry 'fire.'" Actually, Jokopii said that he had seen no one with an Alliance pin standing outside the hall in "the hallway" and that he had only been there for "a few minutes."

Arthur Haapa had testimony attributed to him by the *Calumet News* that he did not give. "He saw no Citizen's Alliance button on any one." Haapa never said anything about a Citizens Alliance pin; the inquest jurors never even asked him about it. It is quite clear that the *Calumet News* was content to print the facts as they wished they were, and to attribute them to witnesses who never said any such things. Presumably they could get away with it because the non-English speaking witnesses did not read the *Calumet News*, and printed versions of the testimony would not be widely available for quite some time.

John Kuppala had his words twisted as well to meet the *Calumet News* editorial slant. When he described what it looked like as people were fleeing the Italian Hall, he testified: "It seem as though everybody was crazy." The *Calumet News* changed this to, "He asked the door keeper what caused this rush and the reply was, 'that the people were crazy.' " Thus, one man's broken-English description of the scene was turned into an official pronouncement of the "door keeper" of the event.

The third day of testimony was the last. On December 31, the inquest jury heard more testimony and then retired to deliberate. The *Calumet News* began its account of what happened on the last day of investigation: "Today's testimony at the inquest into the Italian Hall disaster probe consisted chiefly of a general refutation of the statement that the man who raised the cry of 'fire' wore a Citizen's Alliance button." The paper—in an eerie prediction—said: "It was also established that no one but members of the union, Woman's Auxiliary of the federation or their children could gain entrance to the hall at any time previous to or during the entertainment."

To support that contention, they cited witness John Aho: "The door keeper knew him personally, and he did not have to produce a union card." The *News* skipped the testimony before Aho's—Raymond Berg—who testified:

> **Q: When you got in the hall did you have any trouble getting in?**
> *A: No.*
> **Q: What did you do? Did anyone have to show a union card?**
> *A: No.*
> **Q: Did you have your union card with you?**
> *A: No.*
> **Q: Did anybody ask you anything when you got upstairs?**
> *A: No.*
> **Q: Did you walk right in?**
> *A: Yes sir.*

Aho's testimony that he didn't show a union card to get in—because "the door man knew me"—somehow overruled the directly contrary testimony that immediately preceded it. And, because Aho's testimony could be so easily ignored and contorted, the *News* also threw in for good measure: "No one, he said, had worn a Citizen's Alliance pin." He had never said such a thing, nor had he been asked.

What about the notion that the inquest had found tight security to get into the Italian Hall before the tragedy? There hadn't been any damning testimony on day three, despite the pronouncement of the *Calumet News*.

John Aho testified he was not asked to show a union card to gain entry to the Italian Hall. Raymond Berg did not show a card either; in fact, he did not even bring his card with him to the party. John James walked in unquestioned. Ina Karna was never asked to show a card. Annie Sandretto was not asked for a card and did not have one with her that night. Charles Saari—the man the jurors suggested was watching the door—denied that he was asking anyone for union cards to get into the Hall. Charles Olson said he showed his card to get in, but then pointed out that "there was a lot that did not show their union cards." He then identified Saari as one of the people he showed his card to. John Fretz did not show his union card to get into the Hall. Nine-year-old Battista Brusso got into the Hall with two of his friends and none of them had union cards.

As for the position that proof of union affiliation was required to get in, there was a bit of testimony. A nine-year-old girl name Kate Belcher said she was turned away at two o'clock because her parents weren't affiliated with the union. Annie Rader, a twelve-year-old girl, testified she had to show a union card to a woman at the front door, also at two o'clock. Frank Rouseau, who worked in the building, testified that two women came into the saloon after being told they could not get into the Italian Hall without evidence they supported the union. Rouseau said that when he vouched for the women, they were let in by the woman watching the door.

He then identified the woman at the door as Mrs. Lesch, who also testified. When she was examined, however, the inquest jury did not ask her specifically if people who could not show identification were barred from the party. Instead, they asked:

Q: And if you knew that he did not belong to the Union he would not be admitted into the hall?
A: No, if he did not belong to the Union.

Yet, Lesch testified that she was on stage handing out presents when the cry of "Fire" was raised. She is the only person who appeared to have actually turned people away from the door, and possibly, she was the only person who even asked anyone for identification to gain access to the party. Either way, one wonders why the jurors were so hesitant to simply ask: "Did you ask for identification for every person that tried to get it?" "When you left the door, who took over for you?" Unasked questions have no official answers.

Dominic Vairo was asked if he, too, didn't go upstairs to vouch for people being turned away for lack of union credentials: "No, I never went upstairs." Mary Coscalla said she had to show a union card to get in—but she admitted she was not a member of the union or auxiliary, and the card she showed was a man's.

There were nine witnesses who said it was unnecessary to show union identification to get into the party. Opposing this were two children who were denied admission by a woman who may have been watching the door very early in the day but was not watching the door later (and one person saying he vouched for someone to get past this same woman at the door)—and one non-union member who used someone else's card to get in. From this, the inquest jury drew the conclusion:

> ... that no person or persons was allowed inside of the hall where the celebration was being held without producing a union card or having some member of the union vouch for them before they be allowed admittance.

In law, this is a conclusion drawn "against the great weight of the evidence." Still, the *Calumet News* had successfully predicted—a day in advance—exactly what the inquest would find, even though it was an absurd result.

One wonders what prompted the *Calumet News* to write that there had been such an overwhelming amount of evidence to support the notion that security was tight at the Italian Hall. In reality, the bulk of the evidence went the other way. Was the *Calumet News* protecting the Citizens Alliance—funded by its benefactor, MacNaughton, and comprised of countless friends and allies of the mines and the newspaper?

For readers without a legal background, the issues raised by omissions in the transcript and testimony may not be shocking at first. To those more familiar with the American legal system, however, the manner in which the inquest was conducted was nothing short of derelict. This was compounded by how all hearings of this sort were handled in the early 1900s. There were no recording devices, so testimony had to be recorded by hand. Then, it was typed into transcript form. If someone wanted copies made, they had to type them as well, using the original as a guide. The amount of manual labor required for each copy was tremendous, guaranteeing that mistakes would find their way into later iterations. For instance, copies of the inquest testimony would give different numbers for the dead—seventy-three and seventy-four—within months of the original transcript being created.

The first obvious flaw in the testimony itself is that it was conducted in English without interpreters, while many—if not most—of the people inside the Hall on the day of the tragedy primarily spoke other languages. The only exception was Mrs. Ratz—the Hungarian—who happened to precede a bilingual witness who spoke Hungarian and translated for her. No other witnesses testified through interpreters.

The fact that so many people in the community did not understand English was well known by those on the jury. Everyone in the area knew of the various languages spoken there, and how few understood English. It was even a common theme in MacNaughton's letters to Boston. On one occasion he explained why he declined to speak to a group of non-union miners: "Many of those present would not understand what was being said." He derided a speech given locally by Mother Jones to the striking workers: "Only a very small proportion of the trammers can understand her." Regarding an announcement read to a gathering of strikers at the Palestra auditorium he wrote: "The resolution was undoubtedly written by Miller, and if read in English, as it probably was, at the Palestra, could not be understood by 5% of the people there and the importance or purpose of it could not be understood by one-half dozen of the people there outside of the ring-leaders themselves."

The number of Finns on the list of the dead is telling—forty-nine—and likewise, many of the survivors spoke little or no English. Yet, when they were called to testify, they were questioned in English and they responded— often poorly—in English as well. That many in the Hall did not understand English even came up twice during testimony. Ina Karna recounted how the children were told to enter the stage from one side and then exit the other. First a woman made the announcement in English; then a man made the same announcement in Finnish. Mrs. William Keljo told the jurors how the crowd of children was told to be quiet and calm after the call of "Fire" had been raised. Again, the instruction was given both in English and Finnish.

It was unusual that an inquest was held without interpreters for the foreign-speaking. When this coroner oversaw the inquest into the Seeberville murders in August 1913, five interpreters were used to help witnesses testify. Certainly, the coroner could have found interpreters for the Italian Hall inquest, if he had wanted any. When the United States Congressional House subcommittee came to the Keweenaw a few months later to investigate the labor troubles, they also provided interpreters to many of the witnesses—some of whom had struggled to testify without them at the coroner's inquest. Further, when investigating the shooting of Margaret Fazekas, the sheriff and his deputies took statements from witnesses through interpreters.

What indication do we have that the witnesses would have been better off if they'd testified through interpreters? Recall the first witness, the Italian John Sandretto, who told the jury how he came to be in the Hall:

> *I was tired and dry and was in the saloon for about fifteen minutes with my friend Batista Rastello. Then we was there, take a glass of beer sat down by the table and I hear upstairs big noise, running of children, something like that. I was going up to see for my baby.*

Joseph Czap testified:

> *When he come in holler fire I was out looking for a bondman for Oppman, and I was over there, I don't know the names, Austrians or Croatians, and the fellows started to talk to the man, wanted a bondsman, we come down after. We heard a whistle and as soon as we come in the kitchen we asked "Wheres the fire?"*

Peter Pichittino's testimony is in similarly stunted English. What did he see?

> *Did not see no children and not my wife either. Then all those I seen come out from the stage I don't know, I cant tell, lots of children there waiting for their presents so as soon as this Peter got his pail, I don't know who it was, there was a big bunch I see all these children look after this man for that pail and all at once I turned around myself and looked and see all the people running by the door and did not hear anybody hollering.*

Mrs. Ernesta Mirchisio sounded confused enough to cause a juror ask:

Q: Do you know what the word fire means?
A: Yes sir.
Q: What does it mean?
A: It means fire. That word I know what it is.

Peter Mirchisie's version of events:

> *Just what I see when a big noise like that I look around for the baby, I hear anybody cry I go inside to get my girl; wanted to go back in that little hall that goes back to the toilet, that finally goes to the hall, and went to see if I could get my child, and then I cant [sic] go; and then I go and see for my wife and cant [sic] go either; everybody pushing.*

One is left to wonder how detailed the witnesses' testimony would have been had they testified in their native languages. Clearly, these witnesses had vivid memories and good vantage points to see what they were being asked to describe. They were simply at a loss for words—or language—to express it adequately.

The language barrier was just one of the many problems that the jurors chose to ignore as they plowed ahead with their investigation. Another similar issue arises when a reader of the transcript sees an answer given that needs clarification—yet the jurors do not ask for any. As a result, the witnesses gave vague answers. Presumably they could have given greater detail if they had been asked. One recurring issue relates to doors in the Italian Hall. There were doors to get into the building from the street, doors that entered the vestibule from the adjoining saloon, doors at the bottom of the stairs, doors at the top of the stairs into the hall, doors leading to the ticket room, and other doors scattered about the building.

Antonia Carous said she heard someone cry "Fire" three times:

Q: Where was this voice that cried fire?
A: By the door somewhere.

The jurors do not ask her *which* door. Likewise, Mary Coscalla said she heard a man who "hollered fire" after coming "to the door." They asked her:

Q: Where were you at the time?

A: There was chairs between that door and I was there between those chairs, about twenty or thirty feet from the door.

Likewise, none of the jurors ever asked any witnesses which way the doors at the bottom of the stairs opened. Even though the inquest visited the Hall, no mention was made regarding the direction of the doors' operation.

John Fretz testified he was standing "outside in the hall." Of course, there was Italian Hall, and on the top floor, there was a hallway that ran the length of the floor. Rather than ask him to clarify which "hall" he meant, the jurors asked:

Q: Was the door open or closed?

A: It was opened and closed. People going in and out and it was opened and closed. Spring door.

When Margaret Tomei fled the building, the doors she went through were open. Earlier in her testimony she referred to doors inside the main room by the stage and doors at the top of the stairs. To get to the street, she had to pass through even more doors. Which doors were open? No one asked.

Charles Saari had been asked to watch a door—but not the one the jurors thought. When some of the children received their presents, they sneaked back into line and went through for a second batch. When a woman on stage spotted this, she made the children enter the stage on one side and exit on the other, through doors that took them to a corridor that would force them to re-enter the room toward the rear. Saari was asked to steer children down that hall; instead, the inquest misunderstood what he told them:

Q: Were you at the door taking cards or door-tender?
A: Yes, the outside door.
Q: What were you doing there?
A: Just watching for the children to get their presents and not let them in again.
Q: Any children go out?
A: Yes sir.
Q: Did you watch the door and see that only Union members with their children got inside?

A: No.

Q: Did you ask the people's union cards?

A: No, I did not ask any.

It is painfully obvious from Saari's testimony that he was not the man "guarding" the door to the outside world, keeping non-union people out of the Hall as the jurors had hoped he was. He misspoke—or misunderstood—when he said he was "at" the "outside" door. Either way, the jurors rarely asked follow-up questions, regardless of how vague or imprecise a statement had been. In fact, the testimony is remarkable for how short it is. Many of the witnesses—assuming they were testifying at a regular rate of speech—appear to have spent less than five minutes on the stand. Even the lengthiest portions of testimony take no more than two or three pages of single-spaced question and answer. Evidently, the inquest jurors were merely going through the motions of conducting an inquiry; they were not attempting to discover the truth about anything.

While the issue of the doors was handled haphazardly by the coroner's jury, so was the issue of the fire whistle. The local fire departments in the Keweenaw called firemen to the station by sounding whistles—sometimes referred to as alarms. There was a question raised by *Tyomies* and others about why the fire whistles were blown on Christmas Eve in Red Jacket when there had been no fire. Were the alarms sounded when people outside the Hall heard the commotion? Did someone call in an alarm before the panic occurred? Were the alarms sounded for some altogether different reason, such as a gathering of the Citizens Alliance? These are all questions that should have been addressed by the coroner's inquest. How carefully did the coroner's inquest investigate this issue? Not very; for one thing, the inquest panel didn't seem very interested in which "alarm" witnesses referred to in their testimony and asked few questions about the timing of the whistle.

John Sandretto heard the fire whistles blow after the panic had begun. Charles Meyers was upstairs in the hall when he first heard the "alarm," after the panic was over. He was not asked to clarify, but he was probably referring to the fire whistle, because he had not been in the Hall when the panic started. Dominic Vairo saw deputies after the "alarm was given." He was not asked to specify whether he was referring to the alarm from the fire house or the general alarm raised in the hall above his saloon. Paul Spehar said the Hall was crowded before "the alarm of fire" was raised. Likewise, he was not asked whether he'd heard the cry of "Fire" within the

Hall, the fire whistle, or both. Patrick Ryan came to the Hall in response "to the alarm." Later, he said that he was at the Hall after the "whistles had blown." Were those whistles the same alarm that had called him to the Hall in the first place? He was not asked.

John Sullivan was near a friend's barn a distance from the Hall when the "whistle" sounded. Like most of the witnesses on this topic, he was not asked what time he'd heard the whistle for the first time. Angelo Curto also went to the Hall when the "whistle blew" but was not asked the time of the alarm. Fireman Jacob Kaiser mentioned both the whistle and the alarm and claimed, "I heard them shouting fire at the Italian Hall." Presumably, he meant he heard people in the street near his home saying there was a fire at the Hall, but he did not say what time he heard the commotion.

Mary Lanto was asked: "Was there a jam, a pushing before this alarm or before this rush for the door?" In that case, the word "alarm" most likely refers to the cry of "Fire" raised in the Hall, and not to the fire whistle. Either way, no follow-up questions were asked. Joseph Trudell was down the street when the "alarm blew," an obvious reference to the fire house and not to something within the Hall. Mrs. Czabo heard "the alarm of fire" more than ten minutes after the panic—presumably another reference to the fire whistle. Mrs. Anna Lustig testified that the rush for the door was caused by "the fire alarm." When asked what kind of "alarm," she replied: "A man called 'Fire!' " It was perhaps the only time during the entire inquest that a follow-up question was asked.

Joseph Czap heard the whistle while he was down the street from the Italian Hall but was not asked the time. Louis Wuopia heard the fire whistle blow after he'd exited the building, after the panic had occurred. He was not asked the time of the whistle either.

Finally, it is worth noting the inquest jury's handling of the witnesses who testified they saw a man wearing a Citizens Alliance pin inside the Hall. Although it seems unlikely that any Alliance sympathizer would risk walking into a party held by the union while wearing a Citizens Alliance pin, it would not have been impossible for a Citizens Alliance member to enter the party whether or not they were wearing a pin. With no one checking identification for most of Christmas Eve, anyone could have gotten into the event. Later events would reveal much evidence to support the contention that the man who cried "Fire" was, in fact, wearing an Alliance pin.

This issue has been dissected by people who have studied the Italian Hall tragedy; some argue that if no man was within the Hall wearing the pin, then we must conclude no member of the Alliance was in the Hall that day. That argument is obviously flawed, and flows largely from the way the inquest jury dealt with the issue. They seemed to believe that if they could disprove the "man wearing the pin" theory, then there was no Alliance member in the Hall.

Any rational person reading the transcript in its entirety is left with the distinct impression that one of the inquest's primary goals was to show that there were only union people in the Hall and that there could not have been Citizens Alliance people in the Hall to ignite the panic. Wishing for it doesn't make it so. Likewise, it must be noted that someone wearing an Alliance pin could have been a union sympathizer, in the unlikely role of trying to gain pity for the union.

The direction the inquest was heading—or its lack of direction, really—became clearer when Louise Lesch was recalled to testify. The last question posed to her by the jury was:

> *The purpose of this jury is to find out what caused this and what brought it on and probably the children themselves are to blame? We got to get all the facts we possibly can.*

One might wonder why an inquest convened for the biggest mass murder in Michigan history would perform such a shoddy job. It wasn't incompetence or the lack of legal or medical training on the part of the coroner: The county officials had done an admirable job with the Seeberville murders. In fact, their work in the Seeberville murders, considering the atmosphere of the times, was remarkable. There, the inquest jury had met for four days and brought in interpreters to sift through testimony. They even went so far as to exhume a body to conduct an autopsy. No such efforts were made in the Italian Hall case, even though there were probably more than 700 people who could be called as witnesses. If nothing else, it is remarkable that the Italian Hall inquest took a day less to conduct than the Seeberville inquest.

If not incompetent, could they have been inclined to do a poor job on the Italian Hall tragedy on purpose?

Consider the composition of the local government. Houghton County was run by a board of commissioners. The board comprised eighteen members, most of whom were mine managers—including MacNaughton. And fifteen others were from industries dependent on mining. The board always looked out first for the business of the mines.

The county coroner was appointed by the board of commissioners. Presumably, the same board that hires can fire. The coroner might have thought a proper inquest would implicate the Citizens Alliance and the mine owners who created and financed the Alliance. Clearly, the Alliance was suspected by many in the community of having a hand in the tragedy. If they were innocent, a good investigation could have exonerated them. The coroner might have also suspected the Alliance was behind it and did not want to uncover it, or he might have been told not to dig too deeply into the circumstances of the tragedy.

It is worth noting that the coroner's role in the Copper Country was not necessarily to solve mysteries involving death. Historically, coroners had focused more on explaining how people died—cause of death—and on exonerating prime suspects if they were in positions of power. For instance, in 1895 there had been a fire in the Osceola mine that killed thirty workers underground. Fires in the mines were fairly common because the shafts were shored up with wood, and mining involved the use of flame. When the Osceola fire first started, several mine captains made it safely to the surface and looked for firefighting equipment. When they went back down, they found the mine so filled with smoke that it was impossible to fight the fire. Only then did they suggest to the other workers that they could leave their jobs and make their way to safety. A few hours later, the mine was capped to extinguish the fire, guaranteeing that the thirty men below would perish.

The coroner in that case spent three days listening to testimony—three days seemed to be the standard for an adequate hearing—and drew the conclusion that the Osceola Mine wasn't at fault. The jury's verdict was: "That the deceased came to their deaths by suffocation caused by smoke and gas from a wood fire ... We believe that this fearful loss of life is due to the fact that the deceased did not realize the seriousness of their danger, although from the evidence given to this jury, we find that said deceased were duly notified. We exonerate the mine officials from all negligence in this sad affair." It didn't seem to matter that the coroner's jury was not charged with the job of assigning guilt or innocence: The jury went ahead and announced the innocence of the most likely culprits, without bothering to see what a judge, prosecutor or grand jury might think.

The Houghton County Coroner was capable of conducting a worthwhile inquest. The killings of Tizan and Putrich were an example, but the inquest at their murders was an anomaly. There were so many eyewitnesses who saw the men who did the shooting in broad daylight. And even then, no one was tried for the killing of Tizan. There was only a trial for the murder of Putrich. It may have helped that Prosecutor Lucas was Croatian—as were the victims.

It has also been said that the Italian Hall coroner was so shocked by what he saw the night of the tragedy—six dozen dead, mostly children—that he became physically ill and almost catatonic for the next few days. In interviews decades later, his great-grandchildren described the actions of a man stunned to the point of becoming non-functional. If that is true, it is possible that Fisher's poor performance at the inquest was the result of his mental state. Still, he was assisted by an inquest jury—and no one has ever claimed that they were all in the same stunned condition as Fisher during their three days of hearings.

The final verdict of the inquest into the Italian Hall deaths, in its entirety—other than the listing of the victims' names—was that the victims:

> ... came to their death on the 24th day of December, A.D. 1913, at the Italian hall, in the village of Red Jacket, by the evidence we find, of the witnesses, that the cause of death of the above-named persons was by suffocation, the same being caused by being jammed on the stairway leading to the entrance of the Italian hall, where a Christmas celebration was being held under the auspices of the Woman's Auxiliary of the Western Federation of Miners, and the stampede was caused by some person or persons within the hall, and we further find that no person or persons was allowed inside of the hall where the celebration was being held without producing a union card or having some member of the union vouch for them before they be allowed admittance. We further find by the evidence that the citizens, doctors, firemen, and the sheriff's force are to be commended for their prompt action in their efforts to relieve the suffering.

Although the inquest jury did not exonerate the Citizens Alliance, they came close. Without question, the last sentence of the jury's finding was beyond the scope of what the jury was supposed to be doing. Then again, it was in line with the runaway coroner's inquest juries from the past.

It is also noteworthy that the cry of "Fire" came from near the doorway at the top of the stairs. Although some said it came from outside and others said it came from within the hall, there appears to be a general consensus that centered the cry near the doors at the top of the stairs.

Many inside the hall indicated the cry came from that direction—which could be mistaken as being "outside" those doors. Those at the top of the stairs thought the cry came from within the hall, which could also be just "inside" the doors. Both of these—outside and inside the doors—mesh with a man stepping though the doors and crying "Fire" a few feet inside the hall. Even the *Calumet News*, before adopting the stance that the crime was unsolvable, had published an account that coincided with this.

> *Those in the building who escaped differ, some asserting the cry was first heard from the doorway and others insisting they are certain it came from a man inside the hall, who had been present during the entertainment. Descriptions of this man seem to tally a little better today than on Christmas Eve, however. It seems to be established he had no beard, but a mustache, and was rather a large man.*

The final tally of the dead, according to the inquest follows:

1. Herman Ala	22. Mary Klarich
2. Lempi Ala	23. Kate Klarich
3. Wilma Aaltonen*	24. Matti Kotajarvi
4. Sanna Aaltonen	25. Anna Kotajarvi
5. Sylvia Aaltonen	26. Anna Kotajarvi (girl)
6. Katherine Bronzo*	27. Brida Liisa Kalunki*
7. Ivana Blof*	28. Efia Kalunki
8. Joseph Buttala	29. Anne E. Kalunki*
9. Victoria Burcar	30. Johan H. Karkela
10. Kate Gregorich	31. Mary Krentz
11. Eino Heikkanen*	32. Alper C. W. Lustig*
12. Edward Heikkanen	33. Sula Rubet Lauri
13. Isaac Heikkanen	34. Rafael Lesar
14. Tilma Isola	35. Mary Lesar
15. Ina Isola	36. Arthur Lindstrom
16. Barbara Jesick	37. Lydia J. Luomi
17. Rosie Jesick	38. Mary G. Lanto
18. Jennie Jacolletto	39. Hilda K. Lanto
19. Uno Jokopi	40. Wesley M. Manley*
20. Johan E. Kremanki	41. Elina Manley*
21. Christina Klarich	42. Agnes Mihelchich*

43. Paul Mihelcich

44. Elizabeth Mihelcich

45. Walter Murto

46. Ella E. Montanen*

47. Mathias Montanen*

48. Geza H. Montanen*

49. Johan W. Millykangas

50. Edward Emil Millykangas

51. Abram Niemala*

52. Mary E. Niemala*

53. Annie Papsh

54. Mary Papsh*

55. Elenea Ristell

56. Terresa Renaldi

57. Saida Raja

58. Emilia Rydilahti

59. Heli Rydilahti

60. John Saari

61. Elida Saatia

62. Antonia Staudahar

63. Mary Smuk

64. Nick Cvelkovich

65. Kaisa Tulppo

66. Mamie Tulppo

67. Sandra M. Taipalus

68. Elina Taipolos

69. Lydia E. Talpaka*

70. Edward Takola*

71. Kate Peteri

72. William Piri

73. Hilja Wuolukka

74. J.P. Westola

This list is from Larry Molloy's *Italian Hall: The Witnesses Speak,* which was transcribed from a copy at the Michigan Technological University Archives. This list differs from the official record of the Subcommittee hearings. The Subcommittee was given a copy of the inquest testimony and the inquest jury's findings, which included the same list—albeit with many of the names spelled differently, and some of the names missing or different altogether. For example, the names here with asterisks are spelled differently than they appear in the records of the Subcommittee.

Another striking aspect of the tragedy was how much confusion existed regarding who the victims were and how many people were killed. It seemed that each list—no matter how official—gave a different number of dead and the names were often different. For example, the first list of dead printed by the *Calumet News* on December 26 named seventy-one people; the coroner's inquest named seventy-four. Then, to add to the confusion, the House Subcommittee was given the number of seventy-three—not seventy-four—as the official number of dead. The Subcommittee report reads: "Having the coroner's inquest, and by agreement of the parties who are familiar with the facts, we state that in the stairway at Italian Hall there were killed 62 children and 11 adults, making 73 in all."

On December 26, the *Calumet News* had also reported that "morgues" handled seventy-five dead, which they could not get to balance with their second list—of seventy-two—on the same day in another edition. To add to the confusion, the paper published the list of local undertakers and how many victims each processed:

> *Kallio undertaking rooms*..*40*
> *Richetta and Madronich undertaking rooms*..........................*20*
> *Ryan undertaking rooms*..*8*
> *Peterson undertaking rooms*..*7*
> *Total*..*75*

Seemingly, no one could count the dead accurately. The Peterson funeral home, which was quoted by the *Calumet News* as accounting for seven victims, actually handled the affairs for nine of the victims. According to the records of the Peterson funeral home, they arranged funerals for Erick Piira, the three Heikkinen brothers, Lydia Luoma, the young Niemela couple, Kaisa Peteri and Henry Takala. Since the nine they listed were among those documented elsewhere as having died in the Italian Hall, it calls the rest of the funeral home numbers into question. At the very least, they would add up to seventy-seven, unless the other homes had given numbers that were inaccurately high.

Fewer than twenty names appear on both lists spelled the same way each time. Herman Ala appeared at the top of each. Other names are spelled quite differently: Ilka Bueff—*Calumet News*—appears as Ivance Bolf at the inquest. Some names are so disparate it is unclear if they refer to the same victim: is "Miss Renoldi" the same as Emilia Rydilahti? Or John Karkela and Johan E. Kremanki?

A local Calumet researcher named Peggy Germain has spent decades sifting through the records and history of the Italian Hall, focused largely on sorting out this question. From reviewing the records—including the death certificates—she drew the conclusion there were seventy-three victims. Her list also begins with Herman, but has his last name spelled "Alla."

1. Herman Alla	*8. Katarine Bronzo*
2. Lempi Ala	*9. Victoria Burcar*
3. Sanna J. Aaltonon	*10. Joseph Butala*
4. Sylvia Altonen	*11. Nick Cvetkovick*
5. Wilma Altonen	*12. Jenny Giacoletto*
6. Will Biri	*13. Katarina Gregorich*
7. Ivana Bolf	*14. Edwin Heikkinen*

15. *Eino Heikkinen*
16. *Eli Hiekkinen*
17. *Ina Isola*
18. *Tilma Isola*
19. *Barbara Jesic*
20. *Rosie Jesic*
21. *Uno Jokepii*
22. *Anna Kalunki*
23. *Brida Kalunki*
24. *Efia Kalunki*
25. *Johan Kiemaki*
26. *Katarina Klarich*
27. *Kristina Klarich*
28. *Mary Klarich*
29. *Johan Koskela*
30. *Anna Kotajarvi*
31. *Anna Kotajarvi Jr.*
32. *Mary Krainatz*
33. *Hilja Lanto*
34. *Maria Lanto*
35. *Sulo Lauri*
36. *Mary Lesar*
37. *Rafael Lesar*
38. *Arthur Lindstrom*
39. *Lydia Luoma*
40. *Alfred Lustic*
41. *Elina Manley*
42. *Wesley Manley*
43. *Ella Mantanen*
44. *Mathias Mantanen*

45. *Y. Mantanen*
46. *Agnes Mihelchich*
47. *Elizabeth Mihelchich*
48. *Paul Mihelchich*
49. *Walter Murto*
50. *Edward Myllykangas*
51. *Johan Myllykangas*
52. *Abram Niemela*
53. *Maria Niemela*
54. *Annie Papesh*
55. *Mary Papesh*
56. *Kate Petteri*
57. *Saida M. Raja*
58. *Terresa Renaldi*
59. *Elma Ristel*
60. *Emilia Rydilahti*
61. *Heli Rydilahti*
62. *John Saari*
63. *Elida Saatio*
64. *Mary Smuk*
65. *Antonia Staudohar*
66. *Elisina Taipalus*
67. *Sandra Taipalus*
68. *Edward Takola*
69. *Lydia Talpaka*
70. *Kaisa Tulppo*
71. *Mamie Tulppo*
72. *Hilja Wualukka*
73. *Johan Westola*

Germain pointed out in her book *Tinsel & Tears* that the number of victims varied from source to source and that a figure of seventy-three is her best estimate. She cites the figure of seventy-three from the village and the figure of seventy-four from the inquest and notes that the list from the inquest included Matti Kotajarvi. According to Germain, Kotajarvi identified the bodies of his wife and daughter and somehow, his name was accidentally included in the list of victims.

The issue vexed her to the point that she wrote another book in 2005 which addresses this issue—quite convincingly—and reprints the death certificates of the seventy-three who died at the Hall without question. There is no death certificate for Kotajarvi and another fact that Germain does not mention: Kotajarvi also attested to the personal information of two of the other victims in the disaster. He is listed as the informant for the two Rydilahti children as well as for his wife and daughter, both named Anna. It is impossible that a dead man could serve as a witness both for his own family and that of another, even in 1913 Calumet.

Germain also notes—as do many others who study the Italian Hall—the "nationality" of each victim, with the list made up mainly of Finns and Croatians. This is a bit misleading, however. Although many people in 1913 identified someone who spoke Finnish as a "Finn," most of the victims were American citizens. Of the seventy-three who died, fifty-five were born in the United States. For instance, what nationality was Elma Ristel, the six-year-old whose father was born in Calumet and whose mother was born in Finland? Germain and others call her Finnish—likewise, the "Finnish" Wesley Manley, whose father was born in Calumet and had a mother born in Finland. Manley was certainly a U.S. citizen—he, too, was born in Calumet—even if his mother spoke Finnish.

On January 3, 1914, the *Calumet News* recounted the number of deaths in the area for the preceding year. Despite decreases in violent deaths in 1913, there were "close to one hundred" more burial permits issued in Calumet and Laurium than in 1912. The paper noted the obvious rise in numbers because of the Italian Hall disaster, which the paper pegged as adding seventy-four to the totals.

Prosecuting Attorney Lucas had stated publicly that he would let the coroner's inquest handle the matter of assigning blame for Italian Hall. After all, that process had worked in the Seeberville killings of Putrich and Tizan. But what of the ridiculous conclusion that the inquest could find no one to pin blame on? The witnesses had described the man wearing an Alliance button.

Before Lucas had long to ponder the question, someone made a bold statement to him—by trying to assassinate him. Lucas had taken up offices in Baraga, thirty miles or so south of Houghton, to prosecute some of the strike crimes. Judge O'Brien had moved the cases to get them out of the highly charged mining communities. On January 6, someone left a stick of dynamite by the door to Lucas' office. The explosives were not armed and did not explode, but even *The Daily Mining Gazette* admitted it was an attempt on the prosecutor's life. Who would want to send a message to

Lucas the first week of 1914? It probably wasn't the strikers, because so far, Lucas' prosecution of them had not resulted in many convictions. His most noteworthy activities in the past few months had been his agitation to get the killers of Putrich and Tizan tried for murder. People who thought he would make the same moves after Italian Hall would be the ones with the most to gain from removing Lucas from the scene.

James MacNaughton took a vacation in early January and visited Boston. There he met with Shaw and spent time relaxing. He returned to the Copper Country on January 16, 1914. Upon his return, he wrote to Shaw and said the area seemed quieter. He attributed it to recent grand jury indictments that would soon be handed down—by the grand jury packed with Citizens Alliance members—naming the officers of the WFM for various minor crimes. MacNaughton hoped these would keep Moyer from returning to the Keweenaw anytime soon. He had good reason to believe they might be a deterrent: There would be twenty-nine indictments, most against WFM officials, almost all based on testimony given by mine officials.

The grand jury failed to indict anyone for the kidnapping and shooting of Moyer, primarily because everyone knew it had been orchestrated by the Alliance. In fact, the grand jury announced it would not be indicting anyone for the attack on Moyer, even though witnesses had identified seventeen men from the mob that shot, beat and dragged Moyer to the train station. Some members of the jury claimed the testimony was inconclusive or too muddied to determine guilt, but few believed them. They even failed to indict the two most obviously guilty men: Deputies Hensley and McKeever, the men who kept Moyer on the train after paying for his one-way ticket, and who ordered the porter not to send his telegram until after they'd gotten off the train. The grand jury was particularly derelict in its duty. The kidnapping of Moyer—at the very least—violated O'Brien's injunction. All that had to be proven in that case would have been that any member of the Citizens Alliance had "by any means whatsoever" threatened or intimidated Moyer to compel him to leave the region.

While clearing the Alliance and its allies of the crimes they committed, the grand jury also announced it would indict no one for the shooting of Margaret Fazekas. Witnesses had identified the deputy who shot her; to make it look fair, they announced they would not be indicting anyone for the attack on the deputies, which inspired the man to shoot Fazekas. Again, in the face of overwhelming evidence, the grand jury chose to say they could reach no conclusions.

A few days later MacNaughton wrote to Shaw and mentioned that there might be a congressional investigation into the mines of the Copper Country. He hoped that wouldn't be the case, not because he feared they might turn up anything, but because they might inspire the strikers to hold out longer.

On January 6, Governor Ferris came to the Copper Country and conducted an investigation of his own into the strike. Having heard that the Italian Hall was a mystery no one could solve, and that the coroner had ruled it an accident, Ferris confined himself to the issues of violence and the conduct of the National Guard during the strike. Even there, he found troubling things to examine. The matter of Moyer's deportation struck him as odd. Hadn't there been a grand jury sitting in Houghton during this time, and if so, why hadn't it handed down any indictments? Was it really that big a mystery who was behind Moyer's kidnapping?

Ferris put Sheriff Cruse under oath and asked him a series of questions about the Waddell men. Cruse insisted that although there had been fifty or sixty under his command at one time, all but four who were being held for the Seeberville murders were now gone. Any other Waddell men in the county, he claimed, were there in the employment of private individuals such as the mines. Other than that, Cruse had no idea what might have happened to Moyer.

Ferris asked Judge O'Brien what he thought of the grand jury. O'Brien noted that of the men on it, nine admitted they were Citizens Alliance members. None were members of the WFM.

The WFM and those sympathetic to the strike were suspicious of the coroner's inquest and immediately criticized the process and the verdict itself. The *Miner's Bulletin* of January 7, 1914, editorialized:

> *The coroner's jury impaneled by coroner William Fisher to inquire into the terrible disaster of Christmas eve at Italian hall Calumet met Monday morning, December 29th. Two and a half days were consumed in the examination of witnesses, the majority of those subpoenied (sic) having meager knowledge of the cause of the disaster. About the only information gained being the fact of a rush for the doors with the result already known. Attorney Hilton of the Western Federation of Miners had many witnesses who would have testified to the fact that the man entering the hall and giving the alarm of fire wore upon his coat a "Citizens Alliance" button, but seeing the manner in which his witnesses were brow-beaten, berated and bawled at by many of the jurors as well as by the special prosecutor Nichols, he declined to*

permit any more of them to be placed upon the stand. Seven witnesses examined, stated that they plainly saw the man giving the alarm and that the "Citizens Alliance" button was the first thing to attract their attention. President Moyer's story that the person giving the alarm of fire wore upon his coat a "Citizens Alliance" button was fully borne out by these seven witnesses. All of the witnesses subpoenied (sic) by the coroner were those who were in remote parts of the hall, and others who were not in the hall, but were on the streets or in the saloon and store on the ground floor of the building.

Regardless of what the jury "found" does not in any manner of means make it truth. Many persons were in the room not members of the union, nor were they vouched for by members of the union. A man was stationed at the door but his business was more in the nature of keeping order and the passage way clear, than to inspect the those who entered the hall. Furthermore, it would have been an easy matter for a man to come into the doorway and cry fire regardless of a door keeper. The coroners inquest is regarded by the citizens in general as being the greatest farce ever pulled off in the copper country.

On January 15, 1914, the grand jury returned the indictments that MacNaughton had anticipated. Sixteen officers and members of the WFM were arrested immediately, and a total of thirty-eight were named by the grand jury on charges of conspiracy. Simply put, the WFM officers were accused of conspiring to interfere with nonstriking workers. With the unsolved crimes in the county—most notably the Italian Hall mass murder and the Dally-Jane killings—it was remarkable that they bothered to hand down such a group of indictments. Many of the conspiracy charges were not even felonies.

People familiar with the history of the copper strike would recognize the witnesses who had testified before the grand jury: It was a veritable who's who of the mining industry as well as a rogue's gallery of the thugs they had hired to break the strike. MacNaughton testified, of course, as did Lawton of the Quincy Mine. Denton and Seeber likewise complained of the WFM to the grand jury. Edward Polkinghorne testified—about what was anyone's guess—while awaiting trial for the murder of Louis Tizan.

Moyer was in Colorado when the indictments were issued, so he could not be arrested. The grand jury never indicted anyone for the shooting and kidnapping of Moyer. Under normal circumstances, a defendant charged with a misdemeanor faced little risk of being extradited to stand trial. Notwithstanding that, a special prosecutor who had been brought in for this case—mine management would never allow their enemy Lucas to handle these trials—announced that he planned to have Moyer extradited from Colorado to face the misdemeanor charge of conspiracy in Michigan. And, to make sure MacNaughton knew whose side he was on, Prosecutor Nichols announced to the press: "I believe that Moyer and the others indicted are guilty."

On January 28, the United States House of Representatives authorized an investigation of the strike. Before the announcement, the local newspapers had written numerous articles and editorials about how unnecessary such an investigation would be. At the end of January, the grand jury for Houghton County was officially dissolved. It had returned no indictments for the kidnapping of Moyer, the shooting of Margaret Fazekas, the seventy-three deaths at the Italian Hall, nor the shootings at the Dally-Jane house. The last omission would not rest well with mine management.

The Seeberville Murder Trial

In February 1914, five of the men indicted for the Seeberville murder of Steve Putrich and Diazig Tizan were tried for the murder of Putrich. Raleigh—who was called "the ugly-faced one" by a witness—skipped bail and did not appear for trial. It was of no consequence to him; the $5,000 bond had been posted by the mine for which he worked. The $5,000 bond posted by the mine was equivalent to the salary of a miner for a little more than *five years* of labor at that time. It was a crazy proposition for the mine, knowing that the man was not a Michigan native and that the evidence against him was overwhelming. When it posted the bond, the mine must have known it would never get the money back.

Before the trial, the public relations efforts of the mines paid off with positive press. One newspaper characterized the killers as "young men of good character and agreeable social manners." The men they killed were called "ugly" and "drunk." These reports sidestepped the issue of why these men of good character were shooting wildly into a house filled with unarmed women, children and innocent men.

Court cases in the Keweenaw in 1914 were not known for being contentious drawn-out affairs like modern trials, but the Seeberville murder trial would have been worthy of Court TV. Jury selection became a story unto itself: Prosecutor Lucas convinced the judge to exclude deputies from the jury pool because of their obvious bias. The defense attorneys and the press were flummoxed. Challenging and removing deputies decimated the pool. Even so, eleven of the twelve required were seated by February 4. The *Gazette* complained that only one member of the jury was affiliated with the mines—as if they had the right to pack the jury with friendly jurors.

Just as it had with its coverage of the coroner's inquest, the *Gazette* would not let actual testimony interfere with its interpretation of the case or in its reporting. The headline for the first day's testimony—describing Putrich's actions the day he was murdered—was "CONSUMED TWO CASES OF BEER BEFORE SHOOTING," as if Putrich had guzzled the cases by himself. The *Gazette* failed to mention that the two cases were consumed by ten men several hours before the shooting and that the first witness testified that Kalan, one of the men who had been drinking, was sober. The paper noted that Mrs. Putrich testified through an interpreter. Also, to water down the event, the paper referred to the shooting repeatedly as a "battle."

Amazingly, some of the defendants took the stand and testified. Their stories were bizarre. Cooper claimed he was hit in the head with a bowling pin and that he later found his hat had bullet holes in it. The prosecutor asked him if it wasn't true that he shot the hat himself. Although he denied it, no one believed him. Arthur Davis testified that he, too, was hit by a thrown "club." "The air was filled with clubs and bottles and he became frightened," according to the *Gazette*. Davis' testimony was perjury of the worst kind; in fact, it bore no resemblance to the truth. The *Gazette* boldly proclaimed: "His story of the events leading up to the shooting tallied with all of the stories told by other witnesses." There, the *Gazette* was taking its lead from Davis, for that statement was wholly false.

One of the men was acquitted and the four others were convicted of manslaughter. Many in the community were baffled. The manager of the local mine, who was paying for the legal defense of the killers, fired the attorneys for being inept and hired another firm to handle their appeal. Rees, Robinson & Petermann filed their appearances for the men, replacing the previous attorneys.

Although the Citizens Alliance was outraged, along with pro-mine newspapers, the judge was quite clear on what he thought of the killers:

> *I have tried to find mitigation if it existed. I have made an effort to find something, somewhere, in mitigation for your act. I know too that the jury sat through this trial hoping that from the lips of some witness might fall something that would put at least a drop of humanity into that awful transaction.*

It is not right for a circuit judge to scold convicted men when passing sentence and I do not want to be looked upon as doing so. I have tried to give you boys a fair trial. It was impossible for it to be fairer. If the jury had found your plea of self defense true in this case it would have been a travesty of justice.

The judge also asked the men rhetorically why they had not merely left the yard when they felt someone in the house had thrown something at them; he said it took them longer to draw their guns than it would have taken them to retreat. Still, much of the community was shocked that anyone had been convicted of killing the foreigners at Seeberville.

On February 17, the Seeberville murderers were shipped off to prison. According to the *Gazette*, the murderers "had a good defense for the killing of Putrich and that their innocence" had been shown at the trial. They were just "four luckless young men" being treated unfairly. The headline of the story read: "NOT A DRY EYE AS CONVICTED MEN LEAVE FOR PRISON." The paper claimed the train station was crowded with well-wishers, overcome with sadness to see such fine men being sent from the county.

The convicted murderers' new attorney decided the best route was to simply appeal to the governor and ask for the four men to be pardoned. According to the new attorneys, the men were "trustworthy" as well as "handsome, fine-looking specimens of manhood." Apparently what would pass today for a bad Internet-dating-service description was considered possible grounds for pardoning a murderer. The governor asked Judge Murphy what he thought of pardoning the men. Murphy had actually met with the men around the time of the inquest and confided to the governor: "They are scum." Ferris denied the pardon.

The Dally-Jane Murder Trials

Calumet & Hecla was still having trouble finding labor to cross the picket lines, even in February 1914. Headlines were made across the country when six Romanians were arrested by immigration officials in Calumet. They were working for C&H, which had hired them through an employment agency in Chicago. The incident prompted a flurry of correspondence between MacNaughton and Shaw. MacNaughton closed the chapter by claiming, "When we hired them in Chicago we had no reason to believe they were other than bona-fide residents of this country." He then quickly changed the subject: A "Finn" had recently confessed to the Dally-Jane murders.

Oddly, MacNaughton told Shaw that very few people in the community knew of the confession, and "those who have the information do not care to entrust it to either the Prosecuting Attorney or the Sheriff." He said the confession would be passed along to an assistant prosecutor they trusted and it would implicate Frank Altonen and Steve Oborto, WFM organizers. He did not say how he came to know of the confession before the sheriff or the county prosecutor. It may have been a bit of purposeful deception; the confession was drafted by Waddell men.

Four union men were arrested for the Dally-Jane murders: Nick Verbanac, Hjalmer Jallonen, Joseph Juntunen and James Huhta, who allegedly confessed to the crime. The arrests were made on February 28 and "caused quite a sensation." Frank Altonen and Steve Oborto were apparently omitted from the final draft of the confession prepared by the Waddell men. It was also strange that four men were arrested; the sheriff had originally indicated the shootings were committed by two men, not four.

Prosecutor Anthony Lucas became convinced that the Dally-Jane murders had been committed by Waddell men, fearful that their jobs were about to be eliminated and in an attempt to garner sympathy before their trial for the Seeberville killings. Lucas first heard that someone had confessed to the killings when he read about it in the paper. A copy of a confession was brought to his office, which he immediately found suspicious. The confession had not been taken in a police station, but in the office of the mine superintendent in Painesdale, in the presence of a Waddell "detective." More troubling, Lucas had sought an indictment against a Waddell man named William Malvin. The grand jury balked at indicting him because of his connection with the mines—at least that's what Lucas thought—and Malvin was present when Huhta gave his "confession." It seemed too convenient for Lucas.

Rather than rely on the written statement, Lucas decided to interview the suspect; after all, if he had confessed to the crime, there might not be a need for a trial. When he got to the jail, Cruse refused to let him see the inmate. When Lucas pointed out that the jailers could not keep the prosecutor from seeing a defendant, Cruse relented.

Face to face with Lucas, Huhta recanted. He said the Waddell men had held him captive for ten days and made him an offer: He would sign the confession and they would see to it that he got off with a light sentence. They would also see to it that he got a good job when he was released from prison. The parallels between the Huhta "confession" and the Harry Orchard "confession" were obvious. When Lucas asked which Waddell man prepared the confession, Huhta identified the same man that Lucas had seen at the scene of the crime the night of the killing: Raleigh. Lucas found the coincidence remarkable.

He told the sheriff the confession was implausible and told him why. Lucas said that at that point, "the sheriff swore at him [Huhta] and said, 'you are now lying, you have changed your story, because your mother was in to see you yesterday and told you the strikers were going to kill you when you got out.' " Of course, the only reason the strikers would have been upset with Huhta is if Lucas' understanding was correct.

Lucas wasn't the only one who doubted Huhta's involvement in the killings. Congressman MacDonald told the subcommittee from Washington that he had spoken with people familiar with the grand jury in Houghton County. They had told him: "Do not attach too much importance to that confession." As already noted, when MacNaughton heard of the confession, it implicated two men who were later not mentioned in the confession given to prosecutors. It sounds more like the Waddell men and the mine managers drafted the confession to fit their desires, and not that it was drafted by a man with a guilty conscience who was telling the truth.

Lucas felt he could not prosecute Huhta in good conscience, having heard him retract his confession and knowing the Waddell connection to the investigation of the case. Others within his office pointed out that to refuse the prosecution, after the papers had proclaimed the confession, would be next to impossible. Lucas approached Judge O'Brien and told him of the dilemma. Lucas suggested prosecuting Huhta for filing a false confession but not for the murders. Meanwhile, Sheriff Cruse and others working in the jail—Waddell men—convinced Huhta to retract his retraction.

The Attorney General for the State of Michigan, Grant Fellows, removed Lucas from the case without stating any reasons—Lucas first found out about his removal by reading about it in the local papers. Most likely, the mine interests had appealed for help, claiming Lucas was biased. When the replacement prosecutor brought the case into O'Brien's courtroom, O'Brien said that if they were going to insist on trying Huhta based on nothing more than his confession, he would remove himself from the trial because he believed Huhta was innocent. The case was sent to Marquette for trial. There, the first judge to whom the case was assigned also removed himself from the case. A judge from distant Gogebic County was called in to handle the unpopular trial.

Lucas attended the trial. The four men arrested were to be tried on murder and conspiracy charges, and the basis of the prosecution was to be Huhta's testimony. The morning of the first day of trial, the prosecutor asked for an adjournment. Huhta had *retracted* the *retraction* of his *retraction* of his confession! Apparently, when he was in court and could not be beaten by Waddell men, he was not inclined to take the fall for a crime he did not commit. The judge granted the adjournment and the prosecution took Huhta aside to see if he might change his mind again.

The prosecution of the case was handled by George E. Nichols, a special prosecutor sent up from lower Michigan at the request of the board of supervisors. MacNaughton and company did not want this case handled by anyone local, and the man sent up was a personal friend of the attorney general's. He demanded the princely sum of $50 a day to work in the Upper Peninsula, a figure the supervisors gladly approved.

While being paid on a *per diem* basis, the visiting prosecutor did not feel rushed in bringing the case to a close. In his opening statement, he announced his intention of calling hundreds of witnesses on the theory that Huhta had killed Dally and Jane as part of a conspiracy that began on the first day of the strike.

More than two hundred witnesses were called; their testimony covered things that had nothing to do with the Dally-Jane murders other than a general relationship to the strike. Although defense attorneys objected to the introduction of this irrelevant evidence, the judge allowed most of it to be admitted. After calling his witnesses by the hundreds, the replacement prosecutor then stood and asked the judge to dismiss the charges against the three other defendants because of a lack of evidence. Lucas, watching from the gallery, was shocked: How could the prosecutor not have known before the trial that his two hundred witnesses would not support a case against three of the four defendants?

Writing about the trial later, Lucas pointed out that it was impossible for Huhta to be guilty without the other three; the "confession" attributed to him implicated the other men as clearly as it did Huhta. If the jury believed the confession was real, they should have been able to convict the other three men. Lucas noted how the local papers skipped over this legal nuance, and merely focused on the conviction of Huhta. They also referred to him constantly as a "foreigner," even though he had been born in Calumet.

Huhta took the stand in his own defense and told the court that while he was out of work and drunk one night, the people with whom he'd been boarding suggested they make up a story to get the reward money being offered in the Dally-Jane killings. When the three of them went to the mine manager's office, the other two made Huhta the fall guy in the scenario and someone else wrote up a confession for him to sign. The entire confession was printed in the paper a few days earlier; Huhta would have to have been college-educated in English to have written it as well as it turned out.

> *I did not at this time consider this manner of procedure very strange, inasmuch as occurrences of this kind had taken place several times in gangs, and I was of the impression that it was to take a shot at somebody.*

The closing argument of the defense was interesting in that Huhta's attorney raised the argument of how the Waddell men had been named by witnesses before the grand jury, but that the grand jury had refused to return an indictment. In fact, one of the men named before the grand jury—a Waddell employee—had fled the area and could not be found. This, even after the grand jury refused to indict him. The attorney even pointed out how the grand jury was packed with mining interests and Alliance members. It didn't help: The jury returned a guilty verdict in thirty-eight minutes.

The End of the Strike

After fighting the mines through the entire winter without gaining ground, the WFM decided to hold a vote on whether the strike should continue. Union members voted on April 12, 1914, Easter Sunday, and as many as 6,000 went to the polls. The count overwhelmingly called for a return to work. Official figures were hard to come by. C.R. Hietala said 4,740 workers had voted, with more than 3,100 in favor of returning to work. The Finnish-language *Amerikan Suometar* reported the numbers as 5,997 voting, with 4,560 advocating the end of the strike.

That same weekend, the Citizens Alliance disbanded—which shouldn't have been that hard for such an illusory organization—and re-formed as an "Anti-Socialist League." The League couldn't agitate against the WFM without a strike, so they spent their time attacking *Tyomies* and its advertisers. Later that year, *Tyomies* uprooted itself and moved to Wisconsin. Not long after, the League disbanded.

The annual report for the Calumet & Hecla Mining Co. wouldn't be officially released until May 1914, but 1913 had been a bad year for the company—the strike had impacted it severely. The company produced only forty-five million pounds of copper compared to the sixty-seven million the year before. Likewise, the cost of producing the copper had risen from $.0986 per pound to $.1425 per pound in 1913. At one point in the year, copper had sold for $.14625 a pound, less than half a cent more than it was costing to produce. The company had been walking a fine line, bordering profitability and loss.

To explain its difficult year, Quincy Shaw and other officers told stockholders in the annual reports of their companies:

> *The strike referred to earlier in this report was called July 23 last by the Western Federation of Miners, an organization with headquarters in Denver, Colorado. Less than 15 per cent of the employees joined this union, and many of these were forced to join by intimidation.*
>
> *This organization entered the community with a notorious record of brutality, disorder and crime extending over the past twenty years.*
>
> *The strike was inaugurated with the same brutality, disorder and crime and attempt by violence to prevent the great majority of the employees from continuing work.*
>
> *During the strike a great majority of the employees, by signed petitions, asked the management not to recognize this organization nor to employ its members.*
>
> *The public opinion of 90,000 inhabitants of the copper country, repeatedly expressed in public meetings, representing every class of employment and business, emphatically disapproved the introduction into the community of an organization whose history, principles and recent performances make it a continuous menace to the peace and prosperity of the country.*
>
> *Your management has felt it to be its duty to its loyal employees, to the community and to its stockholders to refuse to have any dealings with this organization and to refuse to employ its members.*
>
> *For a time production was seriously curtailed by intimidation and violence, but at the present time operations are fast assuming normal proportions.*
>
> *On February 21, 1914, the company had in its employ 1,117 men, as compared with a working force of 1,143 men last July.*
>
> *For the directors, R.L. Agassiz, President.*
>
> *Boston February 24, 1914*

Each mine issued its own report with minor variations. A few reports went into greater details regarding the financial situation and the supposed largesse of the parent companies to their workers. The report issued by

C&H said only fifteen percent of the workers in the area had joined the union. While the WFM claimed 9,000 members in 1913, most now think the actual number was closer to 7,000 at the time of the strike. The C&H figures would only have been correct if there had been more than 46,000 mine workers in the range. The mines in the region employed a few more than 14,500 men. It is doubtful, though, that any of the shareholders checked the company's math: While the mine paid hefty dividends, who cared whether the directors of the corporation played fast and loose with their accounting?

As the workers returned to the mines, they discovered they'd been right all along about the new one-man drill and its deleterious effects on the workforce. In 1912, Calumet & Hecla had employed an average of 1,000 men underground. The strike years saw figures in the 700 range. From 1915 to 1918—as the one-man drill was phased in completely—the number fell from 634 to 485.

With all the national publicity the Copper Country was receiving, reporters arrived from around the country to cover the Italian Hall tragedy, as well as the strike. A reporter from Chicago wondered what working conditions were really like and asked a manager if he might be allowed to examine a copper mine. The following article must have upset the union organizers and agitators, for the reporter spoke in glowing terms of how good the working conditions were.

> We walked through underground avenues as capacious as Mammoth Cave. There was no breaking of head against timbers because the drifts in the copper mine are bored through the solid rock and timbering in Amygdaloid at least is unnecessary. The mine was warm, in pleasant contrast to the icy winds that romped around on top of the ground and the air was fresh and free of dust, the torment of a coal mine. We watched miners work with the drills and the trammers shoveling rock and pushing cars. The work was not the kind suited to graduates of Dobs Ferry on the Hudson, but it did not seem especially hard. I would much rather be a miner in the copper country than a street car conductor or motorman or even a policeman. I had heard that the work in the copper mines was of such a man-killing nature that ten years sent a man to the scrap heap.

The reporter then interviewed several of the workers he encountered in the mines and remarked on how young and healthy they looked. His escort had been working the mines for twenty-four years, and another miner he met had been down twenty-five. The men looked younger to the reporter than would be possible for the time they'd spent working. "The copper mines commenced to hold out the hope that somewhere in their dark depths they held the fountain of youth that old Ponce de Leon had so much trouble in searching for ... I felt somewhat displeased that I had not got a job as a drill boy in the Amygdaloid instead of wasting my time at college." Despite finding his dream job underground in the Keweenaw, the reporter wrote his story and returned to Chicago.

In January, the Catholic Church sent a priest to evaluate the situation in the Keweenaw; when he'd seen enough, he wrote a "long and courageous statement" explaining the Catholic Church's position on organized labor. Pope Leo XIII had espoused the philosophy "that just as the stockholders of the mines had organized and were expressing themselves through the directors of their companies, so the workers, too, had the right to organize and, without interference from the outside, to select whomever they wished as their spokesman."

Father Peter E. Dietz wrote a piece that was reprinted in various places, where he discussed the conflicting positions of the miners and the management. "It is difficult to say which of the two extremes is the greatest menace to civilization, but I am inclined to think that unregulated capitalism is the greater offender."

Four men had been convicted in the killing of Steve Putrich. Although the judge sentenced each of them to seven-to-fifteen years, only one would actually spend any significant amount of time behind bars. Convicted in 1914, three of the four were released in 1916, after appeals to the governor by members of the Citizens Alliance—then merely businessmen and mining "interests"—in 1915. Ferris left office in 1916 when he lost the election to a Republican named Albert Sleeper. This change in Lansing would renew the hopes of the mine interests: A Republican would be much more likely to pardon the friends of mine management who had been convicted during the strike.

A noteworthy aspect of the strike was the number of arrests made and who was arrested. The Department of Labor investigated the strike and concluded there were 263 arrests related to the strike. Most arrests were made for "intimidation" and other forms of disturbance, although fifteen people were charged with murder. Of the 263 arrested individuals, all were strikers except for the six men arrested for the Painesdale murders. All other arrests, including the thirty-two for inciting riot, seventeen for resisting an officer, five for riotous assembly, and so on, were of strikers. The Department of Labor drew the conclusion:

> *... when peace officers, deputy sheriffs, soldiers, or Waddell men engaged in conflicts with the strikers and the officers were the aggressors in beating or riding down the strikers, there was no one to arrest the officers. This accounts for the fact that practically all of the cases in the courts of justices of the peace were against strikers.*

Another fascinating aspect of the strike was discovered by Larry Lankton when he researched his book, *Cradle to Grave*. The law firm of Rees, Robinson & Petermann did not get paid for much of their work during the strike. Before the strike ended, at least one mine fired the firm because they felt RR&P was looking out for C&H first, and the other mines' interests later. The Quincy mine simply refused to pay its legal bills to RR&P, taking the position that much of their covert work—funding the Citizens Alliance and defending strike breakers in court—would never be revealed by a law firm seeking payment of its legal bills. Quincy was right; RR&P wrote the legal fees off as a loss in 1915. Perhaps it was a fitting end to the relationship between the devil and its lawyers.

Mine Timbering. Copper mining in the early 1900s was relatively primitive and dangerous, as evidenced by the rough-hewn lumber supports being used here.

Timbering in Copper Mine, Calumet Mich.

Trammer. Tramming—pushing tram cars filled with ore—was a grueling job often assigned to the lowest rank of workers: recent immigrants or those who spoke no English.

Parade Led by Big Annie. Families of striking miners took to the streets to show their support for the strike. They were often led by the wives of strikers and their children. The most famous strike supporter was Big Annie Clemenc, seen here with her trademark gigantic American flag.

National Union Organizers. The Western Federation of Miners strike in 1913 drew the attention of labor organizers from around the country. Some of them joined the daily parades to let the locals know they had support from outside the region.

Judge O'Brien. Patrick O'Brien gained fame in the region as an attorney, suing the mines on behalf of injured workers or the widows of those killed underground. Elected to the Houghton County Circuit Court, he found himself thrust between the parties of the strike.

James MacNaughton. The president of Calumet & Hecla—"Big Jim" to his admirers—ran the all-powerful C&H mine and convinced the other mine managers to follow his lead in fighting the WFM. He ran the Houghton County Board of Supervisors much the same way—looking out for the interests of C&H first.

Prosecuting Attorney Lucas. Anthony Lucas was the first attorney licensed in the U.S. of Croatian descent, and naturally sided with the strikers. Even so, he found himself incapable of pursuing many of the crimes of 1913 because of the more powerful anti-strike forces in the sheriff's department and in the county government.

James A. Cruse, Sheriff.

Sheriff Cruse. James Cruse ran the police force that found itself overwhelmed at the time of the strike. Critics would later point out that he botched investigations into crimes that were committed by pro-management forces. He never arrested anyone for the Italian Hall tragedy or the kidnaping and shooting of union leader Charles Moyer.

Michigan National Guard. Officials in the Keweenaw called for the National Guard at the onset of the strike even though there had been little violence. The governor sent the Guard to the Copper Country largely because they were scheduled for training at the same time. Once in the region, the Guard were seen camping and drilling virtually everywhere in town.

Seeberville. The town of Seeberville was nothing more than two lanes of quickly built boarding houses for workers. Many of these homes were "hot-bunked" with miners taking turns sleeping in the same beds. It was in one of the houses on the right—the building no longer stands—where the "Seeberville murders" took place.

The Dally-Jane House. This house in Painesdale—which still stands—was a boarding house for English-speaking miners, many of whom were not striking. Gunmen fired several dozen shots at the house, killing two men inside. Despite the similarity to the Seeberville murders—where little attention was paid by the media—the local papers began a crusade of strike-bashing as a result of this event. The incident became a catalyst for the creation of the "Citizens Alliance" and was often touted as justification for anti-WFM activities.

Margaret Fazekas the 14 year old
Hungarian girl who was shot in
head at South Kearsarge.

Margaret Fazekas. Fazekas was shot by mine guards during an altercation between strikers, non-strikers and other mine employees. Although the strikers were unarmed, the guards fired repeatedly at them and Fazekas was the only person shot in that incident. While she was in the hospital, mine managers feared she might die and become a martyr for the strikers' cause. She miraculously recovered.

Previous Italian Hall. The Italian Hall where the tragedy occurred was built in 1908 to replace the hall seen in this rare picture. This hall was built primarily of wood and burned to the ground in 1907.

The Italian Hall. This building was erected in 1908 to replace the previous hall that had burned down. At the time it was constructed, the local papers reported specifically on its modern updates which included outward swinging doors. The meeting hall was on the top floor, reached by a staircase beyond the arched doorway on the far left. The ground floor housed Vairo's saloon and a Great Atlantic & Pacific Tea Co. general store.

The Daily Mining Gazette

12 Pages

HOUGHTON AND CALUMET, MICH., THURSDAY MORNING, DEC. 25, 1913

PRICE, FIVE CENTS

VOL. XV.

80 PERISH IN CHRISTMAS EVE TRAGEDY AT CALUMET; FALSE CRY OF "FIRE" THE CAUSE

Half Hundred Children and Thirty Men and Women at Strikers' Festivity Die in Stampede.

MAJORITY CRUSHED TO DEATH IN NARROW EXIT

Shout from Unknown Man Brings Panic and Mad Rush to Stairway of Italian Hall, Where Hundreds Pile in Struggling Mass.

Message from Gov. Ferris

Message from President Shaw

HOUGHTON FOLK QUICKLY PLEDGE $1,500 FOR AID

Citizens in Mass Meeting Take Measures to Relieve Calumet Sufferers.

DEEP SYMPATHY EXPRESSED

While Copper Country Mourns for Its Dead, Moyer Tries to Make Capital of Disaster.

USES CHILDREN'S DEATHS TO BENEFIT HIS STRIKE

Federation President Again Fulfills Roosevelt's Estimate, "Undesirable Citizen," in His Attitude in Present Horror.

COMPLETE LIST OF DEAD

NO GAZETTE TOMORROW

Cry of "Fire" Started Panic.

Piled Over Crushed Bodies

Seventy Bodies in the Townhall

Houghton Relief Committee Appeal

Relief Meetings at Calumet

Headline News. *The Daily Mining Gazette* front page announcing the tragedy. While describing the tragedy on its left side, the paper attacks Charles Moyer on the right. The paper was incapable of remaining unbiased, even when describing the events of Christmas Eve.

TYÖMIES

AMERIKAN SUOMALAISEN TYÖVÄESTÖN ÄÄNENKANNATTAJA

PERJANTAINA 26 P. JOULUK. DEC. 26, 1913.

83 MURHATTU!

Calumetin lakkolaisten lasten joulujuhlasta tehtiin julma kapitalismin uhriteurastus

Tyomies Newspaper. *Tyomies*—the Finnish-language newspaper whose name meant "worker"—pulled no punches in its coverage of the Italian Hall tragedy. "83 MURDERED!" read its headline, while subheadlines and content placed the blame directly on the Citizens Alliance and mine management. Local English-speaking authorities quickly orchestrated the arrest of the entire *Tyomies* staff, including office workers.

Temporary Morgue. The victims of the tragedy were carried the short distance to the Village Hall where a temporary morgue was set up. This photo of the dead children became one of the best-known images of the tragedy.

Citizens Alliance Pin. Many witnesses who testified at the hearings into the event said the man who cried "Fire" wore a pin like this. The pins were given out by a group calling itself the Citizens Alliance who claimed to be disinterested members of the community that merely wanted the strike to end. In reality, the Alliance was funded by mine management and was a tool used by management to escalate violence in the region.

10   Interior of the Italian Hall after the disaster.
Italialaisten haalin sisus onnettomuuden jälkeen.

Hall Interior. This photograph is one of two dozen which were
made into stereo view slides and sold in sets (top). The photo of the
Italian Hall's main room was taken the morning after the tragedy.
Among the overturned chairs and tables is an abandoned baby
carriage sleigh. The hall's balcony is partially visible in the top left of
the photo and the Christmas tree is still standing on the stage. Note
the caption on the bottom right hand side in English and Finnish.

58'-0"

12'-0"

5'-9"

DOWN   DOWN

6'-0"   6'-0"

APARTMENT   APARTMENT

6'-0"   6'-0"

1'-0"

100'-0"

Stairway to
Basement
5'-9"   1'-0"

SALOON   A&P STORE

DOWN

1'-0"

Stairway to
the 2nd
floor

Inner door
to the
stairway   UP

6'-0"

Outer door
to the
stairway   DOWN

6'-0"   6'-0"

DOWN   DOWN

5'-9"

ITALIAN HALL GROUND FLOOR

N

Ground Floor Blueprints. The actual blueprints for the Italian Hall
no longer exist. The drawings on the following pages were made by
an architect in 2006, based on measurements taken at the time of the
event as well as photographs taken in 1913 and in the 1980s before the
Hall was torn down.

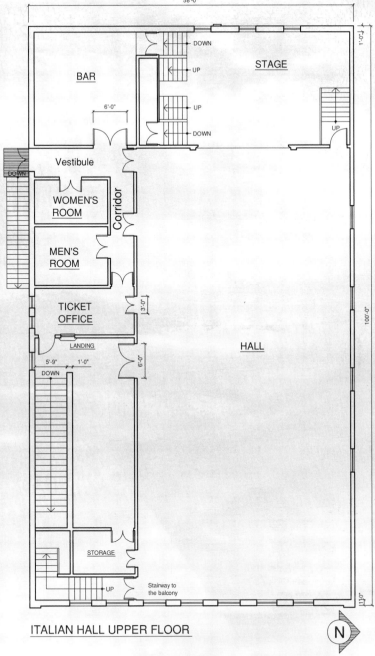

58'-0"

1'-0"

DOWN

STAGE

BAR

UP

6'-0"

UP

UP

DOWN

Vestibule

WOMEN'S
ROOM

Corridor

MEN'S
ROOM

TICKET
OFFICE

3'-0"

100'-0"

HALL

LANDING

6'-0"

5'-9"   1'-0"

DOWN

STORAGE

UP

Stairway to
the balcony

1'-0"

ITALIAN HALL UPPER FLOOR

N

Italian Hall Top Floor. At the time of the tragedy, the top floor of the Italian Hall was crowded with hundreds of children and adults. People were present in almost every part of the floor, but most were crowded into the main hall. When the cry of "Fire" was raised, most headed for the stairs and doors that they had used to enter the hall, unaware of the fire escape on the side, or the ladders on the back of the building.

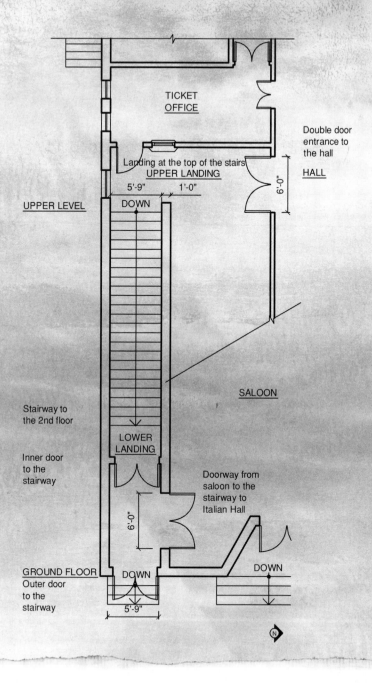

TICKET
OFFICE

Double door
entrance to
the hall

Landing at the top of the stairs
UPPER LANDING

HALL

5'-9"   1'-0"

6'-0"

UPPER LEVEL

DOWN

SALOON

Stairway to
the 2nd floor

LOWER
LANDING

Inner door
to the
stairway

6'-0"

Doorway from
saloon to the
stairway to
Italian Hall

GROUND FLOOR
Outer door
to the
stairway

DOWN

DOWN

5'-9"

N

The Staircase. This drawing is reconstructed from descriptions and photos of the building. The doors at the base of the stairs were removed sometime before the building was demolished in 1984. The door frame at the base of the stairs remained and was clearly too close to the stairs for those doors to have swung inward. The outer doors clearly swung outward in every picture taken of the Hall. There was also a third set of doors at the bottom of the stairs that opened into Vairo's saloon.

The Doors and Stairs. The tragedy centered on the staircase that can be seen behind these sets of doors. More than six dozen people died on the staircase, trampled and crushed in a stampede to get out of the Hall. The small photo on the bottom left was widely circulated in the years after the event and due to its poor composition and focus on the stairs, many people came to believe that the doors opened inward. A much clearer photo (above) shows that both sets of doors opened outward. At the time of the tragedy, no one claimed that the doors opened inward and the photographer was clearly documenting the stairs. That is probably why the clearer photo of the doors was ignored for all these years.

REINO O. NIEMELA,
ORPHAN-AGE- 4 Mo. 2 4 Da.
parents lost in Italian
Hall disaster-Dec. 24, 1913.

One Tragic Family. The Niemela family became symbolic of the tragedy. While the parents died in the stairwell at the Italian Hall, their baby survived. Many people repeated the story that baby Reino was found clutched in his mother's hands as she held him above the crush. Whether the parents actually sacrificed themselves to save their baby is unknown. Reino was adopted by another family who later moved to lower Michigan.

Betty and Abram Niemela
Parents of Little Reino, who
lost their lives in the
Italian Hall disaster, Dec. 24

The Funerals. When officials realized the extent of the calamity, calls were sent out to neighboring communities for more caskets. In the various pictures, the white caskets are for the children. The black held adults.

The Services. Churches filled to capacity overflowed onto the streets and every hearse in the region was called into service.

Processions. Most of the
victims were buried on
the same day, after several
funerals were held. Tens of
thousands of people came
to Calumet to mourn.

Funeral Truck. Organizers of the funerals found themselves without enough carriages to carry the heavier coffins to the cemetery and enlisted an automobile to transport a few of the victims. In 1913, the use of an automobile in a funeral was unusual, and probably viewed as disrespectful in light of the noise it created.

The Cemetery. The number of people attending the funerals was so large that some people even climbed trees to get a better view of the activity at graveside.

Mass Grave. Most of the victims were buried in two trenches dug by striking miners: one for Protestants and one for Catholics on their respective sides of the cemetery. This photograph was probably taken the day after the funeral; the ceremony took so long that it was dark when the last mourners left the cemetery. The photographer must have returned the following morning and taken this photograph before the grave was filled in.

The Mihelchich Children. Agnes, Paul and Elizabeth Mihelchich were all killed in the tragedy. Their father, Joe, had made the news earlier in a confrontation with mining officials. Outside the Italian Hall, a reporter witnessed Joe Mihelchich kneeling in the snow beside his dead children.

The Italian Hall—1980s. In later years, the Hall was used less often and was eventually abandoned. Some locals feared that the crack above the top left window on the face of the building might indicate structural problems. Note that although the face of the building had been altered in the decades since the tragedy, the front doors to the building—including the door handles and hardware—had not been changed. Further, the fire escape on the left side of the building is clearly visible. In earlier pictures, the left side wall of the building was obscured by a building next door.

Demolition. In 1984, the Italian Hall was demolished when funds could not be raised to renovate the building. Despite fears that the building was on the verge of collapse, it proved harder to knock down than anticipated. The arch at the door to the upstairs was saved for a memorial, and someone saved floorboards from the building to make souvenir paperweights. Note the outer doors clearly opening outward. There is disagreement among those who believe inward-opening doors contributed to the disaster: Some say it was the outer doors and some say it was the doors at the foot of the stairs.

The Staircase. These photographs were taken shortly before the building was demolished. There were no handrails in the staircase even though the walls are clearly the same as they were in 1913. The door frame at the bottom of the stairs is visible in the top photo—the frame is far too close to the bottom stair for the inner doors to have swung inward. The view looking up the stairs shows the door to the ticket office and the ticket window. The entrance to the main room of the hall is at the top of the stairs to the right.

The Memorial. After the Italian Hall was torn down, the arch was rebuilt in the center of the lot where the building stood. A photo of the Hall is mounted on a sandstone block behind the arch and a historical marker tells the story of the event. The marker mistakenly says the tragedy was partially caused by inward-opening doors.

WOOD FROM ITALIAN HALL
1908-1984
ITALIAN HALL DISASTER
CHRISTMAS EVE 1913
74 LIVES LOST
37 GIRLS   21 BOYS
11 WOMEN   5 MEN

Italian Hall Floorboards. An entrepreneur saved some of the floorboards from the Hall and made these mementoes. The dates are correct; the number of dead is probably wrong.

Stained Glass. This stained glass depiction of the Italian Hall is in the entrance to St. Anne's church in Calumet.

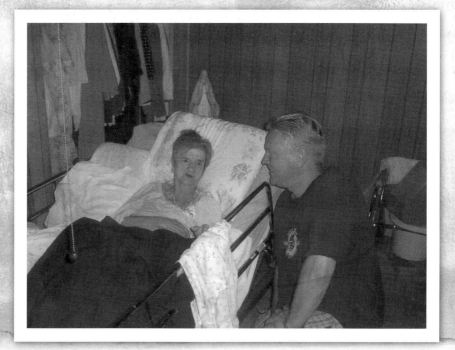

Italian Hall Survivor. Mary Butina was present in the Italian Hall when the cry of "Fire" was raised. In 1913, she was eight years old; she turned 100 the fall after she was interviewed by the author at her home near Painesdale.

PHOTO CREDITS:

Courtesy of the Author: Previous Italian Hall, Citizens Alliance Pin (by Mark Clemmons), Hall Interior, The Mihelchich Children, The Memorial (top, middle, bottom), Italian Hall Floorboards, Stained Glass, Italian Hall Survivor (by Ray Carlson).

Courtesy of David V. Tinder and the Clements Library, University of Michigan: Mine Timbering, Parade Led by Big Annie, The Doors and Stairs (top), The Funerals (top), Day of Mourning (bottom), Funeral Truck (top and bottom).

© 1984 Eric Munch: Demolition (top and bottom); The Staircase (top). Courtesy of Kurzman Architecture LLC, Chicago, Illinois: Ground Floor Blueprints, Italian Hall Top Floor, The Staircase.

© Michigan Technical University Archives and Copper County Historical Collections: Trammer, National Union Organizers, James MacNaughton, Judge O'Brien, Prosecuting Attorney Lucas, Sheriff Cruse, Michigan National Guard (top and bottom), Seeberville, The Dally-Jane House, Margaret Fazekas, The Italian Hall, Headline News, Temporary Morgue, One Tragic Family (top and bottom), The Funerals (bottom), The Services (top and bottom), Day of Mourning (top), The Cemetery Mass Graves (top and bottom), The Staircase (bottom).

Courtesy of the Finnish-American National Historical Archives, Finlandia University: Hancock, Michigan: *Tyomies* Newspaper.

The House Investigation

"There is no middle ground;
you are either for the mine owners or against them."
- CONGRESSMAN WILLIAM MACDONALD -

The United States Congress became involved in the matter when it decided to send a subcommittee to investigate the conditions in the Copper Country—the mines, the strike—and report back to Washington. The House committee announced on February 11, 1914, that it would also take testimony and investigate the Italian Hall tragedy. Among the other topics it covered was the conduct of the National Guard in the area. On February 23, the subcommittee met at Germania Hall in Hancock and called several witnesses, among them Margaret Fazekas. She testified she was on "picket duty" with a large number of strikers the previous September when some deputies told them to "go home." The women with her told the deputies they had as much right to be there as anyone, and perhaps the deputies should go home instead. Fazekas said the deputies drew their revolvers and started advancing toward the unarmed strikers. When they began shooting, she turned and ran, and almost immediately she was shot and knocked unconscious.

This telling of the event was important for one reason: It explained how

Fazekas had been shot in the back of the head. MacNaughton and others had claimed that she must have been shot by strikers. Fazekas spent four-and-a-half weeks in the hospital and eventually recovered. Oddly, her father was not in the area: He had moved away when the strike began, probably to avoid having to pick a side. Her mother was not in the crowd with her, but had given her permission to go out that day.

The hearings lasted for weeks as the congressmen questioned witnesses and officials from both sides of the strike. The rhetoric was extreme at times. Allen Rees, the attorney who represented the mines and the Citizens Alliance told the panel one day of the WFM: "They assaulted and beat up every person who attempted to labor." *Every person.* "Our hospitals were filled with those who were wounded and injured by them, and it required the State troops to restore even a semblance of order and that constitutional protection which the Government has offered through its laws."

MacNaughton took the stand and impressed many, especially those who supported the mines. He complained to Shaw that the testimony was tiring but that he thought he did well. The congressmen questioning him were not completely impressed. At one point, MacNaughton provided the subcommittee with a stack of petitions that he said were signed by his employees, who wanted him not to rehire men from the WFM. When asked who drafted the petition, MacNaughton claimed not to know. They asked him under what conditions they were signed, and he again feigned ignorance. Of course, he didn't want to tell the congressmen that he had his attorneys draft the petition and his mine managers coerce the men into signing.

Other mine-oriented critics ridiculed testimony of strikers. When witnesses told of how Big Annie's flag had been knocked from her hand and trampled by the militia, one critic wrote: "Strikers had carried the American flag in a parade and had used it as a weapon against the militia, finally throwing it on the ground, where it was trodden upon. The strikers afterward displayed the flag and swore that the soldiers had cut it down and thrust their sabers through it. The soldiers were not armed with sabers." Although some of the soldiers did not carry sabers, many officers did. Be that as it may, almost all soldiers with rifles had bayonets—to a person with poor English-language skills, the difference between a "saber" and a "bayonet" might not have been known.

In 1972, Alex Nelson—who had been thirteen at the time of the strike—described his vivid memories of the confrontations between the parades and the militia:

*But they had the American flag there, always the American flag.
Well, we were there all watching, and all of a sudden, somebody
seemed to grab for the American flag to tear it down. With that the
sabres came out from the people on [horseback] and these sabres
came out and that was one of the most impressive things, believe
me, the parade stopped right there. An about turn and back. When
those sabres came out, nobody got hurt and nobody was touched
but it was just authority.*

Later on, William MacDonald, the congressman from Michigan who
started the move to investigate the strike, spoke before the committee.
Although he was not a witness, he had spent much time in the area during
the strike and felt it necessary to get his views before the committee.
He summarized the atmosphere in the Keweenaw: "There is no middle
ground; you are either for the mine owners or against them. If you take
any view except their view, you are against them. They will not admit any
middle ground. If you do not accept as well-founded their absolute right
to control the district, you are opposed to them. That is their view of it."

During MacDonald's appearance, the committee asked him if the mines
had combined or conspired together before the strike had begun. They
acknowledged that the mines had done so once the strike was called.
They were less concerned about that, they explained, than they were
about how the mines appeared to control every other aspect of life in the
Keweenaw. "As you know, after investigating the conditions up here they
have controlled the political offices in the county and in the townships.
The mine owners are the board of supervisors, so far as the control goes,
and they work in unison in all county matters, absolutely. It would be
difficult to say how they could make a combination, under those existing
circumstances, whereby they could gain greater control than they had."

On March 7, 1914, a subcommittee convened hearings at the armory
in Red Jacket to investigate the Italian Hall tragedy. Congressmen Edward
Taylor and John Casey were there to take testimony and report back to the
full committee, which was in Houghton conducting hearings on the mines.
The hearing at the armory was merely to address the Italian Hall tragedy;
the officials sought statements "touching the disaster which occurred at
Italian Hall on December 24, 1913."

This hearing was much maligned at the time, and later, for its apparent
focus on whether or not the person who cried "Fire" wore an Alliance
pin. However, that criticism is misplaced. The congressmen invited

Prosecuting Attorney Lucas to be present and examine witnesses if he so chose, and:

> *If there is any witness present that knows anything about the facts we will be glad to have him present himself and tell us all he knows on the subject referred to.*

The commission had also extended their invitation to "such attorneys as are interested in the investigation generally." Attorney O.N. Hilton provided a list of witnesses to the committee, "but I don't feel like suggesting them, because they were confined entirely to one point [the issue of the Alliance pin], and if the matter is to be heard in conjunction on my part, with the district attorney, in full, at the deference of the committee, I think perhaps the list had better be looked over by him and such selections be made from them as he may wish to make." The politicians pointed out that Lucas had not even arrived yet, and they would gladly take the testimony from Hilton's list of witnesses. They would just allow anyone else who wanted to testify in addition, to do so afterward. Further, many of the witnesses called were not asked about the issue of the Citizens Alliance pin. Perhaps because they had struggled through the inquest testimony—of which they received a copy—or because they had heard the many languages spoken by the witnesses milling about the armory, the committee members started their hearing with the pronouncement: "Now, if there is any citizen present to-day who was present that afternoon, who can speak the English language, we would like to hear what he has to say. If not, we will have to use an interpreter so that we can get the story." Interpreters were not offered to the witnesses at the inquest, and as noted, only one witness over three days of hearings spoke through an interpreter.

As if to emphasize the point, the first witness—"Mrs. Leskella"—used an interpreter. The transcript contains the notation:

> *Mrs. Leskella, a witness, sworn, testified on examination as follows:*
> **The Chairman.** *Did you testify before the coroner's investigation touching the calamity that occurred on the afternoon of December 24 last?*
> *(Here John Laity was duly sworn as interpreter.)*
> **The Chairman.** *Were you a witness before the coroner's investigation?*
> **The Witness.** *Yes.*

Speaking through an interpreter, Leskella's testimony is remarkably clear. "I was standing and a man pushed me, touched me on the chest, and he hollered twice, 'Fire, Fire.' He had a button on his left breast—one of the Citizens' Alliance buttons." She was also adamant that the man wore an overcoat. It is also noteworthy that the men conducting this hearing asked follow-up questions, looking for more detail or clarifications when a witness said something that was not clear.

> **Mr. Lucas.** *Now, where was this man standing that hollered or cried "fire"?*
> **The Witness.** *He came from the back, toward the door.*

The inquest jurors would have dropped the line of questioning here, but Lucas asks more.

> **Mr. Lucas.** *He came from the back? What part do you mean by the back?*
> **The Witness.** *From toward the stage.*
> **Mr. Lucas.** *He came from the main door toward the stage?*
> **The Witness.** *From the stage going out.*

This kind of detail was not sought by the coroner's inquest.

The next witness was Mrs. Lesh (the coroner had called her Lesch). She clarified the issue about watching the door; she had attended the door from two o'clock until three in the afternoon, when she had gone inside to help on stage. Otherwise, her testimony follows her inquest testimony for the most part. She did not address the issue of the Alliance pin, because she had not seen who cried "Fire."

Anna Lustig testified next and described the man who cried "Fire." He had come in from the stairs to the outside, yelled "Fire," and ran out. He was wearing a cap pulled low on his face, and was wearing a Citizens Alliance pin. Her testimony followed closely with that from the coroner's inquest, except she explained herself in greater detail when asked.

John Burcar is one of the few witnesses whose name is spelled the same in both the inquest and the House subcommittee hearings. The thirteen-year-old's testimony was similar at the House hearing as it was at the inquest. He was only a few feet from the man who wore an Alliance pin and yelled "Fire" twice. The man wore a long overcoat and a mustache. After he yelled "Fire," he ran out of the Hall.

Mrs. Hilda Forester testified that she saw a man step into the main room from the landing at the top of the stairs, cry "Fire," and run back out again. As at the inquest, she testified to the committee that the man was wearing a Citizens Alliance button, had a cap pulled low over his eyes and was wearing a dark overcoat.

Frank Schaltz testified he was ten or fifteen feet from the door when he saw a man with a dark coat, a cap pulled low over his eyes, yell "Fire." He said he had seen the man before on the streets of Red Jacket—carrying a club, like a deputy or a Waddell man—but did not know the man's name. The man was wearing a Citizens Alliance button.

Paul Jakkola testified that he was near the top of the stairs when a man ran in and yelled "Fire." He had a mustache, a cap pulled low over his eyes and a Citizens Alliance button on his coat. His testimony was given through an interpreter, presumably from Finnish.

Charles Olsen's testimony at the committee hearing was as impressive as it was at the inquest. He testified that he was looking for his wife and children when he stood on a chair in the middle of the hall to get a better view. As he looked toward the door, he saw a man run in and yell "Fire."

> **The Chairman.** *Did you see the man yourself that hollered fire?*
> **The Witness.** *I see the man. I couldn't help but see him because I was on top of the chair. I was looking at him.*

Like the other witnesses, Olsen described the man as wearing a dark overcoat—he said gray—a cap pulled low over his eyes, and a Citizens Alliance button. When pressed, he admitted he wasn't positive, because from that distance, he could just make out its shape and color. Even so, "I took it for a citizens' alliance button."

The committee spent a good deal of time with several witnesses to verify whether the cry of "Fire" had first been raised near the landing at the top of the stairs, near the main entrance to the Hall. The detail they went into, however, drew different answers from the witnesses than the coroner's inquest had settled for. Peter Lanto didn't hear the cry of "Fire," but when pressed, he didn't think he could have. "I was standing outside of the door and the people inside make noise. I hear nothing about it." At the inquest, they had asked him:

> **Q: Did you hear anybody cry fire?**
> *A: No.*

Later:

> **Q: You are sure you did not hear anybody cry fire in the hallway?**
> *A: No I did not hear anybody tell fire. If I tell that I tell a lie.*

Many had taken this statement to mean that Lanto did not hear anyone yell "Fire" because no one did. However, at the committee hearing, he is asked more detailed questions and gives more detailed answers. He was six feet from the doors into the main room.

> **The Chairman.** *Were you close enough to have heard anyone make an exclamation of any kind inside of the hall if they spoke in a loud voice?*
> **The Witness.** *I was standing over there, but I didn't understand anything.*
> **The Chairman.** *Go ahead.*
> **The Witness.** *They are speaking in English.*

And again:

> **The Chairman.** *Now if anyone had spoken the words, "Fire, fire," in a loud voice in the hall, were you standing near enough to have heard it?*
> **The Witness.** *I could not have heard it.*

Lanto was clearly stating that it was too loud and indiscernible for him to make out what was being said inside the hall, especially since English was not his native language. They also asked him if he had seen anyone go by wearing an Alliance button. The inquest hadn't bothered to ask him. Lanto had seen one person go into the Hall wearing the pin.

As for whether someone at the top of the stairs could have heard someone yelling "Fire" right inside the main doors, the topic came up again with John Jokopie. Standing two or three feet from the door, Jokopie testified that he could hear "noise inside" the Hall but could not make out speaking or talking.

> **Mr. Lucas.** *Well, could you have heard it if he did holler "Fire" in the doorway?*

> **The Witness:** *I couldn't hear it. There was a lot of noise inside and it was possible that I could not have heard it.*

The hearing adjourned for lunch at 12:15 and reconvened at two o'clock in the afternoon. For some odd reason, there were reports that the entire hearing lasted only two hours, but that is obviously not the case; the morning alone lasted two and a quarter hours. The chairman began the hearing by stating for the record that there appeared to be agreement between everyone present that the number of victims was seventy-three, with eleven adults and sixty-two children.

The first witness of the afternoon was Peter Marchesey. At the coroner's inquest, his testimony was almost incomprehensible because of his lack of knowledge of English. Here, they supplied him an interpreter—Paul Tommie—to make sure his answers were as accurate as possible. Marchesey had been in the ticket room at the top of the stairs when the commotion started. They asked him if—while he was in the ticket room—he had heard anyone yell "Fire" in the hall.

> **The Witness.** *There was a certain amount of noise; I couldn't hear if they did make any statement.*

Later:

> **Congressman Casey.** *Did you hear anybody shout fire?*
> **The Witness.** *No, there was a certain amount of noise inside; I couldn't hear.*

And further:

> **The Chairman.** *If anybody cried "fire" out near the stairway, or at the entrance to the stairway, or about the entrance to the stairway descending, would you have heard it?*
> **The Witness.** *I don't believe, because there was a certain amount of noise.*

Marchesey was not asked about the Citizens Alliance pin. The sole result of his testimony was a showing that someone could have yelled "Fire" inside the hall without the people at the top of the stairs hearing it. Contrast that with his inquest testimony—without an interpreter—on the same subject:

Q: When you stood here before you saw this rush of people, did you hear any cry of fire over in the main door?
A: *No.*
Q: If somebody cried fire at this door could you have heard it?
A: *There was a big noise.*

They then changed the question to if he could have heard a cry of fire coming from "the door."

Q: You could plainly hear a cry of fire from this door if there was one?
A: *I might have heard it. There was a little noise before that, but I think I would have heard it before the rush.*

John Boggio likewise chose to testify through an interpreter, a luxury that had not been available at the inquest. Boggio's inquest testimony is almost incomprehensible, whereas his commission testimony is quite clear. He was standing near the main door to the Hall, but the noise level was such that he could not hear if anyone had cried "Fire."

The Chairman. *Did you hear any person that afternoon holler "Fire" in the hall to the people?*
The Witness. *I did not hear it.*
The Chairman. *If such a cry had been made, would you have heard it?*
The Witness. *I could not say if I could hear it. There was noise all around.*

Eli Wiropia—he had been called Louis Wuopia at the inquest—was the last person called at the hearing. He was already on the stairs leaving when the commotion started. He did not hear anyone cry "Fire," and he was not asked about the Alliance pin.

Interestingly, only one person took the commission up on their offer to "come to the stand and make a statement." Jalmer Olsen told a story of witnessing the aftermath. He saw some of the deputies outside the Hall manhandling a Finnish man in the moments after the tragedy.

The subcommittee then toured the Hall and the chairman made a record of what the Hall looked like. The main room was seventy-eight feet by thirty-eight feet in dimension. The front of the building faced east. The stage was twenty feet wide. The doorway to exit the Hall was thirty-eight feet from the front of the building. The hallway that ran parallel to the main Hall was three feet wide, leading from the barroom to the stairway. The main exit door was six feet wide. The stairway was five feet nine inches wide. The vestibule at the top of the stairs was eight feet by ten feet square, and they counted twenty-three steps down to the ground floor. From the door, there were three more steps to the street.

While the chairman was making his measurements and statements, there were about 100 local residents in the Hall, observing. No such measurements were taken by the inquest.

Understandably, *The Daily Mining Gazette* wrote an article the day after the hearing, calling it a failure: "Italian Hall Probe Proves Huge Farce." According to the article, witnesses told such "Varying Stories" that none of them was believed. *None of them*. Further, the witnesses "said nothing whatever that could be taken to strengthen the claim of the federation attorneys" that the man who cried "Fire" wore an Alliance pin. The paper claimed their testimony conflicted and that the WFM had brought in witnesses who were not at the inquest, to no avail. The paper claimed Erick Erickson testified that he saw three men wearing Alliance pins, even though his testimony was that he'd seen two. It didn't matter much; the paper was not above fabricating portions of the story to fit its editorial views.

The *Gazette* further exclaimed that Erickson had been kept from testifying further. "Erickson desired to tell more than he was permitted to tell." That sentence suggests that Erickson was cut off, or not given the opportunity to finish his testimony. The statement of the paper's was baseless, though. Erickson was asked: "Go on and tell us where this man was; tell us everything." The last questions asked of Erickson pertained to men wearing Citizens Alliance pins; Erickson said that he saw men wearing the pins blocking the doors to the Hall after the event. He testified that they weren't helping any, they were keeping people from re-entering the Hall. He stopped testifying because no one asked him any further questions.

"The probe was farcical in the extreme. Witnesses for the federation were uncertain in their stories and there seemed no head or tail to the program." Later, "From listening to the testimony given by the federation witnesses one would gain the impression that they were well coached, too well coached, in several cases, particularly the case of Frank Shaltz, who used big words and language which the ordinary boy of twelve, his age, does not use."

Had Frank Schaltz used big words in his testimony? The only word he used which might be considered out of the ordinary was his use of the word "medium" in describing the man's height. Still, the well spoken— according to the *Gazette*—boy said, "I seen this man before." Sixteen of his responses were either, "Yes, sir" or "No, sir." The *Gazette* was clearly banking on the fact that most people who read the paper would never have the opportunity to read the transcript of the hearing.

The *Gazette* mischaracterized the testimony of other witnesses as well. John Jokopie was the man who stood outside the door and said that the noise level inside the Hall prevented him from hearing anything inside. In fact, he repeated the position that he would not have been able to hear the cry of "Fire" from within the Hall. The *Gazette* wrote: "John Jokopi stood on the landing at the top of the stairs and heard no cry of fire, although practically standing in the doorway of the hall." The *Gazette* likewise spun the testimony of Peter Marchesey, who had also said that it was too loud for him to hear anything within the hall. The *Gazette* reported that he heard no cry of "Fire," despite his proximity to the doors.

The bias of the local papers was noticed by some in the community. The Slovenian Benevolent Societies of Calumet gathered in early March and expressed their collective opinions on the strike and atmosphere of the times. Although they condemned the WFM and its leaders, they went further to condemn the local papers. "We despise all these newspapers and their reporters, condemn them as liars and destroyers of brotherly love between brotherly nations and we protest against all other further insults and attacks."

If the subcommittee hearing transcript is compared side-by-side to the inquest testimony, a few things become abundantly clear. The committee hearing testimony is much more reliable and believable. The inquest jury was not trying to determine the true cause of the disaster; their primary concern was to deflect suspicion from the Citizens Alliance.

The witnesses called were almost unanimous in their description of the man who first cried "Fire" in the hall. He wore a cap pulled low over his eyes, a dark coat, and he cried "Fire" near the entrance to the hall by the top of the stairs, before he ran out of the Hall. He was wearing a Citizens Alliance pin. Some people have counted the witnesses and what they said, to suggest that the more people who saw something would make that thing more likely. For instance, at the inquest, fourteen witnesses did not see a button while seven did. Does that mean the man was not wearing a button? It is axiomatic in the law that the number of witnesses on one side of a quandary are not weighed against the number on the other side to pick a winner. One credible witness is worth much more than ten unbelievable witnesses.

At least eight of the witnesses at the committee hearing identified the man as wearing a Citizens Alliance pin. Some of the others testified they did not see anyone call "Fire"—hence, they could not identify anything about him. And, this is the biggest problem with the fourteen witnesses who "did not see" a button.

For instance, Louise Lesch testified that she had not seen the man who cried "Fire." Still, the inquest asked her if she saw a man wearing a white button near the door or at any time "before this trouble." To that, she answered that she had not—although she had made it quite clear that she was near the stage when the cry went up. She reiterated this at the commission hearing. Not being in a position to have seen the man who cried "Fire," it is unfair to count her as someone who saw no pin. Likewise, John Fretz "did not notice anybody with a button" on. Does he count as someone who can say that the man who yelled "Fire" wasn't wearing a button? He heard the cry but did not see who made it.

Despite the findings by the inquest and the subcommittee that there was no fire—and no one at any of the hearings testified that they had seen fire within the Hall— some writers decided that there had been a fire after all. Elbert Hubbard wrote in May 1914 that "It is thought there was a slight fire on one of the Christmas trees which was decorated with cotton to give the effect of snow, but this fire was quickly put out." No one but Hubbard thought that, but he never clarified his position or his source for this version of the story. He died the next year when the *Lusitania* was torpedoed, so he never had the opportunity to expound on the topic.

In October 1931, James MacNaughton wrote an article: "History of the Calumet and Hecla since 1900." In it, he summarized the 1913 strike into half a paragraph without mentioning the Italian Hall tragedy or the killings at Seeberville and Painesdale.

Lingering Controversies

"Thugs yelled fire and there were dead babies."

- GRAFFITI INSIDE ITALIAN HALL, EARLY 1980s -

The Door Controversy

In the decades following the Italian Hall tragedy, most people repeated a widely held belief that the doors at the bottom of the stairs in the Hall opened inward. This would explain why people became trapped so easily in the stairs, and also why so many people originally thought the doors were being held shut from the outside. It is important to remember that outward-opening doors have not always been the standard. In fact, at the turn of the century, building codes had only recently been changed to require that they open outward for safety reasons.

Strangely, the issue of which way the doors opened was not addressed at either the coroner's inquest or the subcommittee hearings. The most likely explanation for this is that at the time, there was no controversy; everyone knew which way they opened. Although an overwhelming majority of the people who were there or who lived in the community at the time said that the doors opened inward, there were those who argued that the doors swung outward and that the tragedy happened from the crush of people rushing down a moderately steep staircase in a panic. How could such a simple question—which way did they open?—be in doubt more than ninety years later? There are even photographs taken near the time of the tragedy that appear to show them opening inward.

It shouldn't be such a mystery. In 1975, various groups in and around the Calumet area sought to preserve the Italian Hall. At that time, it was owned by a local man named Delbert Masser, but the structure appeared unsafe and was not occupied. Masser had bought the Hall in 1972 for $2,000 from the Fraternal Order of Eagles. The U.S. National Park Service sent an architectural historian out to look at the Hall and evaluate it as part of the Service's "Historic American Building Survey." Kevin Harrington, now a professor of architecture, toured the building in 1975 and wrote an extensive, fourteen-page report. He measured many of the features and sketched the floor plans. He searched the title history for the building and interviewed people familiar with the building.

He was aware of the story of the Italian Hall tragedy—that's why the Hall was being surveyed after all—and he examined the doors in question. Under "Significance" he wrote, "The exit doors at the bottom of the stairs opened inward. People could not get them open and they began to pile up in the stairwell." Elsewhere, he noted, "The door at the bottom of the stairs opened inward." He observed other doors in the building; for instance, the double doors between the landing at the top of the stairs and the hall swung both ways. It seems absurd to suggest that a trained architect—knowing the significance of the operation of the doors—could be wrong on such a simple matter. Yet, Harrington does not write in his report that he observed the state of the doors in 1975. He mentions them in the past tense—how they were—and does not say which way they opened at the time he examined the building.

Another interesting point is found in *The Daily Mining Gazette* from December 30, 1913. The mayor of Hancock, "Stirred by the calamity in Calumet last week," announced plans to address the issue of inward-swinging doors at the next meeting of the village council. In explaining himself, he said: "Moreover there is a state law against doors that open inward. This law above all others should be rigidly enforced." The article never actually comes out and says that the doors at the Hall opened inward, but why was this matter being linked to Italian Hall if the doors at the Hall didn't open inward?

What may have led to the confusion is that there were two sets of doors to pass through to exit from the stairs onto the street. One set was at the very foot of the stairs and did, indeed swing outward. These doors were too near the bottom stair to swing any other way. However, the second set of doors to the street appear in a photograph, apparently hinged to swing inward. Did they? Careful examination of the photograph shows that the doors on the outside of the building swung outward, toward the street. It is necessary to compare a few minor details of the photo to figure out the mystery. There are two doors on the left side of the photo. The one to the farthest left is the outer door, opening toward the street. The door next to it, many people take to be another door that opens inward. It appears to be attached to hinges that are clearly visible in the photo.

However, the second door on the left is actually one of two doors that were at the bottom of the stairs. In the picture, it too, is opening outward. The angle of the photo makes the hinges from the far left door appear to be on this door. If this second door was hinged at this point however, it would mean both of those doors were attached to the same jamb—like a storm door and a regular door. Yet, if you look at the tops of the doors you can see that the door on the far left is much higher than the second door. The difference in the height of the two doors can only be explained by the fact that the second—lower—door is farther back. If you look at the door frame behind the second door (which is closer to the stairway than the front stairs of the Hall) you can see that the second door swings shut into that frame.

Of course, this entire issue is a red herring of sorts. The doors did not contribute to anyone's deaths at the Hall. The earliest witnesses on the scene said bodies were piled up in the stairway and the doors nearest the stairs were not blocked. Still, the debate raged.

The issue of the doors was mentioned in a radio interview given by Dr. Clarence Andrews in 1973. Andrews had just written an article for *Michigan History* magazine about Italian Hall and described the two sets of doors at the bottom of the stairway. Of course, at this time the Hall was still standing, so it should not have been a matter of much debate, at least with respect to which way they opened in 1973.

In 1980, Ted Taipalus—who lost two sisters—returned to the Hall. The building was closed but he found someone who could let him in. He had not been back to the Hall since the tragedy and wanted to visit, in particular to get to the bottom of the issue with the doors. He found that the doors at the bottom of the stairs had been long since removed, although he could tell by marks on the wall where they had been. The proximity of the marks to the bottom stair led him to the conclusion that the doors at the base of the stairs could only have swung outward. However, he wrote that the doors between the street and the vestibule at the bottom of the stairs opened inward! Presumably, despite the fire code that required all doors to open outward, these doors had not been replaced in the sixty-seven years since the tragedy. This observation seems to add to the confusion: there were two sets of doors. Was it that one opened inward and one opened outward?

The Poison Gas Rumor

Memories of the Italian Hall tragedy weighed on the minds of Calumet's citizens and those up and down the copper range. Distrust between the strikers and the mines was amplified by language and class distinctions between different nationalities of the people in the area. The hardest hit group was the Finns; they had lost more people in the tragedy, and they were also the furthest from the mainstream in the community in many ways. Their language—so difficult to learn or understand—kept many Finns separate from other ethnic groups in the community and they tended to stick together as a result. Being set apart from the others allowed rumors to run rampant.

For example, there was a widely held belief among the Finns that the explanation for the deaths in the Italian Hall—suffocation and crushing because of the congestion in the stairway—was a lie. Many believed the deaths were the result of poison gas. As outlandish as it might seem today, an examination of the times and the circumstances of the deaths show how easily the rumor took hold and spread.

Many of the witnesses to the tragedy had not been present in the crush. Word spread through Calumet in the moments afterward, and many arrived on the scene as bodies were being carried out. Some had heard that the fire alarm sounded and that there had been a cry of "Fire," but there was no fire. The bodies being brought from the Hall bore few signs of injury; many appeared not to be injured at all. In 1973, Mary Webb—who was six at the time of the tragedy and had attended the event with her mother—gave an interview where she recounted what her mother had told her about the incident: "There wasn't any fire, but there was poison gas. My mother is eighty-nine today, and she will tell you all about it. It wasn't the fire that killed the people, it was the gas. People dropped dead all over, even people who sat against the wall."

One man recalled years later that as a little boy, he escaped the Hall and ran home. He told his father that there had been a fire at the Hall and his dad dropped what he was doing and went to the Hall to see if he could help. He "walked in and walked through the dead people that were laying there on the floor and on the steps and there were people, the way he stated, still sitting in their seats that were dying, they weren't dead yet, but were dying ... and my oldest sister was laying on a kind-of couch or something, and she was unconscious, not from being stepped on or anything, but she was unconscious for two days and everybody said there was poison on the floor, and that's what my dad told us."

Likewise, another survivor recounted decades later how she had seen the man who cried "Fire," "and all of a sudden a man comes and he has a yellow can, a little yellow can. A can, and he was spreading—and he said 'fire, fire'—and then everybody started running for the door ... Yes, he was going in the aisles and throwing that stuff, you know ... and [her sister] she said that you could just see them laying down."

The best explanation for the poison or poison gas rumor comes from how most of the victims looked when they were laid out for identification. Most bore no outward signs of injury; many still had their eyes open. They looked as if they might just blink, stand up and walk away. Yet they were dead. The only other killer these people had heard of that inflicted such an innocuous-looking death was poison gas. The miners were wary of poison gas in the mines. Working underground in enclosed places it was common for miners to encounter natural gas that was dangerous, as well as carbon monoxide from machinery being run underground or even smoke from underground mine fires. Recent fires in mines had claimed such victims, many being carried out dead, with no signs of injury. Victims of such exposure bore an eerie resemblance to the children carried from the Hall. The resulting rumors and misunderstanding make sense, coupled with the general distrust the workers had of the various forces of the establishment—law enforcement, the Citizens Alliance, the mine managers—all of whom were present in the aftermath of the tragedy.

Among the other stories that gained traction at the time was one that held that someone sprinkled the stairs or the hall with a slippery substance to cause people to stumble down the stairs. It seemed unthinkable to people who were not there that such a crushing pileup of people could occur on the stairway without some kind of nefarious aid.

A survivor recalled years later: "They must have put something on those steps because those people were all piled up on the steps." Walter Lahti, who'd been thirteen when he was at the Hall, said years later about the stairway, "I think it was sprinkled."

The Missing Transcripts

In the 1920s, one of the few copies of the coroner's inquest transcript of the investigation into the Italian Hall tragedy was stolen from the Houghton County Courthouse. In the days before photocopiers, duplicates of a 191-page document were hard to come by. The theft left no copies extant in the Keweenaw, and both sides blamed the other for its disappearance.

The transcript's absence for many years left researchers looking for testimony and often relying on unreliable sources. Italian Hall witnesses were often misquoted; when their actual testimony is compared with what is attributed to them by writers without access to the actual transcript, the differences become obvious. Some of the differences are minor; others so large as to indicate their writers had no access to a copy of the transcript at all. Some researchers merely relied upon the newspapers' coverage of the inquest, presuming that the coverage was accurate. That assumption led to many of the erroneous beliefs about the tragedy in the following decades.

The Answer to the Labor Struggles: Thirty Years Late

The copper industry suffered through the Great Depression as copper prices fell. Mines out west proved more profitable because their operations were closer to the surface. The mines in the Keweenaw were now so deep that their costs soared, even with more modern equipment. Some mines closed; others merged. C&H bought up some of the more productive smaller mines, but saw its own older shafts run out of copper. In 1933, C&H cleared out its mine beneath the streets of Calumet and watched it fill with water. While unions were making inroads in other industries, the mines formed their own management-friendly unions. Many mines created unions that they could run—through placement of friendly officers for example—so they could point to their workforce and claim it was unionized.

During the Depression, various laws were enacted to help the government spur economic growth. One law that affected the mines was the National (Industrial) Recovery Act, which gave the president sweeping powers to oversee industry, and encouraged unionism and outlawed child labor. The National Labor Relations Board was created under the NRA and in 1939, the board inspected the conditions in the Copper Country, and ordered mines there to disband house unions and allow the workers to organize their own unions. In 1942, C&H watched its workers unionize—this time it could not stop them—almost thirty years after the great strike of 1913.

In 1947, Congress passed the National Labor Relations Act after a wave of strikes across the nation, with the usual attendant violence and charges of unfairness from both sides. The federal law guaranteed employees the right to organize and form unions and declared it an "unfair labor practice" for an employer to refuse to bargain with the elected representative of such a union. In essence, the Act outlawed many of the things C&H had done under MacNaughton in its dealings with the WFM. For example, it was illegal to interfere with or coerce employees in any manner with respect to their desire to unionize. It was unlawful to interfere with the formation of a union. Likewise, employers could not hire or fire employees based on their membership in a union.

The new law also created a board to mediate disputes to make sure standoffs didn't occur; no longer could a party refuse to negotiate indefinitely without facing legal consequences. The NLRA worked. After enactment, labor unions in America flourished and became a major portion of the landscape of American industry. Sadly, they came too late to save the WFM.

Enduring Appeal

"See what your greed for money has done?"
- WOODY GUTHRIE, *1913 MASSACRE* -

The Tragedy in Music

Woody Guthrie, the great American songwriter, heard of the Italian Hall and decided to write a song about it. His *1913 Massacre* was filled with inaccuracies, obviously inspired by his pro-labor stance. Some critics of the song complain that he places the tragedy at the "miner's ... big Christmas ball," when in fact it was a party for the children put on by the auxiliary. That point is minor, in light of other statements in the song. If you ask a miner at the party, according to Guthrie: "They'll tell you that they make less than a dollar a day." If a miner told you that, of course, he would have been lying—miners made closer to $3 a day when the strike was called, and the figure Guthrie quotes is one of the misleading figures often touted by the strike organizers who were trying to gain sympathy for the strikers.

Guthrie sang that there were "copper boss thug men milling outside" of the Hall, which may or may not have been the case—that is, assuming he was referring to the deputies or Waddell men. He sang that one of the thug men stuck his head in the door "and he screamed, 'There's a fire!'" This is not necessarily incorrect, for someone very well could have entered the Hall for the sole purpose of falsely announcing the fire. That it was a deputy or Waddell man, however, is no more true than if he'd said it was a member of the Citizens Alliance.

What most rankles those who hear the song today is that Guthrie immortalized the view of the thugs outside, holding the doors shut and laughing "at their murderous joke." This action was the least supported by the evidence, and is most likely far from what actually happened. Guthrie wrote that the "scabs outside" continued to laugh at the people inside the Hall, even as the dead were being unpiled and lined up for identification. Testimony is almost unanimous that the people who saw what happened were universally mortified and stricken with sadness. Many people, even years later, found Guthrie's song insulting—not only for taking such a biased position on who caused the tragedy, but for stating that members of the community could have laughed at such a catastrophe.

In 1974, the topic still upset William Gardener, a local who was six at the time of the incident. He called it a "lousy miserable song" and wished the local radio station would stop playing it "because it is so full of lies it makes me mad every time I hear it."

Big Annie Clemenc followed the workers leaving Calumet in 1914, and moved to Chicago. She left her husband behind and later married a reporter who had been in Calumet covering the strike. She worked in factories and, according to her brother, "… never was the same after the tragedy of the strike and the Italian Hall. She never forgave." She died in Chicago in 1956. Speaking of his sister years later, Frank Klobuchar said:

> She didn't like to talk about the strike and the Italian Hall disaster. It was a real sore spot with her. But she always thought it was the Citizens Alliance that was responsible. She said, "I was there. I know what happened." You know how soldiers are about the war? How they saw such horrible things that they just won't talk about it? Well, that's how Annie was. She didn't want to talk about it.

In 1980, the Michigan legislature honored Big Annie by declaring June 17 "Annie Clemenc Day," and she was the first woman inducted into the Michigan Women's Hall of Fame. Her portrait—holding her huge American flag, of course—was put on display in the State Capitol building.

The 21st century saw the Italian Hall tragedy immortalized in opera form. The piece was called "The Children of the Keweenaw," and focused on Big Annie as a lead character in the telling of the story. It was written as an opera in two acts by Paul Seitz and Kathleen Masterson; Masterson wrote the libretto. The opera was performed at the Calumet Theater, the opera house built a hundred years earlier in the heart of the then-rich Copper Country. The opera had been commissioned by the Pine Mountain Music Festival and premiered in 2001.

As could be expected, the opera had its critics. The composers purposely attempted to give an overview of the story with the understanding that no single story would ever be accepted as true by everyone. The first person on stage sings: "What's true for me may not be true for you." Further, an opera is not intended to be a documentary or investigative piece. What Seitz and Masterson accomplished was beautiful: They captured the feeling of the community from having suffered such a tragedy and presented it in a context showing what the times were like when these people lived.

The character of Annie says to MacNaughton, in a moment of perfect literary license: "Sheep do not require their shepherd. It is the shepherd who requires the sheep."

The End Of Calumet & Hecla

After World War I ended, the copper mines saw a drop in business. Production was down and so was the demand for copper. The mines tightened their belts and Calumet & Hecla even sold off many of its company-owned homes. While C&H retained title to the real estate they sat on, the structures were put up for sale for prices ranging from $5 to $12. For those who believed the argument the mines had made about the high quality of the housing they provided, it was probably shocking that most of the houses were torn down to recycle their lumber. A few were moved, but most were dismantled or destroyed.

The Copper Country began to dry up in the years following World War II. The Quincy mine closed in 1945, and the few mines that remained open were forced to dig deeper and work harder for copper. The WFM lost any chance of negotiating for the miners when they voted to end their strike in 1914. Labor organizer Bill Haywood later complained:

> *An important strike occurred on the Upper Peninsula of Michigan involving all the copper miners of that district. By this time the Western Federation of Miners had died, with the blade of conservatism plunged deep into its heart. The prestige of the W.F.M. was a thing of the past. Its revolutionary preamble had been changed for one emasculated of*

all revolutionary pretense, the last clause of which is: "To endeavor to negotiate time agreements with our employers and by all lawful means establish the principles embraced in the body of this constitution."

Meanwhile, another union began to organize the miners in the region. Haywood was wrong: It wasn't violence that would cause the unions to get bargaining power. It would require changes in the law, where employers were required to recognize unions and negotiate collective bargaining agreements when a majority of workers combined and demanded them.

The United Steelworkers Union started activities in the Keweenaw in the 1950s, and by 1955, had enough confidence in the laws and their membership to make demands of the mine owners. By 1968, Calumet & Hecla had been bought by Universal Oil Products, and the two sides faced off over a new contract. The miners called a strike on August 21, 1968. At this time, there were perhaps 1,200 workers on strike at the mine.

State and federal mediators tried to settle the strike and brought a compromise position to the union. The owners of the mine said the offer would be their last, and if it was rejected, they would merely close the mine rather than keep negotiating. In May 1969, ninety-five percent of the strikers voted to reject the offer. The mines remained closed and Calumet & Hecla ceased mine operations . The 1,200 striking miners never returned to work. Perhaps there was some justice in the miners shutting the mines down for good—rather than caving in—as they were forced to in 1914.

Survivors of the Tragedy

In the early 1970s, the approaching sixtieth anniversary of Italian Hall rekindled memories among the diminishing population of those who had been there or lived in the area. Two major sources of firsthand reports came into existence because of interest in the story and the local Finnish college, Suomi (now Finlandia University), conducting an oral history project among local Finns. Interviewers from the school met with locals and interviewed them on a range of topics, and allowed the subjects to speak freely about anything that might be of interest to people wondering what life was like growing up in the Keweenaw. The sessions were recorded and later transcribed; the transcripts and their indexes are now in the Finlandia archives. A cursory review of the indexes shows that the Italian Hall played a major role in the memories of people who lived in the region in 1913.

Arvo Pyorala mentioned the tragedy when speaking of the strike. His family lived on a farm but he remembered going into Calumet and seeing the parades of strikers and the militia. He said: "And they got trampled going down these steps because the door was locked that they couldn't get the door open and they still think to this day that it was the mining companies' own stooges that hollered this false alarm."

James MacDonald had been a newspaper carrier in Red Jacket and was returning from his route on Christmas Eve when he heard the news. One of the other boys told him: "Oh, there is going to be an 'extra'—there was a lot of people killed at that Italian Hall." While waiting for the extra to be printed, he wandered over to the Hall and saw the dead children being removed. "It was a pitiful sight."

In 1973, Dr. Clarence Andrews wrote a paper about Italian Hall and delivered it in a radio interview on the local radio station, WMPL. After reading the article, the host and Andrews spoke on the air to people who had memories of the event. Sixty years later, their memories were old, but vivid. One man told of how a stranger had saved his life by picking him up and putting him under his arm and carrying him to the back of the hall where he went down a fire escape. "But that one man, whoever he was, I would like to thank him a million times."

Mary Webb told the hosts of the show how she had been six years old at the time of the tragedy. Although she was in the Italian Hall kitchen and survived, she became deathly afraid of the dark and developed a stutter that she attributed to the experience. When asked about the direction of the doors, she was adamant, "And, I do know about the door opening in—it did not open out!"

Walter Lahti likewise described the inward swinging doors. He was thirteen at the time of the tragedy and had been caught in the stairwell for an hour and a half as the bodies were untangled. Interviewed on the show, Lahti wished he knew the name of a boy who was near him in the crush; the boy told him to remain calm and not "holler" like the others. Lahti credited the boy's advice for helping save his life. He described the feeling of being suspended in the mass of bodies on the stairs. For a while he had been held off the ground by those around him and he thought the floor beneath them had given out. When he was pulled from the mass, he ran to the back of the building and jumped out the kitchen window.

Mary Mosack (nee Kenttala) also went on the air and told how she was one of the few children taken to local hospitals after the calamity. She had been near the top of the stairs when the cry of "Fire" went up and she got swept along with the crowd. Her brother made it out of the building, but Mary was caught. She passed out and awoke in the hospital. Her father was also caught in the crush and survived. His memories—passed along to his children—were more gruesome. He was stuck in the stairway and he saw John Westola, a Finnish insurance man, die in the crush. Westola was a good friend of her father's and he felt terrible that he could do nothing to help his friend. At the hospital, there wasn't a mark on her body that she could see, "but my head was covered with heel marks."

Alex Nelson was thirteen at the time, and did not attend the party; his family belonged to the Citizens Alliance. He had been in Hancock and returned to Red Jacket by streetcar when he saw the commotion near Italian Hall. He went over and saw the bodies being removed from the building. He took "one look" and went home. He mentioned knowing that the doors of the Hall opened "in."

Edmund Raymond's memory of the event sounds like hearsay, but is interesting for its tone:

> **Q: Do you remember the Italian Hall incident?**
> *A: Ja, I do remember something. I remember a girl she was there, five years old.*
> **Q: What happened exactly?**
> *A: Well, it was gangsters hired by the company. Somebody purposely yelled out: 'Fire', they cannot put a finger on the man, but they had seen a man walking away. Sombody [sic] from outside opened the doors and yelled out 'Fire!' and then closed the doors, many people died in that, but by jees I don't know how many.*

Jean Nicholas was seven at the time of the strike, and remembered wearing a Citizens Alliance button to school. She didn't know exactly what it meant at the time, but many of her classmates—children of strikers—knew. They chased her home, yelling at her and taunting her. Her father was a deputy at the mines. She also vividly remembered MacNaughton's Eye, the searchlight erected to keep watch over Red Jacket at night. "It was frightening to children to see that light."

Henry Snabb turned seven on Christmas Day 1913, and was in the Hall on Christmas Eve. Speaking to an interviewer in 1973, he recalled the confusion as his father held him back after the stampede started:

> *We stayed there for some time after and I remember people laying around that they had hauled up from the bottom of the stairs ... a lot of them dead I suppose and a lot of them just passed out and lot of*

people were working on them. I remember it pretty well. You know, when you're seven years old you're already beginning to realize things ... so I remember quite a bit about it.

Norman Trezise was returning to his home in Tamarack, near Red Jacket, when a neighbor told him something had happened at Italian Hall. He saw the bodies laid out in the village hall and saw James MacNaughton among the people present. According to Trezise, MacNaughton offered the services of the C&H carpenter's shop to construct caskets for all the dead, but others there turned the offer down.

Some of the archive transcripts are of interviews with others who played a role in the region. W. Parsons Todd, a former manager of the Quincy mine, spoke at length in defense of the mines and their actions during the strike. He did not mention Italian Hall but he did talk about the imported workers from New York. According to Todd, the train car full of men who escaped and ran away had done so because the union found them higher paying jobs in Chicago. He did not offer any evidence to support his notion that the union "induced them all to leave."

The year 1973 was not only the sixtieth anniversary of the Italian Hall tragedy; it was also the seventieth anniversary for *Tyomies*, the newspaper whose staff was arrested for its coverage of the incident. *Tyomies* published a "Seventieth Anniversary Souvenir Journal." It included various articles on the history of Finns in America, the story of *Tyomies*, and of course, the tumultuous times of the strike of 1913-1914. Without apology, *Tyomies* explained what happened at Italian Hall on Christmas Eve 1913.

The strike was bitter. National guardsmen were called to protect the strikebreaking activities. There was terror and killing of strikers. Most infamous was the incident when the company hirelings provocatively hollered "fire" to cause a panic among strikers' children attending a Christmas party at the Italian Hall in Calumet, December 25, 1913. 86 children died, half of whom were children of Finnish miners.

The date was off by a day, and the number of dead was off by a dozen or so, but the rest of the facts were arguably correct. This time, no one was arrested for the report.

In 1981, a copy of the stolen coroner's inquest transcript was brought in to the Calumet Village Hall. It "magically" appeared on the desk of village manager Dan McCormick. McCormick didn't know what to make of it. At first, no one claimed to know where it came from but everyone knew what it was. This copy of the transcript bore markings on its face sheet that indicated it was originally stored at the Houghton County courthouse, which would link it to the one stolen sixty years earlier. McCormick also noticed that the copy bore distinctive marks on each page—similar to photocopies made in the Village Hall at the time, on a copier that was malfunctioning and leaving a telltale smudge on every copy it made—which led him to believe that someone within the Hall had copied it first, then returned the copy but kept the original.

Newspapers reported the return of the transcript, but no one would say who had returned it. McCormick left the person who returned it as "unnamed" and told the paper that he talked to the person but had no more information about the transcript's whereabouts the previous sixty years. The story in the paper didn't mention that the person returning the transcript was a young woman who was related to another village employee who worked in the Hall. McCormick never found out the complete story of how the transcript copy came to be in the possession of the people who returned it, but he guessed that they were related somehow to whoever had stolen it. The motives of the thief remained unknown.

Later Memories of Italian Hall

The Italian Hall disaster stayed in the minds of the people who remained in the area, even seventy years later. When a man named Leslie Chapman mentioned to an acquaintance in 1982 that he'd heard a confession fifty-eight years earlier, it made local headlines in *The Daily Mining Gazette*.

The March 16, 1982, *Gazette* recounted the "ITALIAN HALL CONFESSION" and how Chapman had happened upon Lawrence Westola on the streets of Calumet shortly before. When Westola told Chapman that his father had died in the Italian Hall, Chapman mentioned that someone had confessed to him about yelling "Fire." Chapman said that he had been in Butte, Montana, for a court case involving the copper industry when a man approached him and asked him if he was from Michigan. The man told him he wanted to get something off his chest. According to Chapman in 1982, he said:

> *I've got a confession to make. Do you remember the tragedy they had in 1913 in Calumet, where all those people died? Well, I was there at the time with my partner. We were both single men and drunk and thought we'd have some fun. As we walked by the hall, we decided to yell "fire" and watch the people come down. We didn't know it would turn out*

bad. We both left town afterward. My doctor told me I have a few weeks to live as I have tuberculosis and I want to get that out of my mind.

The *Gazette* said Chapman asked the man his name but the man wouldn't give it to him. The paper called Chapman to confirm the story as told to Westola, and the paper said he did.

Wilbert Maki, author of *Stairway to Tragedy* about the Italian Hall, read the *Gazette* article and followed up with Chapman. Maki interviewed Chapman at his home in 1982 and recorded the conversation. This time, Chapman recalled the conversation like this—"I" being Chapman, "He" being the mystery man:

> He said, *"Yes, I know, but I'll tell you what happened."*
>
> *I said, "I know what happened, when all those people died, men, women and children."*
>
> *He said, "My partner and I got drunk and we were having lots of fun. Everybody was happy. My partner said, 'Let's have some fun.' He said, 'We'll holler 'fire' and watch them scramble.'"*
>
> *The man related that both being drunk, they didn't realize what would happen.*
>
> *He said, "That's been bothering me and I haven't got long to live. I noticed in the paper that somebody was coming out here from Calumet. That's why I'm here. I want to tell you exactly what happened. Both my partner and I were drunk."*
>
> *The man looked awful bad.*
>
> *He came beside me and made this confession. That's what really happened. Of course, there was no fire.*

Maki asked Chapman why he hadn't told people this story previously, and Chapman said that "people out here aren't interested in this story." Chapman then told Maki that "he had the man's name on a piece of paper, however, he misplaced it. He could not recall the name of the man." Chapman died in 1982.

Unfortunately, Chapman was either lying or mistaken when he recounted the story in 1982. He had told the story previously to an interviewer at Suomi College in 1972, while being interviewed for the college's oral history project. There, the subject of the Italian Hall was only one of many that he discussed, and the interviewer—Paul Jalkanen—asked only the simplest questions and let Chapman respond as he desired. There, he said:

When I was out in Butte I was staying at the Finley motel and I was sitting in the lobby about the fourth or fifth day I was there and this fellow came over and sat down beside me and asked me if I'm from Michigan? He said are you lost out here and I said no I'm out here on a Federal case. He said I was an orderly up there. He said you know you had a bad strike up there about 60 or 70 people died up there in the Italian Hall. Well the fellow who died here at the hospital, he confessed that he was the one who hollered fire. I asked what did he say. He told me that he and two other guys were drunk and they were going to have some fun and see some people scatter. The one guy said I'll holler fire and you'll see some people scatter to get out of this place. So he hollered fire.

Well just then they paged me to come over to the Federal Courts. So I never had a chance to talk with him anymore. I looked for him after because I wanted to get his name and address and find somebody else who worked at the hospital at the same time to get two signatures on the statement that that was true.

When asked by the interviewer if Chapman ever found the man again, he replied, "No." So, in 1982, Chapman said he spoke with the man who yelled "Fire." In 1972, he said he spoke to the man who heard a confession from the man who cried "Fire." In ten years, Chapman lost the man in the middle. Further, in ten years he changed the number of men in the drunken party from three to two and also added the fact that he had the man's name "on a piece of paper" when in 1972 he had said he had not gotten the man's name and could never find him again.

Whether Chapman actually met someone in Butte who told him *they* knew who had confessed to the crime is not the issue here. Chapman's later—embellished—version of events is just not believable. The fact that it was printed in the paper at all shows the incredible amount of emotion this story still garners in the Keweenaw. Be that as it may, Chapman having met someone he couldn't name fifty-eight years earlier, who told him that they had heard a deathbed confession from someone they couldn't name does not add anything to the story.

Rebels on the Range
In 1984, Arthur W. Thurner's book, *Rebels on the Range* was published. Thurner was a professor in Chicago who had grown up in Calumet and did intensive research into the copper miner's strike of 1913-1914. Part of that

story, of course, is the tragedy at the Italian Hall. In telling his version of events—in an otherwise remarkable history book—Thurner relies heavily on the contemporary press accounts and the coroner's inquest, to the exclusion of other sources. This led Thurner to the mistaken conclusion that the tragedy was nothing more than "sheer *accident.*" He argued that the man who first raised the cry of "Fire" did so because he really thought there was a fire in the Hall. Thurner is one of the few sources to suggest there really had been a fire in the Hall.

Thurner bases this conclusion on very sketchy evidence and, of course, does not name the man who made the innocent mistake of thinking there was a fire, and starting the panic by crying "Fire." He even wrote the author in 2005 and said he found it odd that "NO ONE ever really confessed to calling 'Fire!' " Presumably, if his suggestion were correct—it was an innocent mistake—that person would have been more likely to come forward and admit it. Especially if, as Thurner suggests, there were witnesses prepared to testify that there was, in fact, evidence of a fire in the Hall that night.

While investigating the tragedy, Thurner interviewed a survivor in 1978. Frank Shaltz was twelve when he was trapped in the stairwell of the Italian Hall, and he also testified at the House subcommittee hearing. Although seventy-seven at his meeting with Thurner, Shaltz was impressive with his memory and youthful appearance. He told Thurner that no one had been checking for union cards when he arrived at the Hall with his friend that evening. Later, he said he had a good view of the man standing near the door, crying "Fire" and waving his hands. The man wore an Alliance button; he was as certain of it in 1978 as he had been in 1913. Thurner mentioned to Shaltz how the newspapers had suggested that Shaltz had been coached in his testimony answers. "I was not. I told the truth," he replied.

Still, Thurner made many statements that clearly adopt the position taken by the coroner's inquest and other pro-management parties. He called Albert Lanto the "official doorkeeper for the day" at the Italian Hall. He does not give a citation for the source of this incorrect statement. Lanto never mentioned being the "official doorkeeper" in the inquest testimony nor in the subcommittee hearing. In fact, at that second hearing, he testified that he saw a man pass by him wearing a "Citizens Alliance" pin. If Lanto had been the official doorkeeper, it would seem odd he would stand idly by and watch an Alliance member wander into the Hall. Where Thurner found information to support this statement is unclear—the statement appears to be baseless. Worse, it appears to support the "inquest" version of events over the "subcommittee" version.

Thurner also wrote: "People did not die in the stairway because they were trapped by doors that opened inward ..." To support that contention, he relies on the coroner's inquest testimony of a few people who said that when they got to the scene, they found the doors open. As with all of the testimony from the inquest, there are several problems with this. The testimony of many of the witnesses was muddled, often due to language problems, and because the witnesses were never asked to clarify things they said. Dominic Vairo is one of the people he cites for the contention that the doors swung outward. What did Vairo say?

> **Q: Then what did you do next?**
> *A: When I heard everybody holler fire I tried to go upstairs from the front and as soon as I got up the hall was jammed.*
> **Q: Did you go up then?**
> *A: Up the saloon.*
> **Q: You opened the door by the saloon, the main doorway, and the hall was filled with kids? Who was pulling them out?**
> *A: I don't know. I tried to pull out a few of them myself but could not. The kids were all hollering.*
> **Q: You could not pull any of them out?**
> *A: No.*
> **Q: Was that front door open?**
> *A: Opened that time.*

At that point, Vairo went through the back of his saloon and climbed up into the Hall from the rear. Yet, what exactly did Vairo do? Although his testimony is vague, he started in his saloon and "opened the door by the saloon." Presumably, that is the door between the saloon and the vestibule at the bottom of the stairs, not the doors from the street into the Hall. If that had been the case, Vairo would have had to exit the saloon, walk outside the building, and then go to the doors at the front of the Hall. It makes more sense that he went to the closest door—the one between the saloon and the stairs.

If Thurner was splitting hairs, his statement might be true. The direction the doors opened probably did not play that large a role in the deaths of the seventy-three victims. From most accounts, the bodies were piled up on the stairs and the mass of bodies did not reach the outer doors. But, Thurner does not address how Vairo—who he found credible—could have heard the cry of "Fire" when he was downstairs, while Thurner found that the cry of "Fire" could not be heard by people at the top of the stairs to the hall.

Thurner simply dismissed the subcommittee's hearing. He wrote that the hearing only lasted a "couple" of hours—it lasted a full day—and that it excluded "all witnesses who did not both see the button and hear the cry." This statement is patently false. The congressmen running the hearing announced that anyone could testify, and Hilton—who Thurner quotes as saying that witnesses would be "confined" to the topics of the button and the cry of "Fire"—also said that he welcomed any and all who wanted to testify and that he didn't want an "unfair" hearing.

Further, the hearing *was not* confined to the topic of the Citizens Alliance. Lesh, Saari, Mary Lanto, Peter Lanto, Jokopie, Marchesey, Boggio and Wiropia were not asked about the Alliance button, and none of them testified regarding the button. Thurner also wrote that one of the witnesses said he saw "five men wearing Alliance buttons." This statement is not borne out by any of the witnesses at the hearing. In 2005, corresponding with the author, Thurner explained that upon closer examination of this issue, he might have "misread this testimony." He referred to Erick Erickson who said he saw two people wearing Alliance buttons—later those two were standing with three others—but he did not say that the other three were wearing buttons. Erickson specifically said that he saw only "two buttons."

It is possible that Thurner, who relied heavily on newspaper coverage of the events for some of his facts, accepted as true *The Daily Mining Gazette* version of Erickson's testimony. The paper had reported that he saw three men wearing buttons, when in fact, he had specifically said he had seen only two. Of course, it is still a far stretch to go from three buttons to five.

Thurner's heavy reliance upon coverage from the local newspapers is problematic. He did not address the fact that many of the newspapers were either owned or heavily influenced by the mine owners. Nor did he even address their bias, a shocking omission in light of how twisted their coverage has been shown to be when the transcripts are compared with the newspaper accounts of the same testimony. And the newspapers' coverage of the events crept into Thurner's story in less obvious ways. For instance, Moyer was unquestionably kidnapped—a rather serious crime—but Thurner adopted the newspaper's version and repeatedly called the event a "deportation."

And, when it supported his thesis, Thurner adopted the newspaper coverage over the inquest testimony. According to Thurner, Matt Saari spoke at the funeral home the day after Christmas to a reporter. Thurner wrote that Saari "flatly contradicted the report being circulated that a bearded man wearing a Citizens' Alliance button had entered the hall and caused the panic. He said no one had come up the stairway and raised the alarm at the door. He had been at the main entrance and he said the cry came from within the hall in a section occupied by 'a group of men and women who were sitting together at one side of the hall.' " Thurner appears to have found that statement in the *Calumet News*, the paper that acted as the unofficial mouthpiece of the mines. And the paper did not say its reporter spoke to Saari; the reporter claimed to have spoken to someone else who said they spoke to Saari.

A couple of days later, Saari testified before the inquest—testimony that Thurner treated as gospel previously. What did Saari testify to when he was under oath and his words were being written down?

> **Q: Did you hear any cry of fire?**
> *A: I hear something like that but I did not take notice of it. I had a newspaper and started to read that and then I looked inside where they gave the candy and see no fire. I thought they were fooling and started to read again but the people were going out so fast I thought there must be some kind of trouble.*
> **Q: How many times did you hear somebody cry fire?**
> *A: I could not say that.*
> **Q: Did you hear someone say fire?**
> *A: Yes.*
> **Q: Was that before or after they started to go out?**
> *A: Before it was like that.*
> **Q: Where did you hear that cry of fire come from?**
> *A: I could not say what part because I was reading that paper. I can't tell you that.*

Thurner's version of the Italian Hall tragedy was embraced by many in the community. Perhaps it was the extensive research that had gone into the book that convinced readers that Thurner's opinion must have been correct. Sadly, much of it does not withstand scrutiny. Thurner concluded that there really was a fire in the Italian Hall, perhaps a chimney fire that later extinguished itself. "There were reports by men on the street outside the hall shortly after the panic began that there had been a chimney fire at Italian Hall." For that statement, Thurner referred his readers to four pages of the inquest testimony, none of which addressed a chimney fire, or even men on the street. Careful readers are left to wonder where the allegation came from. Thurner also wrote:

> *Herman Bibber, at his home next door, had seen smoke rising from the hall and he became convinced the building was on fire. When he called the Red Jacket Fire Department to report a fire, he was questioned about the certainty of it for the department had been bothered by a series of false alarms. He said he was sure there was a fire.*

For that, he cites the Coroner's Inquest, "p. 61." Page sixty-one of the Coroner's Inquest begins in the middle of Jacob Kaiser's testimony, which is page fifty-three of Molloy's later transcription. Kaiser said he lived near the Hall and heard "them shouting fire at the Italian Hall." He went over to the fire hall and while he was there the phone rang. The person on the phone said there was a fire at the Hall, although Kaiser did not identify the caller and he could not even tell if it was a man or a woman. Elsewhere in his book Thurner refers to Herman Bibber, although the only place Bibber was reported was in the local newspapers; he did not testify at the inquest, at the subcommittee hearing, nor did anyone else mention him by name. Thurner's adoption of the "Bibber" story came from the newspaper coverage, as evidenced elsewhere in his footnotes. Bibber's version of events was highly suspect though because he never testified under oath and, as we have already seen, witness statements in the local newspapers were more likely fiction than fact.

Was Bibber "convinced" there was a fire? In 2005, Thurner wrote the author and indicated that he had found references to Bibber in two different local papers, but that his notes (Thurner did not photocopy his sources) made no mention of Bibber actually phoning the fire hall. Thurner suggested the author "recheck this story in the [*Calumet News*]." The *Calumet News* story of Bibber reads in its entirety:

> *Herman Bibber, whose residence is in the rear of the hall, estimates that a hundred or more of those in the building escaped by reaching the fire escape, the top platform of which is only a few inches from an upper porch of the Bibber residence. As rapidly as children appeared on the fire escape, they were lifted across onto the porch, then down through the house to safety. Those in the Bibber home had no realization until afterwards, however, of the extent of the calamity occurring at the other end of the building.*

No mention was made of Bibber notifying anyone of the fire. Thurner wrote the author further: "The figure of Bibber is intriguing. Why was he not summoned as a witness? Assuming he *did* telephone the Red Jacket Fire Station to report he 'thought' he saw smoke coming from the Hall, his testimony would be valuable. But Bibber 'disappears' from the proceedings."

Although Thurner pointed to the *Calumet News* in his letter to the author, Bibber was mentioned in the *Gazette*, where he was reported to have been "the man who telephoned the fire alarm to the Red Jacket department [and] thought he saw smoke issuing from the building." The *Gazette* does not make Bibber seem as certain as Thurner did and does not even say why it thought Bibber may have called anyone that night.

In his final analysis, Thurner proposed:

> *The explanation that the panic might have occurred through sheer accident apparently occurred to very few people in those bitter days of December when strikers and Alliance members waged war on each other.*

Thurner was wrong in saying it had occurred to "very few people." The paragraph referring to Herman Bibber in the *Gazette* on December 27, 1913, was directly above a headline that read: "Purely Accident." The column begins with the contention that officials "are now convinced that the catastrophe was the result of accident, pure and simple." It was not "very few people" who thought it was an accident; it was the newspapers controlled by the mines that promoted that notion, two days after the event, while witnesses were coming forward to blame the Citizens Alliance.

It seems no one bothered to sift through the evidence and see how Thurner's conclusions about Italian Hall held up to scrutiny. After all, much of what he wrote about the copper industry and the unions before the strike appears accurate. It might have been a long-held desire to put the matter to bed: By saying no one was to blame, the community could finally drop any old grudges and move on. Although it might be a noble desire—to exorcize the blame we wish to place—we cannot exonerate everyone just to make the matter go away.

Some of Thurner's conclusions were drawn before others had made startling discoveries in this field. For instance, Thurner wrote that it really was a mystery as to who organized the Citizens Alliance. "What appears to have happened is that an anonymous group of businessmen, when the labor conflict stalemated, took hold of an idea which had been afloat in the community as a potential means of combating the WFM and declared the existence of the Citizens' Alliance." Thurner apparently didn't know about evidence that showed the mines funded the Alliance, arranged the rallies, paid the legal fees of Alliance members, paid to print the Alliance papers and even supplied the speakers for the Alliance rallies. The organizers may have wanted to remain anonymous, but history found them out.

While investigating the Italian Hall, Thurner set out to locate a copy of the coroner's inquest transcript and discovered that no copies could be found. The one that should have been at the Houghton County courthouse was missing—stolen in the 1920s—and none of the copies that were given to the House subcommittee could be located. Thurner found a copy in "private" hands, but never disclosed whose hands those were. He later gave his copy of the transcript to the Michigan Technological University Copper Country Archives. That copy is missing a page, the same page that is missing from the copy that magically reappeared at the Village Hall in Calumet. Clearly, Thurner's copy and the Village Hall copy were both made from the same copy that had been stolen from the Houghton County courthouse.

American Heritage

In 1986, *American Heritage* magazine published a story on the Italian Hall tragedy that was a mixture of facts and errors. It appears that many of the mistakes in the article are the result of its author relying too heavily on newspaper coverage and not having access to the inquest transcript. For instance, in addressing the rumors of the deputies holding the doors shut, the author wrote:

> *That rumor was baseless and quickly disproved by the inquest where scores of witnesses testified that deputies had worked to exhaustion trying to get people out and to untangle the bodies on the stairwell.*

Although many people use the word "score" flippantly to mean "many," it actually means twenty. Scores—plural—would technically mean forty or more, but how many people testified at the inquest that the deputies "had worked to exhaustion" rescuing people? Sandretto said he saw deputies standing around by the door; he did not know what they were doing there. Theresa Kaisor said she saw deputies in the Hall, with no mention of what they were doing there. Charles Meyers said he saw no deputies that evening that he could remember. Dominic Vairo saw deputies on the street keeping people from going into the Hall but does not mention them working to save anyone. Big Annie Clemenc said she saw deputies carrying in the dead but does not mention how hard they worked. Flora Wright saw no deputies. Neither did John Fretz. Patrick Ryan saw deputies holding people back but did not see them helping with the recovery. Albert Lanto saw no deputies that evening. Angelo Curto likewise saw deputies holding the crowd back. Jacob Kaisor testified that the deputies did not arrive until "after," and does not mention them helping at all. Margaret Tomei escaped the Hall and saw deputies heading toward the Hall, but did not see them try and help. Caesar Bono was one of the few who testified about trying to untangle the bodies and help those in the stairwell. A man from the saloon and "another fellow" were there with him, but there were no deputies there that he saw.

Joseph Trudell is one of the few who saw the deputies helping: He mentions "the firemen and the deputies were taking them out" referring to the dead and injured. John Rastello did not see deputies when he first heard the commotion, but he saw them later outside the Hall. He was not asked what the deputies were doing and he did not say. Mrs. Czabo testified that she saw the deputies holding people back from entering the Hall, and also that the deputies were compounding the problem by not letting people leave the Hall. Mrs. Forster testified that she saw deputies near the stairs, but does not mention them helping anyone. John Jokopii testified that he saw no deputies until after the rescue efforts were started. He does not say if they took part, and he was not asked. Louis Wuopia saw deputies guarding the doors but does not mention them helping anyone. Theresa Burcar saw deputies at the scene but was never asked what they were doing there. Peter Jetta said he never saw deputies clubbing anyone, but was never asked if he saw deputies doing anything else. James Vivian saw no deputies even though he was there, helping to untangle the bodies. Peter Pichittino saw deputies but did not say they were helping. Mrs. Mirchisio said she did not know if she saw any deputies that evening. These are all the witnesses who mentioned the word "deputy" or "deputies" in their testimony. Of more than three score witnesses who testified, only one—Trudell—mentioned them helping at all.

Where did the idea that "scores" of deputies worked "to exhaustion" to help the rescue efforts come from? It came from the local newspaper coverage. The *News* and the *Gazette* made the stories up from whole cloth to make the deputies and mine management look good. This could just have been part of the propaganda battle they had been waging all year, or it could have been more. Just as they had anticipated the need of inventing and pushing the notion that only union members could get into the Hall, they may have seen the need to promote the deputies as the saviors in this calamity. Clearly, they weren't the heroes the papers made them out to be.

Otherwise, the *American Heritage* article is relatively accurate. It was published shortly after the Hall was torn down, and called attention to the event on a rather broad stage.

The Legend
The "official" version of events was adopted by many others. For example, the local writer Clarence J. Monette writes regional histories, such as *The Copper Range Railroad.* In a passing reference to the strike, he wrote:

> *On July 14, 1913, written demand for recognition of the Western Federation of Miners was made to all the mining companies. No other specific demands or grievances were set forth. Ample evidence before and since that date has shown that this organization represented no more than a small minority of men. Recognition was refused and on July 23, 1913, the Western Federation called a strike. They then inaugurated all the violence and intimidation which had made the strikes of this organization notorious everywhere. The mines were closed, many men left the district, and others under the reign of terror then prevailing joined this organization. After the arrival of the State National Guard, operations were resumed, but were hampered greatly by strike conditions. Improvement came slowly but persistently.*

The bulk of that paragraph is false. He claimed no demands were made, while the letter sent to the mines spoke of "the demand for higher wages, shorter hours, and other things, in this letter." The evidence indicated that a majority of the miners were sympathetic to the union; it is ludicrous to argue that a "small minority" called the strike and got the rest, presumably a "great majority," not to cross the picket lines. Mine management even admitted in court documents—one of the rare occasions when they were forced to tell the truth—that there were only 4,000 miners who wanted to cross the picket lines. As for "inaugurating" violence, history shows that the imported Waddell men and the deputized miners were just as culpable—if not more so—as the WFM in bringing violence to the area. Monette does not mention the Putrich boarding house murders or the Italian Hall either, when claiming that the violence of the times was the fault of the WFM.

Many other writers refer to Thurner or Lankton (who relies almost exclusively on Thurner for his version of the Italian Hall) for background facts on the strike and Italian Hall. For example, an article about the stereo photo cards of the tragedy in *Stereo World* magazine in 1992 stated their context: The union was a "vocal minority" and "a later inquest found no evidence to support" the notion that the Alliance was involved in the tragedy.

In their attempts to put the matter to closure, residents of the Keweenaw were tempted to believe various theories floated in later years, including some far-fetched "death bed confessions" that were widely publicized in the local media. Chapman's story was discussed above. In 1993, *The Daily Mining Gazette* boldly pronounced it had solved the mystery, eighty years after the fact: "The man who cried fire at Italian Hall," the headline teased. The sub-head explained, "Resident claims prankster made deathbed confession." Although the similarity of this story to Chapman's should have been obvious to the reporter, the paper ran the story on its front page with extensive and unbelievable detail.

According to the *Gazette*, its reporter interviewed a man who was on his own deathbed in 1993 and had come forward to tell of the story he'd heard told by another man on his deathbed in the 1930s. In this multiple-deathbed scenario, "Bill" demanded anonymity from the reporter. Although he was just days away from death, he told the reporter to protect his identity because he feared *someone might try and kill him*. Much more nonsense was attributed to Bill.

Bill claimed that besides himself, there were "two county sheriffs, two judges, an attorney, a priest and an undertaker" who witnessed the confession. Bill claimed that the eight men then made a pact not to disclose the confession until seven of the eight had died. The eighth man was then to make the facts known—presumably on his own deathbed—so the community could put the matter to rest. How each of the men could guarantee they would die predictably was not the biggest problem with the story, however.

According to Bill, the confession was made in the 1930s—while the matter was still fresh in everyone's memory. The sheriffs, judges and the attorney present would all have been under a duty to disclose the confession because of the fact that as a possible murder prosecution, the Italian Hall disaster was still a pending criminal investigation. When asked about that notion, Bill said: "The sheriff wanted it disclosed, but the judge said no." In Bill's world, a sheriff chose not to solve the crime of the century because a judge—not in court or in any official capacity—told him not to.

Much more of the story is unbelievable and bizarre. According to Bill, the man who confessed to the crime was on his deathbed in the 1930s and was eighteen at the time of the tragedy in 1913. The "dying" man would have been in his late 30s or early 40s. When asked how the man died, Bill *guessed* the death was caused by heart failure. It seems odd that a man in his late 30s would know he was within days of dying, have the foresight to gather together a regular who's who of witnesses to vouch for his story, but not tell them what he was dying of.

Bill claimed that the man felt terrible after the incident, and "worked through the night helping to remove the dead." Bill did not explain how this could have been the case when so many people testified that they saw the man who cried "Fire" and presumably would have recognized him if he came back into the Hall afterward to help with the rescue efforts. Bill also claimed that the man helped dig the graves at Lakeview and then devoted his life to community service. "He was well-liked." Despite taking up several columns in the *Gazette*, "Bill's" story is nonsense. That it was even printed is remarkable, except when one considers how deeply the story affected the community, even eighty years after the event.

The *Gazette* also carefully pointed out that "Bill" was not his real name, but said he had been a federal employee for twenty years, suffered a stroke in 1993, lived in Baraga County and one can guess that he would have had to be about eighty years old in 1993. The 1990 census counted 7,954 people in Baraga County, with only 697 aged seventy-five years old or older. Assuming that half of those were men, one would guess that a search for "former federal employees who have had strokes this year and are over 75 living in Baraga" would have narrowed the list of people who might be Bill to a very small number. Assuming that the reporter didn't just invent Bill out of thin air, there must have been quite a few people in the Keweenaw who knew who Bill was after the story ran.

Despite that, no other stories ran about Bill, except a follow-up a few years later about how no new details had been learned. Then, the *Gazette* reiterated that Bill had refused to give the reporter the name of the man, because he "did not wish to speak ill of the dead." As silly as that reasoning is—how "ill" can you speak of someone who was responsible for the deaths of seventy-three people?—the *Gazette* stood by its story because the reporter believed Bill was telling the truth. Even so, they had no way of knowing if the man Bill had spoken to—assuming there really was such a man—had been telling *him* the truth.

Finally, Peggy Germain, the researcher who has studied the Italian Hall with an eye toward determining an accurate count of the victims, wrote another book in 2005. There, she claimed that she also knows who cried "Fire." She does not disclose the name, however:

> *For those of you who believe that knowing the name or names of the fire caller or callers will bring you comfort and closure, trust me when I say that it doesn't. I would willingly divulge this information if it would bring any of the dead back to life.*
>
> *I recall the telephone conversation with an elderly man from L'Anse when I learned who called "Fire." He told me that everyone knew who called fire at the time but kept silent. I believe he told me the complete story, because six decades is a long time to keep a secret. Also, since there is no Statute of Limitations on murder, it wasn't safe to name the fire callers until they were dead, since they could have been prosecuted for these crimes.*

Germain writes that she is not disclosing the name of the perpetrator of Michigan's largest mass murder because it won't bring anyone "comfort and closure" or bring the dead back to life. She also indicates that "everyone" knew the identity of the mass murderer, but for some odd reason, no one would name him because everyone wanted to keep that person "safe." Germain's story, as sketchy as it is, sounds too much like the story of "Bill" to be credible. In any case, Germain and the others never said they spoke to the person who confessed to the crime—they spoke to someone who said they knew who did it. Lawyers call those stories multiple hearsay; everyone else can just call them unsubstantiated rumors.

It is also important to remember that it is easy for someone to confess to something they did not do. Although it seems odd that anyone would, a person on their deathbed may have incentive to confess to crimes they did not commit. They might be covering for someone else; they might think that by confessing to a tragedy like the Italian Hall they will help the community heal. Or, as in Chapman's case, they just might like the attention they get from telling stories. Boring stories don't make headlines; stories that purport to solve the state's largest mass murder are front-pagers.

The Memorial

The Italian Hall fell into disuse and disrepair over the years. In 1945 the building had been bought by the local chapter of the Fraternal Order of Eagles for $3,200. In 1972, they sold it to a local businessman named Delbert Masser for $2,000. The declining price mirrored the building's health. It was not occupied in the early 1980s, and some began to question whether the building was a hazard.

Efforts had been made to gain recognition for the building and its place in history. In 1974, the building was examined for the Historic American Building Survey. Historian Kevin Harrington examined the building in great detail, inside and out, and also did extensive research on it. He found out the names of the architects who designed it, and also traced the chain of title back to 1882.

Harrington walked through the building. Immediately inside the front doors he found graffiti: "Thugs yelled fire and there were dead babies." He did the best he could to observe and record what he saw. "The ceiling of the stage could not be adequately observed since there is no longer electricity serving the building ..."

People in the area noticed that a large crack was forming on the front of the building, directly above the southernmost window, one story above the door to the upstairs hall. The Village of Calumet hired an engineer to inspect the building to see what it would take to save it: The news wasn't good. It would take more than $50,000 to make it safe for occupancy. The village did not have that kind of money.

Some locals, including Peggy Germain, formed the Friends of Italian Hall and tried to raise money to save the building and restore it, but their efforts fell short. The building was demolished in 1984. A large crowd gathered to watch as the wrecking ball was put to the Hall. Ironically, the first few strikes bounced off; the old Hall was tougher than predicted. But, eventually, the building came down.

A local entrepreneur saved floorboards and made souvenirs. The small wood blocks are about the size of a bar of soap, and bear the inscription: "WOOD FROM ITALIAN HALL." The dates 1908-1984 are listed below, along with a reference to Christmas Eve 1913, and the loss of seventy-four lives. According to the language on the block, there were thirty-seven girls, twenty-one boys, eleven women and five men who perished in the Hall that day.

Some funds were raised by the Village of Calumet to buy the parcel the Hall sat upon to erect a memorial to the tragedy, and the pillars and archway that framed the front door of the Hall were saved. They stand alone now on the spot where the Italian Hall stood, along with a historical marker placed by the State of Michigan. The park was dedicated on November 13, 1989, in a ceremony that concluded with a singing of the hymn, *Silent Night.*

The marker on the site reads:

ITALIAN HALL

On December 24, 1913, area copper miners had been on strike for five months. The miners were fighting for better pay, shortened work days, safer working conditions and union recognition. That day, during a yuletide party for the striking miners and their families, someone yelled, "Fire!" Although there was no fire, seventy-three persons died while attempting to escape down a stairwell that had doors that opened inward. Over half of those who died were children between the ages of six and ten. The perpetrator of the tragedy was never identified. The strike ended in 1914.

Arguably, the marker is correct. Some may quibble with the issue of the doors. The matter will probably never be resolved because of the overwhelming belief in the community that the doors opened inward, even as photographs and other evidence indicate otherwise. The wording on the marker was drafted by Peggy Germain and Theresa Spence, and the sign became Michigan Historical marker number 1337. Some have suggested placing another marker on the spot with the names of those who died. Such a roster is problematic: To carve the names in stone would require agreement on the spellings of the names, as well as consensus on how many people actually died in the calamity. When Seitz and Masterson composed the opera "Children of the Keweenaw," they were criticized for adopting the position that seventy-four had perished. This is the number adopted by Arthur Thurner and many others, but there are stronger arguments for seventy-three. Some argue for other totals based on the conflicting lists of victims, disagreement among funeral home records and illegible death certificates. The controversy will probably prevent any such marker being created. Of course, the marker could be installed, recognizing that arguments over spellings of names and the number of dead would inevitably follow—no matter what information was eventually used.

What Actually Happened

Simply put, what happened at Italian Hall was this: A man wearing a Citizens Alliance pin ran in, cried "Fire," and ran out. His actions killed seventy-three people. Some will react negatively to that conclusion, for it seems inconceivable that anyone would aim to do such a thing. But that is the other huge misconception that causes students of the tragedy to stumble: The man didn't have to intend for anyone to die. The likely scenario is that he merely wanted to create a disturbance to disrupt the festivities. After all, the mines and their allies knew that anything pleasant strengthened the miners' resolve to continue the strike. The Christmas Eve party was the kind of thing that would delay the miners from wanting to come in from the cold and get back to work.

When the "disturbance" killed seventy-three people, it probably shocked the man who had done it—and certainly his employer or others who knew what he was up to. Why else were the papers so willing to distort the truth and misreport what happened in the days following the tragedy and at the inquest? Why was the law so quick to arrest the entire editorial staff of *Tyomies* and shut the paper down, when the bulk of their reporting was more accurate than that of the *Calumet News*? The only logical explanation is because of the cozy relationships between mine management, the newspapers, the Citizens Alliance, local law enforcement, the county board of supervisors and the grand jury. All were implicated in the killings at one level or another, as co-conspirators or accomplices after the fact. But there was just no chance for justice in 1913 Calumet for the children of striking miners.

Epilogue

The name Calumet comes from the French, where it describes a wooden shaft or baton used in ceremonies and religious observances. The term appeared in America when settlers labeled the ceremonial pipe used by some Native Americans as the "calumet." In popular use, the item was sometimes called a peace pipe. Ironically, the area known for the largest mass murder in Michigan history bears the name of an instrument of peace.

Notes and Sources

A few comments are needed to clarify some of the issues that arose during the preparation of this book. Many people will dislike the conclusions I reach, largely because they conflict with much of the popular literature on the topic. However, I hope readers will note why I differ from the opinions of many who have written before me.

The most obvious error made by students of the Italian Hall tragedy is a reliance on local newspaper reports for factual explanations of the event. However, the newspapers of the day and region were wildly inaccurate—often on purpose—and should never be the starting point for this investigation.

Likewise, there were several investigations into the tragedy and a few hearings where witnesses testified under oath. Luckily, transcripts survive. The problem is that the transcripts are not of equal value, as some historians appear to believe. The coroner's inquest was botched worse than any other legal proceeding of its sort in Michigan. People can debate all they want about the reason why it was botched, but that is not the point.

On the other hand, the House subcommittee hearing was well conducted and appears today—more than ninety years later—as the transcript of a well-run hearing. Those interested in the topic should obtain copies of the two transcripts and compare them. If you want to reach the height of absurdity, read them alongside the coverage of the same hearings in the *Calumet News*. The bias for the first transcript and against the second hearing seems to have its roots in the newspaper coverage of the day. Those who read them without preconceived notions—or, heaven forbid, having their minds polluted by the newspaper coverage—will reach the same conclusion I did.

I enjoyed *Rebels on the Range* when I first read it after I had begun researching this topic, because I was impressed with the amount of detail in Arthur Thurner's book. Problems surfaced, however, when I compared his statements and attributions to primary sources that I located. I found his dismissal of the House subcommittee hearings to be so baseless that I located Thurner and wrote to him about it. Most glaringly, I found his claim of "five" men wearing Alliance buttons to be so far from the testimony that I could not imagine where he had found such a thing.

Thurner wrote to me and explained that he had possibly misread the testimony but he stood by the rest of his book. He and I exchanged correspondence for a while and he even gave me a copy of his notes from interviewing Frank Shaltz. We disagree on many things regarding the Italian Hall, which is fitting considering that very few people anywhere agree completely on the story. I think the difference in our opinions comes from the fact that I attempted to examine the story with the starting point being that nothing was proven and I would examine as much as I could before reaching conclusions. Thurner and other natives of the Keweenaw often seem to start from the position of what they've grown up knowing—community knowledge—and then seeing which evidence supports or attacks that position. Too often, the evidence that goes the wrong way is ignored.

By this, I do not intend to demean Mr. Thurner and I hope that readers do not take it that way. I merely want to set the record straight and find it frustrating that half of my battle has been in correcting the errors others have made before me. I am not confining my comments to Mr. Thurner. For instance, the articles in *The Daily Mining Gazette* of anonymous deathbed confessions come to mind as well.

One problem is that inaccurate history acts similarly to a computer virus: it spreads exponentially. In February 2005, Dale Killingbeck's *Michigan Triumphs and Tragedies* was published, including a chapter on the Italian

Hall. Generally accurate in its twenty-four-page treatment, the chapter includes many inaccuracies traceable to prior mistaken histories: Union members checked each person before they could enter the Hall. Witnesses from within the Hall saw a boy whose hat was "a blaze" being carried toward an exit. The coroner turned the investigation over to a grand jury. Herman Bibber saw the building on fire, and Edward Manley of the Waddell-Mahon agency was a hero. These facts all appear to have originated from Thurner's *Rebels on the Range*, and do not stand up to scrutiny.

I visit the Keweenaw every summer and in 2005, I stopped by many of the sites I've written about. Ray Carlson, my relentless researcher, introduced me to Mary Butina of Seeberville. Mary had been in the Italian Hall on Christmas Eve 1913, and was one of the few surviving witnesses to the events of that evening. She was eight at the time and I was amazed to meet someone who had actually been there. While I researched the subject, it had always been cold and distant in a way. Mary gave the story a human face. While visiting her home, she showed me her wedding portrait on the wall. Taken in 1921, the pictured showed her standing next to her groom in a dress with another fascinating connection to history: The dress was made in Hancock by a seamstress who had survived the *Titanic* sinking in 1912—the year before Italian Hall.

The next day, I visited the Copper Range Museum and struck up a conversation with Norma Vezzetti, the volunteer running it that day. When I told her that I was researching Italian Hall, she told me of her family connections to the events of 1913. Her father, Caesar Lucchesi, ran a livery in South Range. During the strike, he was deputized by the Copper Range mine but managed to stay away from too much violence and confrontation.

Some childhood friends of Vezzetti's had been in the Italian Hall on Christmas Eve 1913. Ina Mikkola and her brother went to the party with a friend who was blind. All three children were elementary school age, and when the cry of "Fire" went up in the hall the blind girl grabbed her two friends by the hand and insisted they stand still until someone official told them how to get out of the building. While other children headed for the exits, Ina, her brother and their friend stayed behind and survived.

Stories like these survive because they are such an important part of the fabric of the Keweenaw community. I suspect they would live forever with or without books like this.

Acknowledgements

Thanks to Jari Liukkonen at Finlandia, Oakland University Kresge Library, Library of the State of Michigan, Archives of the State of Michigan, Peggy Germain, Larry J. Molloy, Michigan Technological University library, Kevin Musser, Paul Seitz and Kathleen Masterson, Arthur W. Thurner, Margaret Kurzman, Amanda Kurzman, Dave Reinard, Tom and Mary Spademan, Gerald Vairo, Jean Ellis, Jim Stimac, Erik C. Nordberg, Mary Butina, Norma Vezzetti, Debbie Pindral, Deborah Frontiera, Dale Killingbeck, Melissa Coulter, Adam Alexander, John Sedor, Dan McCormick, Daryl and Simone Samano-McDaniel, Bruce and Maureen Dutra, Susan Cone, Village Clerk of Calumet, Brad Curtin, Peter Werbe, Jay Brandow, Tony Bausano (proprietor of Copper World, Calumet), Konnie LeMay and *Lake Superior* magazine.

Although I had been staring at photos of the doors to the Hall for months, it took my brother Rick only a few minutes to look at the picture and explain to me what it showed. I attribute his insight to his coming to the problem without the preconceived notions that I had when I looked at it.

Ray Carlson is a retired schoolteacher from Painesdale who assisted me in researching this book. While I worked on the manuscript in the lower peninsula, I would e-mail Ray with requests for information and copies of documents from the MTU and Suomi archives. Inevitably, he would find what I needed and also discovered items I had not expected. Without him, this book would have taken many more years to write. He was also kind enough to show me around town when I visited in August 2005. Although I am familiar with the area, Ray introduced me to the people at MTU and also to the Butinas, whom I would never have located on my own.

Ken Ross and Louis Galdieri are the producers of a documentary on the subject, *1913 Massacre*. I met with them on a very cold Sunday in February 2006, and talked with them at the memorial arch. Later, we sat down and discussed the Italian Hall and my research on the topic while they filmed my answers. Ken and Louis were fabulous to talk to because they showed an interest in the topic that was as great as any I'd seen during my time spent in the Keweenaw.

Also, I must thank the people who are saving the Champion Shaft house No. 4. Most of the mines in the Keweenaw have been abandoned and the buildings above them are often neglected. The Champion Shaft No. 4 was saved from the wrecking ball by locals interested in preserving it. Next door to the shaft is the Captain's House, also being restored. This is the house where the deputies and guards received their orders to go and get John Kalan the afternoon of the murders in Seeberville. If you are interested in learning more about this particular mine and the efforts to save what is left of it, visit www.copperrange.org.

If you visit Painesdale, you can visit the Champion Shaft and Captain's House. From there, you can look up the street to where the road dips at the sign for Seeberville. A hundred yards or so past the sign on the right-hand side of the street is a small, vacant, overgrown lot where the Putrich boarding house used to stand. Ask the people at the Champion Shaft museum and they can point these things out for you.

Bibliography

Books

Berlitz, *Finnish-English Dictionary* (1981).

Ella Reeve Bloor, *We Are Many* (1940).

R.L. Dodge, *Michigan Ghost Towns of the Upper Peninsula* (1973). Reprinted 1996.

Peggy Germain, *False Alarm—1913 Italian Hall Disaster and Death Certificates* (2005).

Peggy Germain, *Tinsel & Tears* (1984).

Bill Haywood, *Bill Haywood's Book* (1929). Reprinted 1958.

Dale Killingbeck, *Michigan Triumphs and Tragedies* (2005).

Larry Lankton, *Cradle to Grave* (1991).

Armas K.E. Holmio, *History of the Finns in Michigan* (2001).

Wilbert B. Maki, *Stairway to Tragedy* (1983).

Larry Molloy, *Italian Hall: The Witnesses Speak* (2004).

Clarence J. Monette, *The Copper Range Railroad* (1989).

Angus Murdoch, *Boom Copper* (1943). 2001 edition.

Arthur W. Thurner, *Calumet Copper and People* (1974).

Arthur W. Thurner, *Rebels on the Range* (1984).

Seventieth Anniversary Souvenir Journal, Tyomies (1973).

Magazine Articles

Clarence A. Andrews, " 'Big Annie' and the 1913 Michigan Copper Strike," *Michigan History* (Spring 1973), p. 67, fn. 26.

William Beck, "Law and Order During the 1913 Copper Strike," *Michigan History* magazine (April 1970).

Francis John Dyer, "The Truth about the Copper Strike."

Diana Paiz Engle, "Standing Tall With Big Annie," *Michigan History* magazine, July/August 1999.

Alison K. Hoagland, "The Boardinghouse Murders: Housing and American Ideals in Michigan's Copper Country in 1913," *Perspectives in Vernacular Architecture*, Vol. XI 2004.

Lee Laney, "The Italian Hall Disaster," *Stereo World* magazine, May/June 1992, p. 10.

Anthony Lucas, "Anthony Lucas Recalls Important Events During His Fifty Years of Law Practice," *Copper Country Review*, January 1966, February 1966, March 1966.

Peter Clark MacFarlane, "The Issues at Calumet," *Collier's*, (February 7, 1914).

James MacNaughton, "History of the Calumet and Hecla Since 1900," *The Mining Congress Journal*, October 1931.

William A. Sullivan, "The 1913 Revolt of the Michigan Copper Miners," *Michigan History* (September 1959), p 300.

Michael F. Wendland, "The Calumet Tragedy," *American Heritage*, April/May 1986.

"A Catholic View of the Copper Miners' Strike in Upper Michigan," *Survey* vol. 31, 1914.

"In the Copper Country," *The Fra* magazine, May 1914.

"Western Federation Strike in Michigan," *The Canadian Mining Journal*, January 15, 1914.

Newspapers

Calumet News
Copper Island Sentinel
The Daily Mining Gazette
The Detroit News
New York Times
The Mining Journal
Truth
Miner's Bulletin
Chicago Daily Tribune
Chicago Record Herald
Grand Rapids Herald

Archival Materials

"1907-1913 RJFD Records of Fire Alarms," (Log books from Calumet Village Hall for Red Jacket Fire Department.)

63d CONGRESS: SENATE DOCUMENTS, "Strike in the Copper District of Michigan," (1914).

Affidavit of mine superintendent, (several) courtesy of the MTU Archives.

Affidavits of Mary Chopp, Bridget Brown, and Jenevive Sandretto, MTU Library Archives.

Baltic Mining Co v Houghton Circuit Judge 177 Mich 632 (1913).

Calumet and Hecla Mining Co. [Annual] Report For the Year Ending December 31, 1912, 1913, 1914.

Charlotte Kessler, "Handwritten Diary," courtesy of MTU Archives and Copper Country Historical Collections.

"Conditions in the Copper Mines of Michigan," statement of Hon. William J. MacDonald.

Coroner's Inquest, Louis Tijan, commenced upon August 22, 1913, Archives, State of Michigan, p. 43.

Correspondence between Quincy Shaw and James MacNaughton, Archives of MTU.

Correspondence from John W. Black to Governor Ferris, dated January 16, 1914, courtesy of State of Michigan Archives.

"Employment Slip," of A. Johnson. Courtesy of MTU Archives.

"Ground Lease to Employee," State of Michigan Archives, records of the Copper Strike, 1913.

Historic American Building Survey: Italian Hall HABS No. MI-425.

"Memorandum of Conversation Between Mr. Moyer and the Members of the Committee Consisting of Dr. Thometz, Joseph Wills, John H. Rice, Mr. Shumacher, James T. Fisher and A.E. Petermann, December 26th at 8 p.m. at the Scott Hotel in Hancock." MTU Archives.

Michigan Compiled Laws (MCL) 52.202, MCL 52.213a.

Moyer v Peabody, 212 US 78 (1909).

"News From Calumet," (translation of *Tyomies*) furnished by J.W. Black to Governor Ferris, courtesy of State of Michigan Archives.

"Notice to the Public," signed by Charles H. Moyer, undated, courtesy of MTU Archives and Copper Country Historical Collections.

"Operative No. 1 Reports," MTU Archives.

Oral Histories, Suomi College (now Finlandia University)

"Personnel of Houghton County Grand Jury," State of Michigan Archives, single page document.

"Proceedings of meeting of Citizens Alliance and others at the Amphidrome in the village of Houghton, Houghton County, Michigan on the 10th day of December 1913." MTU Archives.

Program for the Dedication Ceremony, Italian Hall, dated November 13, 1989.

"Report of the examination and testimony of witnesses on the occasion of the visit of Governor Woodbridge N. Ferris to the Upper Peninsula of Michigan, January 6, 1914." Courtesy of the State of Michigan archives.

Report of the Osceola Consolidated Mining Co. of Michigan for the Year Ending December 31, 1913. Author's collection.

U.S. Congress House Committee on Mines & Mining: Conditions in the Copper Mines in Michigan (hearing before subcommittee pursuant to House Resolution, 63rd Congress, 2nd Session, 7 parts) 1914. pp. 2064-2098.

"Strike in the Copper Mining District of Michigan," Report of the Commissioner of Labor Statistics in Regard to Strike of Mine Workers in the Michigan Copper District, January 29, 1914.

"Strike Investigation," Copper Country Commercial Club, 1913.

"To Hell With the Law," flier, undated. Courtesy of MTU Archives.

Transcript of Radio Broadcast, WMPL Hall Disaster, courtesy of Finlandia University.

"Translation from *Tyomies* Friday, December 26, 1913," courtesy of MTU Archives.

Unlabeled transcript of testimony taken August 15, 1913, Archives of the State of Michigan.

United States Code (USC), 29 USC Chapter 7 § 158, National Labor Relations Act of 1947.

Other

"Children of the Keweenaw: An American Opera," libretto by Kathleen Masterson (2001).

Interviews by author: Gerald Vairo, Mary Butina, Jean Ellis, Norma Vezzetti, Dan McCormick and Peggy Germain.

Correspondence with author: Cyndi Perkins, Arthur W. Thurner.

Ted Taipalus, unpublished article, "The Italian Hall, Calumet, Michigan Tragedy: A Personal Account," July 1980. Finlandia Archives 977.4 IT.

Notes

INTRODUCTION

The details of the event are given here as an overview. With 700 or more people either in the Hall or outside at some time during the evening, a coherent story is almost impossible to nail down.

SEEDS OF DISCONTENT
The Copper Country

The early history of Calumet and the Copper Country is best told in Angus Murdoch's *Boom Copper* and Arthur W. Thurner's *Calumet Copper and People.*

The Italian Hall is not well described in literature, but there are sources that give its dimensions and some of the more intricate details of the building. The Historical American Building Survey: Italian Hall HABS No. MI-425 is one such source.

The state of the copper industry in 1913 is described well in the *Strike in the Copper Mine District of Michigan*, the document created by the House subcommittee that investigated the industry, the strike and the Italian Hall in 1914. Hereafter, it is merely called *The Strike* p. 12.

Calumet & Hecla

The detailed descriptions of Calumet & Hecla and its labor relations is found in *The Strike.* p. 119.

The ground-lease language is excerpted from an example of the Calumet & Hecla's version, found in the State of Michigan Archives.

Statistics for the numbers of homes rented by C&H etc. is found in *The Strike*, pp 113-117.

How Calumet & Hecla built various buildings in town, *The Strike*, pp. 124-125; details of the Opera House, from "Standing Tall With Big Annie," by Diana Paiz Engle, *Michigan History*, July/August 1999, p. 17; "The Calumet Tragedy," by Michael F. Wendland, *American Heritage*, April/May 1986, p. 40, and Murdoch, p. 151.

MacNaughton's biographical information from Arthur W. Thurner's *Rebels on the Range* (1984), p. 44 and "In the Copper Country," *The Fra*, May 1914, p. 34. Roster of University of Michigan football team from www.umich.edu.

The Unions

On why MacNaughton was hired by Calumet & Hecla, *Cradle to Grave*, Larry Lankton (1991), p. 201.

On the rising costs of copper mining, *The Strike*, p. 105.

On MacNaughton and C&H's leadership role in the copper industry of the Upper Peninsula, as well as the history of corporate spying in the area (especially that of J.A.P.), Lankton, pp. 209, 211 and 127-128.

Comparing the value of a man to that of a mule, Helen Torkola, interviewed by Paul Jalkanen, August 7, 1972, Suomi College Oral History Project, courtesy of Finlandia University archives, p. 18.

The discrimination against Finns and census figures are found in Lankton, pp. 212-213.

History of the Miscowaubik Club can be found at www.miscowaubik.org.

O'Brien's biography leading to his time on the bench is told in "History of the Finns in Michigan," by Armas K.E. Holmio (2001) pp. 116-119.

The quote about eliminating Finns in the mines is found in Lankton, p. 214.

The Copper Mines

Description of the mines and how they worked is found in *The Strike*, pp. 103-104.

The labor shortage is described in Thurner's *Rebels*, p. 37, and in *The Strike*, p. 26.

Unsafe mine conditions and worker injuries are detailed in *The Strike*, pp. 109-110.

Fatality rate of 61 per year from Lankton, p. 111.

Description of daylight hours and when the workers saw daylight, Arthur Oinas, interviewed by Art Puotinen, August 3, 1972, Suomi College Oral History project, courtesy of Finlandia University archives, p. 8.

The Western Federation of Miners

"Contracts were formerly let ..." *The Strike*, p. 11.

MacDonald's dealings with the mines on behalf of workers is from "Conditions in the Copper Mines of Michigan," statement of Hon. William J. MacDonald, p. 7.

Regarding the situation in the copper mines out west and the Citizens Alliance are from Bill Haywood, *Bill Haywood's Book*, 1929, reprinted 1958, pp. 80, 97, 104.

The rising profits and wages at C&H are from Calumet and Hecla Mining Co. [Annual] Report For the Year Ending December 31, 1912, as are the comments regarding implementation of the

one-man drill.

The hiring of women by C&H is covered in Lankton, p. 191.

The role of the one-man drill in rallying membership to the WFM is described in *The Strike*, p. 7.

The use of mules for tramming is mentioned in Calumet and Hecla Mining Company [Annual] Report For the Year Ending December 31, 1912.

The circumstances surrounding the strike vote, the text of the ballot, and the comment about the control of the papers are all from *The Strike*, pp. 27, 39-40.

The editorial leanings of the local papers and the mine management influence on the non-local papers is described in Lankton at 214 and 226. As for *Tyomies*: The name was spelled *Työmies*, but in English—as in court documents for instance—it was spelled *Tyomies*. The name meant literally "worker," "wage earner," or "working man" but from the Finnish it had a connotation of the lowest strata of the working class. Some translated it as "wage slave" which it might have tended toward, but was not a literal translation.

On MacNaughton and his involvement behind the scenes with *Paivalehti*, including his Boston correspondence, see Holmio, p. 118 and Lankton, pp. 214-215.

The pastor who took sides is described in Holmio, p. 289.

The figure of 7,085 for the membership of the WFM in 1913 is from Thurner's *Rebels*, p. 46.

The propensities of the Cornish and Scottish workers is from *The Strike* at p. 40.

The makeup and the role of the board of supervisors, as well as the description of Waddell-Mahon, is found in *The Strike* at pp. 136, 53, 44.

The interactions between the local WFM and the headquarters in Denver is detailed in Thurner's *Rebels*, pp. 41-42.

The letter from the WFM to mine management—as well as how the managers reacted to it—is from *The Strike*, pp. 41-42. A few sentences that do not impact the letter's meaning have been omitted from the text.

All correspondence quoted or mentioned here, unless otherwise specified, is from letters or telegrams between MacNaughton and Shaw, courtesy of Michigan Technological University Archives and Copper Country Historical Collections. These will be identified by date only, such as this, which was dated 7/15/1913.

"My present feeling ..." Correspondence, 7/15/1913.

TENSIONS GROW
The Strike

"Approve not acknowledging letter ..." Correspondence, 7/18/1013.

The timing of the beginning of the strike is from *The Strike*, p. 40.

The number of workers, strikers and how the

first confrontations took place is from *The Strike*, pp. 42-43.

The mine manager who took his own poll is described in *Strike Investigation*, by the Copper Country Commercial Club, p. 55.

"In connection with this tournament ..." and "The day seems much like 4th of July ..." Correspondence, 7/23/1913.

"Subjugation on arson ..." and the translation are found at www.hu.mtu.edu/yup/strike/ telegrams/350-001.tele_1.gif. Many of the documents found on this site are available from the Michigan Technological University Archives and Copper Country Historical Collections.

"MacNaughton had received permission ..." "Law and Order During the 1913 Copper Strike," by William Beck, *Michigan History*, April 1970, p. 279, note 13.

The "identical affidavits" can be seen at MTU Archives and Copper Country Historical Collections where they are labeled, "Affidavit of mine superintendent."

Details of the "cheap handguns" and the story about their distribution is from: "Three guns mementoes of strife," by Lee Arten, *Copper Island Sentinel*, August 20, 1981.

The full story of Big Jim and his quotes is found in: "The Czar of the Copper Country," by Frank M. Sparks, *Grand Rapids Herald*, September 14, 1913.

"Two hundred men ..." and "A mob of between four and five hundred..." are quotes from www. hu.mtu.edu/yup/strike/telegrams/350-001. tele_2.gif and www.hu.mtu.edu/yup/strike/ telegrams/350-001.tele_3.gif.

MacNaughton's first news of the strike, "we are swearing in deputies," "they will be permitted to carry clubs," and "The suspense we have ..." are from the letter he wrote to Shaw that day, Correspondence, 7/23/1913.

MacNaughton describes his "council of war" and everything leading up to Cruse's telegram in Correspondence, 7/27/1913.

The text of Cruse's telegram is found at *The Strike*, pp. 49-50.

MacDonald's criticism of the calling of the troops and of Waddell are from his "Conditions in the Copper Mines," pp 9-10.

J.W. Black's panicked telegram is found in Beck's article, p. 281.

Ferris' response to the Cruse telegram and the number of troops at his disposal are from *The Strike*, p. 50.

"If the governor refuses to send troops ..." Correspondence, 7/24/1913.

Waddell's hiring and that he advertised that he could break strikes is from *The Strike*, p. 53.

"... any possible advantage to see ..." is from Correspondence, 7/24/1913.

The meetings of the mine managers and the "made no effort" quote are both from *The Strike*, pp. 42, 45, 51.

"Taps" at sundown is from Virginia A. Cooper, interviewed by Betty Berry, August 6, 1973, Suomi College Oral History project, courtesy of Finlandia University archives, p. 9.

"Hum Nutmeg ..." from www.hu.mtu/jup/ strike/telelgrams/350-001.tele_4.gif.

Shaw's response "Some of the papers ..." and "The worst part ..." from Correspondence, 7/24/1913.

"Everything quiet here today ..." from www. hu.mtu.edu/yup/strike/telegrams/350-001.tele_ 5.gif.

"You leave those men alone ..." Beck, p. 278.

"Procession of about eight hundred..." Correspondence, 2/25/1913.

The Parades

Description of Big Annie is from Engle, p. 17.

The role of women in the strike—and MacNaughton's shock at their involvement—is from Lankton, pp. 230-231.

MacNaughton's exhaustive report on the strike is from the nine-page letter he wrote: Correspondence, 7/27/1913.

The leanings of the Keweenaw County sheriff and of the Ahmeek Village president are from Beck, p. 283, note 21.

"Rest assured that the sympathy ..." Correspondence, 7/27/1913.

Moyer's Supreme Court is immortalized in the reports of the United States Supreme Court: *Moyer v Peabody*, 212 US 78 (1909).

MacNaughton's thoughts on imported gun men and the strangers on the streets is from Correspondence, 7/27/1913.

Ferris' statements about the calling of the National Guard are from *The Strike*, p. 51.

MacNaughton's letter regarding his talk with the Calumet businesses is in Correspondence, 7/31/1913.

The date the Waddell men were hired is from *The Strike*, p. 53.

"There were only two mines ..." is from *The Strike*, p. 42.

Hepting's communications to General Abbey are from *The Strike*, p. 51.

The anecdote about Hepting not shooting back is from William A. Gardner, interviewed by Doris Helgren and Larry Harju, August 5, 1974, Suomi College Oral History project, courtesy of Finlandia University archives, p. 1432.

Shaw's comment about Hepting is from Correspondence, 7/31/1913.

The actions of Quincy's president are detailed in Correspondence, 7/29/1913.

MacNaughton's letter about meeting with Lawton is found in Correspondence, 7/30/1913.

Lawton's quote, "I understand ..." is from Correspondence, 7/29/1913.

Shaw's letter regarding the Waddell men and other detective agencies is found in Correspondence, 7/29/1913.

Ferris' letter, "I don't like …" is from Beck, p. 279.

"This thing may rather …" and "We are getting the local Union …" are from Correspondence 7/31/1913.

Attempted Resolution

Ferris' letter is quoted in MacNaughton's Correspondence 7/31/1913, as is the story of Joe Mihelchich.

"Nothing new …" Correspondence, 8/2/1913.

The effects of the strike on non-striking workers who chose to leave the area is from Thurner's *Rebels*, p. 47.

The efforts of the WFM to involve the Department of Labor in the strike are detailed in Thurner's *Rebels*, p. 61.

That Ferris told Abbey he was working on the issue, Thurner's *Rebels*, pp 60-61.

MacNaughton's observation on Abbey's position is from Correspondence, 7/31/1913.

Details of the relationship between MacNaughton and his attorney are from Lankton, p. 231.

That MacNaughton first heard of Judge Murphy's appointment in the papers is from his own Correspondence, 8/10/1913.

"The Board of Supervisors will meet …" Correspondence, 8/10/1913.

MacNaughton's impressions of Murphy are from Correspondence, 8/13/1913.

"Chastised them …" Thurner's *Rebels*, pp. 60-61.

"From all I find out …" and "If the Governor …." are from Correspondence, 8/13/1913.

Ferris' reaction to Murphy's report are from Thurner's *Rebels*, p. 61.

How the WFM agreed to a meeting and the managers did not is detailed in Thurner's *Rebels*, p. 61.

Under Military Rule

The flooding mines is described in Thurner's *Rebels* at p. 53.

"A plague of rats …" Charlotte Kessler, "Handwritten Diary," courtesy of MTU Archives and Copper Country Historical Collections.

The topic of letting the mines flood was found in Correspondence, 8/4/1913 and 8/6/1913.

MacNaughton's letter regarding Cruse's letter about hiring deputies is Correspondence, 8/10/1913.

Waddell's payment by the Houghton County Board of Supervisors is from *The Strike*, p. 58.

The language of the strike poster is from *The Strike*, p. 49.

MacNaughton's Eye is described in several places, including in *The Strike*. The quote, "the strikers had shown no disposition …" is from *The Strike*, p. 49.

The reference to "Seen by the Searchlights," is from Thurner's *Rebels*, p. 66.

On MacNaughton's espionage efforts and the banks, Lankton, p. 229.

Ferris' warning to Cruse, *The Strike*, p. 52.

MacNaughton's optimism can be seen in www.hu.mtu/jup/strike/telelgrams/350-001.tele_10.gif.

The story of the WFM members meeting with Terzich rallying them, as well as their meeting with MacNaughton the next day are told in Thurner's *Rebels*, p. 64.

MacNaughton told Shaw of the demands made by the WFM members in Correspondence, 8/6/1913.

The billy club manufacturing is described in Thurner's *Rebels*, p. 95.

Shaw's rebuke is found in www.hu.mtu/jup/strike/telelgrams/350-001.tele_11.gif.

"Perhaps $100,000 a year" is from "The Czar of the Copper Country," by Frank M. Sparks, *Grand Rapids Herald*, September 14, 1913.

MacNaughton's comments about his salary and other lies told about him and the requests for money is from Correspondence, 8/6/1913.

The details of Cruse and the deputies to "aid" him are found in *The Strike*, pp. 53-55.

MacNaughton's telegram about the 1,800 person parade and "When this idleness …" Correspondence, 8/10/1913.

MacNaughton and whether or not C&H was involved in hiring Waddell is found in *The Strike*, p. 55. Thurner wrote *Rebels on the Range* in 1984, one of the few books that addresses Italian Hall in any detail. There, he suggests MacNaughton was telling the truth and, in fact, did not know of Cruse's hiring of the Waddell men until after the fact. Thurner, p. 48. This is highly implausible. MacNaughton had met with Waddell along with the rest of the board of supervisors, and it is inconceivable that Cruse—whose budget was overseen by the board—could hire 52 men of his own accord and *then* tell the board he had done so.

"We have Croatians …" and "We do this …" is from *The Strike* p. 55.

That Ferris would "confer with the devil" is from Thurner's *Rebels*, p. 84.

MacNaughton's "back to work" campaign, meeting with the board of supervisors, the discussion of C&H's finances, and "We now have a very good …" are from Correspondence, 8/13/1913.

FIRST BLOOD

Murder on the Range

The details of the events leading up to the Putrich boarding house murders are from the coroner's inquest, Louis Tijan, commenced upon August 22, 1913, Archives, State of Michigan, p. 43. Kalan's name is sometimes spelled "Kollan" or "Kaln."

Raleigh's involvement is also detailed in *The Strike*, p. 69.

That the men grabbed Kalan but did not tell him he was under arrest is from an unlabeled transcript of testimony taken August 15, 1913.

Polkinghorne, p. 9. This transcript was found in the State of Michigan Archives, filed along with the coroner's inquest for Louis Tijan, although it is clearly taken on the 15th, a week before the inquest. Further, at the inquest, the deputies refused to testify.

Thurner also discusses some of the facts of this incident, although he gets some of the details wrong. Thurner's *Rebels*, p. 70.

More details of the ambush and a good description of the sequence of events is found in "The Boardinghouse Murders," p. 1. Testimony was taken the day after the incident, and the deputies testified—in a case against Kalan. Since some of the men refused to testify later at the coroner's inquest, this testimony is important. The case is referenced in the inquest transcript; Attorney Kerr asked Humphrey Quick if he had testified "the other day ... in the case of the People vs. Kalan et al, in Justice O'Sullivan's court?"

Many continue to promote the theory that Kalan was being "arrested" and resisted, igniting the incident. For example, Thurner writes on p. 71, "Polkinghorne ... said, 'You're under arrest.'" That is not true.

Polkinghorne testified:

"I said, 'I want you.'

He said, 'No, you can't take me.'

I said, 'Come on, don't make any trouble.' I then got up and took hold of him by the arm and he started back."

Polkinghorne never claimed to have told Kalan he was under arrest. That statement came from Cooper—the man who killed the unarmed Putrich—who was clearly lying. He also testified that he was hit by a block of wood, that the men in the house were throwing "things" at him, and that he only shot Putrich after Putrich had shot at him. "I shot where that shot came from." Then "A lot of shots came from inside [the house]." Again, Cooper's testimony was almost entirely fictional and is utterly unbelievable. After all, there were no guns in the house and a dozen witnesses said no one fired a gun from the house.

"Gun smoke so thick it was impossible to see" is described in coroner's inquest, Louis Tijan, commenced upon August 22, 1913, Archives, State of Michigan, pp. 32, 51.

The lack of guns in the house is from *The Strike*, p. 69.

"They didn't have anything to shoot ..." is from "The Boardinghouse Murders," p. 1.

The throwing of stones and bottles into the yard is from *The Strike*, p. 69.

The warrantless search of the house, along with Lucas' visit to the scene of the killing and the preliminary exam the next day are from "Anthony Lucas Recalls Important Events During His Fifty Years of Law Practice," by Anthony Lucas, *Copper Country Review*, January 1966, pp 3-4.

The murder indictments are described in *The Strike*, p. 69.

The impact of language and race on job placement is explained in *The Strike*, p. 69.

"Pretending not to understand English ..." is from *The Daily Mining Gazette*, 2/15/1914. One wonders if MacNaughton's attorney tried yelling at the Italian in English, to see if that made the language more understandable.

The funerals for "our murdered brothers" is recounted in *The Strike*, p. 69.

The moral high ground concept is from "The Boardinghouse Murders," p. 2.

The telegram of the 18th, "very large demonstration" "When Judge Murphy read it," "I can assure you" and the accusation that Murphy was misleading Ferris is Correspondence, 8/18/1913.

"The county Prosecuting Attorney Lucas ..." quote is from Beck, p. 285, note 32.

"Today a man we call 'Slippery' ...", "I am keeping track ...", "Women acted as pickets ..." and "It was a most complete back-down ..." are all found in Correspondence, 8/18/1913.

The intent of the mine managers to meet again is from Correspondence 8/22/1913.

All information and descriptions regarding the activities at the inquest are from coroner's inquest, Louis Tijan, commenced upon August 22, 1913, Archives, State of Michigan, pp. 3, 10, 12, 22, 34-35.

MacNaughton's trip to Wolverine and Mohawk is recounted in his Correspondence, 8/26/1913.

MacNaughton's reaction to Murphy's report is from Correspondence, 8/28/1913.

Treatment of strikers who had been beaten while in custody is from Thurner's *Rebels*, p. 111.

Lucas' observations of the treatment of arrested strikers is from "Report of the examination and testimony of witnesses on the occasion of the visit of Governor Woodbridge N. Ferris to the Upper Peninsula of Michigan, January 6, 1914." Courtesy of the State of Michigan archives. p. 27.

MacDonald's comments on reasons for arresting strikers are from his report: "Conditions in the Copper Mines of Michigan," statement of Hon. William J. MacDonald, p. 15.

Court Intervention

Statistics on convictions and arrests are from Thurner's *Rebels*, p. 114.

The WFM's trip to court seeking an injunction is from Lankton, p. 135.

Judge O'Brien's rulings and comments, the quoted language from the Waddell-Mahon poster, the pay rate of the strike breakers, and information regarding which counties hired the strike breakers and which did not is from *The Strike*, pp. 57-59.

MacNaughton's telegram about the parade and the "discontented" is Correspondence, 8/23/1913.

"More picketing ..." is Correspondence, 9/3/1913.

The amount of money spent on Waddell men and the payment of their bills is from *The Strike*, pp. 58-59.

The story of Margaret Fazekas is largely from the transcript of "The People vs. John Lavers," November 21, 1913. Margaret's last name is spelled variously as Frazakas or Fazekas depending on the source. The spelling used here is the most common among court documents. Some of the story is retold in *The Strike*, p. 70.

MacNaughton's thoughts on the Fazekas shooting, as well as "I would not submit ..." "just last night" and the quoted passage, "It may be that ..." are all from Correspondence, 9/2/1913.

MacNaughton's "vow" is found in Correspondence, 9/13/1913.

Big Annie's confrontation with the militia, as well as the story of what happened after the military investigation into the incident is recounted in Thurner's *Rebels*, pp. 94-95.

Big Annie's first car ride is from WMPL Hall Disaster, p. 8.

The details of the injunction and O'Brien's statement "This court will protect ..." are from the Michigan Supreme Court reports: *Baltic Mining Co v Houghton Circuit Judge* 177 Mich 632 (1913).

"O'Brien's Socialistic tendencies ..." are described in MacNaughton's Correspondence, 9/29/1913.

The statements of the Michigan Supreme Court and various language from the appeal, as well as the number of 4,000 (men willing to work) is from *Baltic Mining Co v Houghton Circuit Judge* 177 Mich 632 (1913); this story is also recounted in *The Strike*, pp. 60-61.

MacFarlane's article is The Issues at Calumet," Peter Clark MacFarlane (1914) p. 10.

The Black letter is Correspondence from John W. Black to Governor Ferris, dated January 16, 1914, courtesy of State of Michigan Archives.

MacNaughton's concern about his image and about getting the "facts" out are found in his Correspondence of 9/12/1913 and 9/13/1913.

The MacNaughton-Moffitt meeting is described in Correspondence, 9/15/1913.

"Palmer was more friendly..." and "although I have not taken the trouble ..." are from Correspondence, 9/21/1913.

MacNaughton's report on the status of the Copper Country Commercial Club report is from Correspondence, 9/15/1913.

Imported Workers

The story of the imported Germans and the contract and affidavit they signed, the arrest of one by the Waddells and the treatment of them as "prisoners" is from *The Strike*, pp. 63-65.

The "bizarre" stories are verified in "The 1913 Revolt of the Michigan Copper Miners," by William A. Sullivan, *Michigan History* (September 1959), p 300.

The stories of the workers quitting and escaping are found in *The Strike*, p. 66.

That gunshots were fired at a train with no injuries is found in Correspondence, 10/25/1913.

The employment slip with the traced-over signature is merely labeled, "Employment Slip," of A. Johnson. Courtesy of MTU Archives.

O'Brien's handling of the arrested strikers *en masse* is described in *The Strike*, pp. 61-62, and MacNaughton's comments on the actions are in Correspondence, 11/2/1913.

The eviction proceedings against Putrich are detailed in "The Boardinghouse Murders," p. 11.

"I never say I don't pay ..." is from Thurner's *Rebels*, p. 103.

MacNaughton's comments on the sheriff being a "dummy" and the story of the woman intending to blow up the *Gazette* office are found in Correspondence, 10/5/1913.

The "Notice to the Public," is signed by Charles H. Moyer, undated, courtesy of MTU Archives and Copper Country Historical Collections.

The report of the CCCC is "Strike Investigation," by the Committee of the Copper Country Commercial Club of Michigan 1913, courtesy of MTU Archives, p. 1.

That this was not the first strike in the area is from Lankton, p. 198.

Information from the "Strike Investigation" is from pp. 56, 85.

Shaw's request for names to send free subscriptions is found in Correspondence, 10/24/1913.

MacNaughton sending the reports to Moffitt is recounted in Correspondence, 10/29/1913.

Shaw's desire to exile the WFM leaders is Correspondence, 10/16/1913.

Further Relief Efforts

The opening of commissaries and the effect of this on the local store owners' attitudes is from Thurner's *Rebels*, p. 103.

Ella Bloor's story is from her autobiography, *We Are Many*, Ella Reeve Bloor (1940), p. 121.

MacNaughton griping about O'Brien and also recounting his meeting with O'Brien are from Correspondence, 11/2/1913.

"There was a great deal of ..." is from Correspondence, 11/16/1913.

MacNaughton's meeting with the "mutt" from the bank and complaints about the "miscarriage of justice" are from Correspondence, 11/2/1913.

The mild weather of this winter is recounted in Beck, p. 287, note 39.

That the local press thought O'Brien a traitor is found in "The Issues at Calumet," by Peter Clark MacFarlane, February 7, 1914, republished by Helen Holman Smith (1980), pp. 14-15.

BLOODY DECEMBER
The Second Round of Boardinghouse Murders

Details of the Dally house are found in "The

Boardinghouse Murders," p. 7.

Nicholson's account of the shooting is from "Under Fire," by Kenneth A. Nicholson, www. copperrange.org.

Lucas' visit to the crime scene, as well as his "personal observation," and comments about who he thought was responsible are from his account: "Anthony Lucas Recalls Important Events During His Fifty Years of Law Practice," by Anthony Lucas, *Copper Country Review*, February 1966, pp 4-5, also *Mining Journal*, 11/23/1914.

Newspaper accounts of the Dally home are from "The Boardinghouse Murders," p. 7.

The Citizens Alliance

The formation of the Citizens Alliance is described in Beck, p. 287; the pledge is from "Citizens Alliance Membership Pledge," courtesy of MTU Archives.

MacNaughton's first comments on the Alliance are from Correspondence, 11/9/1913 and 11/16/1913.

When the WFM became aware of the Alliance is from Beck, p. 287, note 40.

The language quoted from the Alliance newspaper is from *TRUTH*, 12/2/1913. That it was paid for by Calumet & Hecla is from Lankton, p. 233.

The *Miner's Bulletin* language is from *Miner's Bulletin*, 12/2/1913, quoted in William A. Sullivan, "The 1913 Revolt of the Michigan Copper Miners," *Michigan History*, September 1959, p. 308.

How Orchard's "confession" came to be published is detailed in Correspondence, 12/2/1913 and 12/3/1913.

The use of Orchard's confession in Colorado is retold in, *Bill Haywood's Book*, 1929, reprinted 1958, p. 209. This created a problem for the prosecution; Orchard had confessed to numerous crimes and with Haywood's acquittal, *someone* had to go to jail. Orchard was tried and convicted. He was sentenced to execution, but his sentence was commuted to life in prison. One wonders whether he would have been tried if his testimony had resulted in the conviction of Haywood. See http://www.law.umkc.edu/faculty/projects/ftrials/haywood/HAY_N66.HTM

"Foreign agitators ..." headline is reprinted in Beck, p. 289, note 44.

That Rice was a member of the Citizens Alliance: *The Daily Mining Gazette*, 12/24/1913. He is listed as a member in an article published in his own paper. Presumably, if he was not a member, he would not let them say he was.

The "publicized threat" and the language are from a legal document; appears to be the motion for injunctive relief sought by the WFM. It quotes portions of the paper verbatim. Courtesy of MTU Archives.

The details of the alliance rallies, who spoke at them and who funded them are from Lankton, p. 235.

MacNaughton's description the Alliance is from Correspondence, 11/16/1913.

That the newspapers pretended the Alliance was not affiliated with the mines, and the figures from marches are in Lankton, pp. 233, 235.

MacNaughton's telegram regarding the Dally-Jane killings, including the quoted portion and his request to Shaw that he write a letter are from Correspondence, 12/8/1913.

The details of the speeches from the Alliance rally including the quoted portions are from "Proceedings of meeting of Citizens Alliance and others at the Amphidrome in the village of Houghton, Houghton County, Michigan on the 10th day of December 1913." p. 5, courtesy of MTU Archives.

The Alliance "raids" are described in Beck, p. 289.

The presence of Waddell men and deputies at the raids is from "In the Copper Country," *The Fra* magazine, May 1914, p. 43.

Petermann's statements are from Beck, p. 289.

The "poisonous slime" quote is from Thurner's *Rebels*, p 128.

That Petermann's speeches were reprinted is from Beck, p. 289.

The injunction obtained by the WFM—including the language which is quoted in full—can be found in: Injunction, two pages, dated December 10, 1913 (on second page), courtesy of MTU Archives.

O'Brien's instruction to the attorneys to obey the injunction is from *The Daily Mining Gazette*, 12/24/1913.

The Citizens Alliance Grand Jury

The bias of the grand jury, including the quote, "That will not do ..." is from "Conditions in the Copper Mines of Michigan," statement of Hon. William J. MacDonald, p. 15.

Ferris' findings of the grand jury are within his "Report of the examination and testimony of witnesses on the occasion of the visit of Governor Woodbridge N. Ferris to the Upper Peninsula of Michigan, January 6, 1914." Courtesy of the State of Michigan archives, p. 25.

The makeup of the grand jury is found at "Personnel of Houghton County Grand Jury," State of Michigan Archives, single page document.

It was commonly known that MacNaughton's chauffeur was on the grand jury: MacFarlane, p. 19.

"We hope shortly ..." Correspondence, 12/15/1913.

The pledge quoted here was also found in Beck, p. 287.

"From all indications ..." is from Correspondence, 12/17/1913.

The quote from the spy report "Clyde Taylor and Witmer ..." is found in "Operative No. 1 Reports," MTU Archives.

The Daily Mining Gazette story on the sheriff's

Christmas presents ran on 12/24/1913.

The *Calumet News* and *The Daily Mining Gazette* reports of the Citizens Alliance in court and the "plug uglies" ran on 12/24/1913.

The members of the Alliance purportedly represented by Rees, Robinson & Petermann was reported in *The Daily Mining Gazette* of 12/24/1913.

DEATH'S DOOR
Christmas Eve

Bloor's arrival in Calumet and her meeting with Big Annie are told in her autobiography, *We Are Many*, Ella Reeve Bloor (1940), pp. 121-122.

The *Calumet News* predictions of a good Christmas and of the status of local charities—as well as the piece about the new doors being placed—was published on 12/24/1913.

The history of the Hall is from the *Calumet News*, 10/13/1908.

Details of the festivities leading up to the cry of "Fire" are from "Conditions in the Copper Mines in Michigan," pp. 2068, 2076.

The number of children in the Hall has been given in many sources, one being the *Calumet News* of 12/26/1913.

Details of the event inside the Hall in this chapter, up to that of Ted Taipalus, are from "Conditions in the Copper Mines in Michigan," pp. 2074, 2085, 2088, 2090.

The account of Taipalus is his: "The Italian Hall, Calumet, Michigan Tragedy: A Personal Account," July 1980. Finlandia Archives 977.4 IT.

Henry Snabb's account is by: Henry Snabb, interviewed by W.E. Anderson, August 7, 1973, Suomi College Oral History project, courtesy of Finlandia University archives, p. 1154.

"The deputies are coming ..." Petchetino's observations, and Lustig's comments are from "Conditions in the Copper Mines in Michigan," pp. 2067, 2075, 2072.

Lahti's story was retold from WMPL Hall Disaster, pp. 43-44.

Jalmer Olsen's story is from "Conditions in the Copper Mines in Michigan," p. 2096.

The story of William Nara is from "The Italian Hall Disaster," by Lee Laney, *Stereo World* magazine, May/June 1992, p. 10.

An example of a union-printed handbill as referenced here is "TO THE PUBLIC," handbill, undated, referring to the agreement of management to adopt an eight-hour workday beginning in January 1914. Courtesy of the MTU Copper Country collection.

The Nara photographs have been republished many times in various formats. Some of them can be seen in Laney, p. 10.

The fire alarms that night and the run to the Italian Hall are recorded in "1907-1913 RJFD Records of Fire Alarms," (Logbook of Red Jacket Fire Department, entry dated 12/24/1913. Courtesy of Calumet Village Hall.)

The *Calumet News* Revised List of Dead, and the story of three taken to the C&H hospital and the "One little girl was laid out ..." are from the 12/26/1913 edition.

Taipalus' account is from "The Italian Hall, Calumet, Michigan Tragedy: A Personal Account," July 1980. Finlandia Archives 977.4 IT.

Vairo's account is from his grandson: Gerald Vairo, interviewed by author on July 27, 2005.

Slanted Reporting

"Arrests are expected ..." the block quote and the yelling and clamoring are all from the *Calumet News* article of 12/26/1913.

The Daily Mining Gazette gave the names of the agencies in its 12/25/1913 edition.

The "Deputies, mounted police ..." quote and the condolence messages from the mayor of Detroit and governor of Wisconsin are from *Calumet News*, 12/26/1913.

The spy report on the WFM for Christmas Day is "Operative No. 1 Reports," 12/25/1913. MTU Archives.

The gathering of money and the offer of aid to the WFM was widely reported, as was Moyer's response. These quotes are from the *Calumet News*, 12/26/1913.

Shaw's telegram and its subsequent printing in the newspaper are Correspondence, 12/24/1913 and *The Daily Mining Gazette,* 12/25/1913.

"Cases of poverty ..." is from the *Calumet News*, 12/26/1913.

"$1,000 REWARD" and "80 PERISH ..." are from *The Daily Mining Gazette*, 12/26/1913.

Translations of Finnish to English are by Berlitz, *Finnish-English dictionary* (1981).

The Daily Mining Gazette's attacks on Moyer and "It is generally known ..." are from the issue of 12/25/1913.

The report of *Tyomies* was widely covered elsewhere and is mentioned in Thurner's *Rebels*, p. 157.

The Detroit News stories ran on 12/25/1913, as did that of the *New York Times*.

The History of *Tyomies* is from Holmio, p. 280. Thurner's *Rebels* discusses the *Tyomies* article and its contents on p. 157, and the *Calumet News* quoted the article in its 12/27/1913 edition.

The history of Italian Hall, the resolution adopted by the community leaders, and the assembled committee were all from the *Calumet News*, 12/26/1913.

Lucas' statement, which is block-quoted, is from the *Calumet News*, 12/27/1913.

Language quoted from death certificates is from Death Certificate of Eli Heikkinen, as reprinted in Peggy Germain's, *False Alarm* (2005) and other certificates in her book generally.

Calumet News coverage to clear the Alliance was in the 12/27/1913 edition, the affidavits referenced are Affidavits of Mary Chopp, Bridget Brown, and Jenevive Sandretto, Michigan

Technological University Library Archives.

The quote regarding Annie Clemenc is from the *Calumet News*, 12/27/1913. The author quoted is Thurner in his *Rebels*, p. 152.

The Daily Mining Gazette article on Big Annie is from 12/30/1913.

The Daily Mining Gazette's coverage of "children are dying," "That any set of men ..." and "it was proven by the investigations ..." are from the 12/27/1913 edition.

Whether *Tyomies* accused the deputies of "murder," is from Thurner's *Rebels*, p. 166.

The arrests and arraignment of the *Tyomies* men is from the *Calumet News*, 12/29/1913.

"The copy of the translation ..." quote is from *The Daily Mining Gazette*, 12/28/1913.

The translations of the *Tyomies* articles are from "News From Calumet," (translation of *Tyomies*) furnished by J.W. Black to Governor Ferris, courtesy of State of Michigan Archives. Likewise, Clarence A. Andrews noted in his 1973 *Michigan History* article that he could not find a copy of the article either. Another translation exists "Translation from *Tyomies* Friday December 26, 1913," courtesy of MTU Archives.

The full text "but the first question" quote is from the "News From Calumet" translation.

The use of the fire whistle by the Alliance and it being written about in the local papers are detailed in Thurner's *Rebels*, pp. 131, 134 and the *Chicago Daily Tribune* article was published 12/30/1913.

TWISTED JUSTICE
Moyer's Kidnapping

Moyer's claims that witnesses would testify regarding the Alliance role in the tragedy are quoted from the *Calumet News*, 12/27/1913.

Moyer's statement that the money was offered by unclean hands and the Alliance response to that statement are from Murdoch, p. 226.

The sheriff's party that visited Moyer with Alliance members is a well-known story; here the best details are found in Beck, p. 291.

The composition of the group is also known and found in several sources, including "Western Federation Strike in Michigan," *The Canadian Mining Journal*, January 15, 1914, p. 56.

The intent of the party and what was said in the meeting were recorded by a member: "Memorandum of Conversation Between Mr. Moyer and the Members of the Committee Consisting of Dr. Thometz, Joseph Wills, John H. Rice, Mr. Shumacher, James T. Fisher and A.E. Petermann, December 26th at 8 p.m. at the Scott Hotel in Hancock." MTU Archives.

The quote, "take care of its own ..." is from *The Detroit News*, 12/27/1913.

Moyer's refusal to renounce his statements is from Beck, p. 291.

"He was then asked ..." is from the Memorandum of Conversation.

From the mob entering Moyer's room to the time he was at the train station are described in the *Calumet News*, 12/27/1913.

Moyer's train ride and the details of who was there and what happened on the train are from Thurner's *Rebels*, p. 161-162.

Calumet News event coverage and the quote of the hotel manager were published on 12/27/1913.

"Moyer was not shot in hotel ..." and the block quote are from the *Calumet News*, 12/28/1913. Arthur Thurner, in a letter to the author in 2005, admitted the "local press ... were decidedly opposed to the strike, to the Western Federation of Miners, and were capable of distorting facts in their accounts of 'what happened' during the entire strike."

The "inhuman monster" story appeared in *The Daily Mining Gazette*, 12/28/1913.

Cruse's statements regarding Moyer's kidnapping are from the *Calumet News*, 12/29/1913.

Elbert Hubbard's fictionalized version of events was "In the Copper Country," *The Fra* magazine, May 1914, p. 43—although he presented it as if it were true.

Moyer's medical condition is from *The Detroit News*, 12/27/1913, as was his statement that the shooting was accidental.

The signed statement was reported in the *Calumet News* 12/27/1913.

MacNaughton's telegram to Shaw of the kidnapping is of 12/27/1913; Shaw's response, "How much of this is a frame-up ..." is Correspondence, 12/29/1913.

The WFM handbills posted shortly after the event: "To Hell With the Law," flier, undated. Courtesy of MTU Archives.

The Funerals

The marching of the miners to the cemetery to dig the graves is reported in the *Calumet News* 12/27/1913, and the dates of burial were reported in *The Daily Mining Gazette*, 12/28/1913.

The sleigh "stacked with coffins" is from the Taipalus account as is the description of the twelve coffins in the church.

"The papers anticipated ..." is describing the *Calumet News* coverage of 12/27/1913.

The coffins being carried three miles is from Taipalus.

Descriptions of the funeral procession are from the *Calumet News* 12/27/1913, and 12/29/1913.

"It is not charity we want ..." is from Thurner's *Rebels*, p. 167.

Darrow's fear is recorded in "Operative No. 1 Reports," 12/27/1914.

Iron workers coming to protect their "fellow workers" is from Bloor, p. 126.

That Mrs. McGrath broke her arm is recorded in the *Calumet News*, 12/30/1913.

The story of the Gaumont Film Co., and the missing film is from *The Daily Mining Gazette*,

12/30/1913.

The recovery of the film is from "Film Thief Foiled," *Miner's Bulletin*, January 7, 1914.

Lankton suggests that the film was shown in theaters around the country at p. 239. It is unclear, however, if it was the film being shown or if it was the slides of the Nara photos.

The Coroner's Inquest

Fisher's background is from Jean Ellis, interviewed by author on July 27, 2005. Ellis is the great granddaughter of William Fisher.

Members of the inquest jury are from *The Daily Mining Gazette*, 12/25/1913. Various spellings occur even for these names; those used here are from the *Gazette*.

Headline, "Man who cried fire ..." and the quoted text, "He testified ..." are both from the *Calumet News* of 12/29/1913.

Sandretto's testimony in the block quote is from *Italian Hall: The Witnesses Speak*, Larry Molloy (2004), p. 17. All page numbers of inquest testimony are from Molloy.

Kaisor's testimony, that of the Meyers couple, and the rest through Big Annie's testimony are from Molloy, pp. 20-21, 25, 22-30, and 31.

"The newspaper" that accused her was the *Calumet News*, 12/29/1913.

Testimony of Coscalla and Fretz are Molloy, pp. 40, 42, 48.

The *Calumet News* headline, "Did not wear ..." ran on 12/29/1913.

The headline of the *Chicago Record Herald* ran on 12/30/1913.

The various quotes and headlines of the *Calumet News* were published 12/30/1913.

Rader's testimony quoted is Molloy, pp. 69-70.

Auno, Antila, and Mrs. Mihelchich are Molloy, pp. 69, 70, 72, 75, and 77.

Calumet News, "She saw no fire ..." "wore whiskers" and other criticisms of these witnesses was published 12/30/1913.

Ratz, Czabo, and Lustig testified at Molloy, pp. 78, 79, 82.

Forster testified at Molloy, p. 87.

Jokopii testified at Molloy, p. 88; Haapa at pp. 91-91; Kuppala at p. 93.

Further criticism by the *Calumet News* occurred on 12/31/1913.

Berg testified at Molloy, p. 118. Aho at 119.

The following are Molloy references: Aho, p. 120; Berg, p. 118; James, p. 117; Karna, p. 111; Sandretto, p. 106; Saari, p. 103; Olson, pp. 101-102; Fretz, p. 48; Brusso, p. 46; Belcher, p. 108; Rader, p. 68; Rouseau, p. 29; Lesch, p. 127; Vairo, p. 28; "that no person or persons was allowed ..." p. 140.

MacNaughton's comments, "Many of those present would not understand ..." is Correspondence dated 8/6/1913; "Only a small portion ..." 8/10/1913; "The resolution was undoubtedly ..." 8/13/1913.

Karna's testimony regarding bilingual announcements is Molloy, p. 111 and Keljo's is p. 61. It should be noted that at least 55 of the 73 victims were American-born U.S. citizens. The issue of "nationality" goes more toward the native language of the victim and to what class of Calumet society they were from.

The use of interpreters at the previous inquest is well documented. One reference is "The Boardinghouse Murders," p. 5.

Statements made with the assistance of interpreters are affidavits dated October 1, 1913 and September 25, 1913 (regarding the shooting of Margaret Fazekas), courtesy of the MTU Archives.

More Molloy references regarding the unclear testimony: Sandretto, p. 17, Czap, p. 90; Pitchittino, p. 125; Mirchisio, p. 129; Mirchisie, p. 131; Carous, p. 33; Coscalla, p. 39; Fretz, p. 47; Tomei, p. 61-62; Saari, p. 103. In a legal setting, this question is objectionable as being "compound"; that is, it is asking two questions—were you at the door taking cards and/or were you a door tender? A simple yes or no does not tell you which question is being answered. The transcript is full of questions like this as well.

Also, Mrs. Louise Lesch said she "went to the door and there was some Finnlander there" she told "don't let them in. They had their candy and would not get any more." Molloy at 57-58. She is clearly referring to children—not adults—and the Finn was probably Saari, who said he was watching a door to direct children who'd gotten their candy.

On the matter of the fire alarm and whistle, Molloy's references: Sandretto, p. 17; Charles Meyers, p. 23; Vairo, p. 28; Spehar, p. 35; Ryan, p. 48; Sullivan, p. 51; Curto, p. 52; Jacob Kaiser, p. 53; Mary Lanto, p. 55; Trudell, p. 66; Mrs. Czabo, p. 81; Lustig, p. 83; Joseph Czap, p. 90; Wuopia, p. 95.

The quote including "the children themselves are to blame" is Molloy, p. 128, emphasis added.

The office of the coroner is an archaic one in Michigan today. It was replaced with the office of a medical examiner in 1969. MCL 52.213a. Other than the title change, not much else was done to the office. For the most part, the coroner or medical examiner is charged with, among other things, investigating violent, unexpected or medically unattended deaths. MCL 52.202. The Italian Hall tragedy was all three.

The Osceola mine accident and inquest are from Lankton, p. 124.

The state of mind of the coroner is also well known. This is retold by Jean Ellis, interview with author. This point about Fisher's reaction has been widely reported in the press as well, but not at the time: these stories were most common in the 1990s, and as such are not as trustworthy as contemporary reports.

The "came to their death" portion of the inquest is quoted from "Conditions in the Copper

Mines," p. 2098, although it also appears in Molloy and others.

The *Calumet News* story that included, "Those in the building who escaped ..." ran on December 26, 1913.

The final tally is taken from: "Conditions in the Copper Mines," p. 2097 and from Molloy pp. 12-13. The quote, "Having the coroner's inquest, and by agreement ..." is from "Conditions," p. 2091.

The *Calumet News* articles on the number of dead and the funeral homes ran on 12/26/1913. The Peterson Funeral Home records can be viewed at http://www.mfhn.com/houghton/petersonfuneral/ accessed 7/15/2005.

Germain's list is from her book, *Tinsel & Tears*, Peggy Germain, pp. 37-40, as well as her *False Alarm—1913 Italian Hall Disaster and Death Certificates*, (2005).

The *Calumet News* ran its story on the previous year's fatalities on 1/5/1914.

The Daily Mining Gazette reported on the dynamite left at Lucas' office on 1/7/1914.

MacNaughton's correspondence at the beginning of the year is dated 1/18/1914.

The indictments and who testified to support them is found in MacFarlane, p. 19.

More on the indictments and who they named—and did not name—is found in Thurner's *Rebels*, pp. 184-186.

MacNaughton mentioned a potential investigation in Correspondence, 1/22/1914.

Ferris' investigation is recorded in a transcript, January 6, 1914 (the transcript says 1913, but that is a typographical error), Archives, State of Michigan.

The block quote of the *Miner's Bulletin* was first published on 1/7/1914.

The returned indictments and who testified to support them were reported in the *Daily Mining Journal*, 1/16/1914.

Nichols' statement, "I believe that Moyer and the others ..." was reported in *The Daily Mining Gazette*, 1/18/1914; they reported the authorization of the investigation by the House of Representatives on 1/28/1914.

The Seeberville Murder Trial

The Daily Mining Gazette's coverage of the jury selection for the Putrich killing and the coverage of the first day's testimony was published on 2/4/1914.

The reactions of the public, the Alliance and the judge's comments are from the *Daily Mining Gazette*, 2/15/1914.

"Not a dry eye ..." and the other coverage of the killers leaving for prison came from the *Daily Mining Gazette*, 2/18/1914.

The reporting of the "They are scum" quote is from "The Boardinghouse Murders," p. 6.

The Dally-Jane Murder Trial

"When we hired them ..." and that he had

heard of a confession is from MacNaughton's Correspondence, 2/27/1914.

Huhta's alleged confession was widely reported as were the arrests of the four men. There is more information on this at "Under Fire," by Kenneth A. Nicholson, www.copperrange.org.

"Law and Order During the 1913 Copper Strike," by William Beck, *Michigan History* magazine (April 1970) p. 289, note 47.

The "caused quite a sensation" quote is from Correspondence, 2/28/1914.

Lucas' feelings about the Huhta arrest is from "Anthony Lucas Recalls ..." by Anthony Lucas, *Copper Country Review*, March 1966, p. 3.

That Malvin was present when Huhta's confession was made, *Mining Journal* 11/17/1914.

The story of Lucas at the jail and his dealings with the sheriff are from "Anthony Lucas Recalls ..." by Anthony Lucas, *Copper Country Review*, March 1966, p. 3.

"Do not attach too much importance ..." is quoted in "Conditions in the Copper Mines ..." p. 16.

Lucas's attendance at the trial and all of his observations on this matter are from "Anthony Lucas Recalls ..." by Anthony Lucas, *Copper Country Review*, March 1966, p. 3.

The labeling of the defendants as "foreigners" is from "The Boardinghouse Murders," p. 16, note 14.

Huhta's "confession" is quoted from the *Mining Journal*, 11/20/1914, and the *Calumet News*, 11/18/1914. These articles also detail the closing arguments of the case.

The quick return of the verdict was reported in the *Mining Journal*, 11/23/1914.

The End of the Strike

The number of members in the WFM and how they voted, as well as the fate of *Tyomies* is from Holmio, pp. 290-292.

The facts and figures of the preceding year are taken from the annual Report of the Osceola Consolidated Mining Co. of Michigan For the Year Ending December 31, 1913, author's collection.

Employment figures for 1913 and 1914 are from *The Strike*, p. 8.

Falling employment due to the one-man drill's implementation is from Lankton, p. 241.

The Chicago reporter's story was reprinted by the *Calumet News* on 1/2/1914.

The report of the Catholic priest is detailed in Holmio, p. 289. The Dietz piece was published, "A Catholic View of the Copper Miners' Strike in Upper Michigan," *Survey*, vol. 31, 1914, p. 521.

The fate of the men convicted for killing Putrich is detailed in Beck, p. 285, note 31.

The discussion of violence—or lack of it—during the strike and the quote, "when peace officers ..." is from *The Strike*, p. 74.

That the law firm was never paid by some of the mines is found in Lankton, p. 240.

THE HOUSE INVESTIGATION

The House committee announcing it would look into the Italian Hall tragedy was reported in *The Daily Mining Gazette*, 2/12/1914.

Margaret Fazekas' testimony was preserved: House subcommittee hearings at Germania Hall, February 23, 1914, Archives State of Michigan.

The testimony of Rees is recounted in "The Truth about the Copper Strike," by Francis John Dyer, p. 237.

MacNaughton's testimony is recounted in "Conditions in the Copper Mines," p. 13.

The argument that soldiers did not carry sabers and that Big Annie was lying is from Dyer, p. 244.

Thurner says it was a saber, p. 92. Also, Alex Nelson's statement: Alex Nelson, interviewed by Paul Jalkanen, July 28, 1972, Suomi College Oral History project, courtesy of Finlandia University archives, p. 3.

MacDonald's statement "There is no middle ground ..." is from "Conditions in the Copper Mines," p. 4; his statements about the mines in collusion is from p. 8.

The quoted language from the hearings at the armory are from "Conditions in the Copper mines," "touching the disaster," "if there is any witness," and O.N. Hilton's statements p. 2064; Leskella, p. 2065-2066; Mrs. Lesch, p. 2068; Lustig, pp. 2071-2073; and Burcar, 2076. Burcar's testimony is often described as confused because he claimed to have been near the stage and near the door at the same time. However, in his subcommittee testimony, he clarifies that he was coming from the stage, down the hallway toward the doors when the cry of "Fire" was heard. p. 2076.

More from the armory hearing are found at: Forester, pp. 2078-2079; Schaltz, p. 2081; Jakkola, p. 2083; and Olsen, pp. 2085-2086.

Lanto's inquest testimony is Molloy, p. 50.

More from the armory hearing are found at: Lanto, p. 2088; Jokopie, p. 2091; their count of the victims is noted at p. 2091; Marchesey, p. 2091.

Marchesey's inquest testimony is found at Molloy, p. 132.

Boggio's armory testimony is p. 2093; Wiropia, pp. 2095-2096; the dimensions of the Halls and counting of the steps is p. 2098. "Conditions in the Copper Mines in Michigan," p. 2098. There is some debate on how many steps there were, but the point is meaningless. It actually depends on how one counts steps: Do you count the landings at the top and bottom of the stairs? Many people counted how many steps a person would take climbing the stairs, and naturally counted the "last" step taken, which is to step onto the top landing. Not counting the two landings at the top and bottom of the stairs, there were 22 steps.

The article calling the probe a "farce" is *The Daily Mining Gazette*, 3/8/1914. The corresponding pages of testimony for Erickson are 2089-2090.

Schaltz' testimony is p. 2081-2083. There is also some confusion on the part of whether Schaltz had testified at the inquest or not. Although he told the subcommittee members that he had testified at the inquest, his testimony does not appear in the transcript. Further, the *Mining Gazette* wrote that he was one of the subcommittee witnesses who had not appeared before the inquest.

The Daily Mining Gazette's criticism of the hearings, and the Slovenian statement, "We despise all these newspapers ..." is from 3/8/1913.

Elbert Hubbard's story of a fire on the stage is: "In the Copper Country," *The Fra* magazine, May 1914, p. 43.

MacNaughton's article is "History of the Calumet and Hecla Since 1900," by James MacNaughton, *The Mining Congress Journal*, October 1931, pp. 474-477.

LINGERING CONTROVERSIES
The Door Controversy

Harrington's report is The Historical American Building Survey: Italian Hall HABS No. MI-425. There is a copy at the MTU archives.

The Clarence Andrews interview was broadcast and transcribed. WMPL Hall Disaster, p. 9.

Taipalus' visit is documented at Ted Taipalus, "The Italian Hall, Calumet, Michigan Tragedy: A Personal Account," July 1980. Finlandia Archives 977.4 IT.

The Poison Gas Rumor

The following persons spoke on the WMPL program; their transcript pages are as follows. Webb, p. 30; "Another little boy ..." is p. 48; "yellow can," p. 27; "They must have put something on the steps ..." p. 34. These stories regarding poison gas and something placed on the floor were recounted sixty years after the fact, on WMPL in Hancock. The callers were screened, that is, the host of the program and his guest spoke to them to hear their stories off the air and then called them back to interview them on the air. The guest on the show, Dr. Clarence Andrews, was a professor at Michigan Tech who had recently published a paper on the tragedy. Unfortunately he did not ask any follow-up questions on these issues, presumably because he knew they were not true. Even so, they are a fascinating insight into the mindset of the survivors of the tragedy.

Lahti, p. 44.

The Missing Transcript

That there were no copies of the transcript available, "1913: A year of disaster, mystery and strife," by Lee Arten, *Copper Island Sentinel*, August 20, 1981.

The Answer to the Labor Struggles:
30 Years Late

See Lankton generally for the history of copper mining in the Keweenaw, and the history of unions there during the Depression and beyond. For the laws that were enacted, see the National Labor Relations Act of 1947, 29 USC Chapter 7 § 158 ("Unfair labor practices").

ENDURING APPEAL
The Tragedy in Music
William Gardner, who was upset by the Guthrie song: William A. Gardner, interviewed by Doris Helgren and Larry Harju, August 5, 1974, Suomi College Oral History project, courtesy of Finlandia University archives, p. 1432.

The story of Big Annie after the strike is from "The Calumet Tragedy," by Michael F. Wendland, *American Heritage* magazine, April/May 1986, p. 48. Wendland does not say if he interviewed Frank Klobuchar himself or read the interview elsewhere; the magazine does not provide footnotes or indicate sources. Although the article is well written and often quoted by those researching this topic, it is also the source of mis-quotes: Wendland did not appear to have a good copy of the inquest transcript to work from and his quotes of witnesses contain many—albeit usually minor—mistakes.

Stories of the opera appeared in many local newspapers. "Tragedy focus of new Play," The *Mining Journal*, January 14, 2001; "Premiere anticipated," *The Daily Mining Gazette*, February 10, 2001.

The words are from the opera: "The Children of the Keweenaw: An American Opera," music by Paul Seitz, libretto by Kathleen Masterson (2001), pp. 11, 40.

The End of Calumet & Hecla
That the homes were mostly destroyed: "Michigan Ghost Towns of the Upper Peninsula," R.L. Dodge (1973) reprinted 1996, p. 134.

The quote of Haywood's is from his autobiography, p. 277.

The story of the United Steelworkers coming to the region is from *Stairway to Tragedy*, Wilbert B. Maki (1983), p. 93.

Survivors of the Tragedy
Arvo Pyorala, interviewed by Art Puotinen, July 13, 1972, Suomi College Oral History project, courtesy of Finlandia University archives, p. 3

James MacDonald, interviewed by Paul Jalkanen, July 24, 1972, Suomi College Oral History project, courtesy of Finlandia University archives, pp. 5-6.

"But that one man ..." from WMPL, p. 23; Webb, p. 31; Lahti, p. 30; Mosack, p. 46. Alex Nelson, interviewed by Paul Jalkanen, July 28, 1972, Suomi College Oral History project, courtesy of Finlandia University archives, p. 4; Edmund Raymond, interviewed by Eero Ranto, July 2, 1973, Suomi College Oral History project, courtesy of Finlandia University archives, p. 5; Jean Nicholas, interviewed by Paul Jalkanen, August 4, 1972,

Suomi College Oral History project, courtesy of Finlandia University archives, pp. 14-15; Henry Snabb, interviewed by W.E. Anderson, August 7, 1973, Suomi College Oral History project, courtesy of Finlandia University archives, p. 1154; Norman Trezise, interviewed by "Troopers Harju and Helgren," July 28, 1972, Suomi College Oral History project, courtesy of Finlandia University archives, p. 1491, It is possible that Trezise was retelling—inaccurately—the story of the union saying it would "bury its own dead"; W. Parsons Todd, interviewed by R. J. Jalkanen, October 1974, Suomi College Oral History project, courtesy of Finlandia University archives, p. 1849.

"Seventieth Anniversary Souvenir Journal," *Tyomies* (1973), p. 16

The recovery of a transcript for the Italian Hall inquest is reported in "1913: A year of disaster, mystery and strife," by Lee Arten, *Copper Island Sentinel*, August 20, 1981; Dan McCormick, interviewed by author on October 25, 2005.

Later Memories of Italian Hall
The twisted story of Chapman's confession reports are found in "Italian Hall Confession," by R.C. Peterson and Carl Peterson, *Mining Gazette*, 3/16/1982; *Stairway to Tragedy*, Wilbert B. Maki (1983), pp. 81-83; and Leslie Chapman, interviewed by Paul Jalkanen, August 3, 1972, Suomi College Oral History project, courtesy of Finlandia University archives, pp. 12-13.

Rebels on the Range
Thurner's statement that the tragedy was a "sheer accident" is on p. 174 (emphasis in original). Thurner wrote the author in 2005 and stated that this was a *suggestion* and not a *conclusion*.

Thurner's correspondence with the author occurred in 2005.

The Schaltz interview was contained in a written report, supplied to the author by Thurner in 2005. "Italian Hall Tragedy, Interview with Mr. Frank Shaltz, July 29, 1978," courtesy of Arthur Thurner.

That Lanto was the "official" doorkeeper, p. 141.

That Lanto had actually seen a man wearing an Alliance pin, "Conditions," p. 2088.

Vairo's testimony is from Molloy, p. 27.

Erroneously that the hearing only lasted a "couple" of hours, Thurner's *Rebels*, p. 217.

"That anyone could testify ..." "Conditions ..." p. 2065.

Erroneously, that someone saw "five men wearing Alliance buttons ..." Thurner, p. 217.

That he may have "misread" the testimony, Arthur Thurner, correspondence with author, dated July 23, 2005.

Erickson's testimony, "Conditions ..." p. 2089.

Thurner's use of the word "deportation" instead of "kidnapping," p. 164.

Thurner's reliance on newspaper coverage

over better sources: Thurner, *Rebels* (1984) p. 157. The *Calumet News*: "Matt Saari, father of one of the boys who lost his life, told Chief of Police Trudell yesterday that he was at the top of the stairs at the time and saw no one come up the stairs giving the alarm which started the panic." *Calumet News,* 12/26/1913.

Saari's inquest testimony is Molloy p. 37.

"There were reports ... chimney fire ..." Thurner, p. 168.

The "Herman Bibber, at his home," block quote is Thurner, p. 169.

The correspondence from Thurner is dated 7/29/2005.

The Daily Mining Gazette report that mentions Bibber is 12/27/1913.

Thurner's "explanation" quote is his, p. 174.

"Purely accident" is from *The Daily Mining Gazette* of 12/27/1913.

In correspondence with the author in 2005 Thurner hinted that not all history can be found in documents or other forms of concrete evidence:

Carl Becker, noted US historian wrote about 1926 in his Everyman his own Historian *that the most important history is that which the common man carries around in his head—reminding us once again that political/social/economic tendencies cause ordinary people to believe what they believe to be the truth. That conclusion certainly applies to the testimony of men/women on both sides vis-à-vis Italian Hall.*

That statement, coupled with the fact that he grew up in Calumet and lived there until 1946, might indicate Thurner's justification for inserting "community beliefs" into his narrative, even though they are unsupported by concrete facts.

This author would note, however, that Thurner (born in 1924) was not a witness to the Italian Hall, and as such, is removed from the event just as much as any other historian investigating it today.

Thurner's erroneous statement about the Citizens Alliance is p. 123.

The *American Heritage* piece is "The Calumet Tragedy," by Mike Wendland, *American Heritage* April-May (1986) p. 48.

Did the guards help? The Molloy references here are: Sandretto, p. 19; Kaisor, p. 20; Meyers, p. 23; Vairo, p. 28; Big Annie, p. 32; Wright, p. 45; Fretz, pp. 47-48; Ryan, p. 49; Lanto, p. 51; Curto, p. 53; Kaisor, p. 54; Tomei, p. 62; Bono, p. 63; Trudell, p. 67; Rastello, p. 72; Czabo, pp. 81-82; Forster, p. 87; Jokopii, p. 89; Wuopia, p. 95; Burcar, p. 727; Jetta, pp. 109-110; Vivian, p. 113; Pichittino, p. 125, Mirchisio, p. 130.

The Legend

Monette wrote this in *The Copper Range Railroad,* by Clarence J. Monette (1989), p. 52.

The *Stereo World* article is "The Italian Hall Disaster," by Lee Laney, *Stereo World* magazine, May/June 1992, pp. 7, 9.

"The man who cried fire ..." *The Daily Mining Gazette* 1/26/1993. Population data derived from fact finder at U.S. Census website: www.factfinder. gov. In 1990, the population of the county was almost perfectly 50-50 male to female ratio, although in the older age ranges the numbers probably varied—with even more females to male (making Bill even easier to identify).

Correspondence with Cyndi Perkins, former editor of *The Daily Mining Gazette.* Email to author, on July 26, 2005. The author attempted to get more details of this story, and corresponded with the editor of the *Gazette* who allowed the story to run. She said she gave it the go-ahead—without being able to verify any of the facts—because the reporter had a reputation as a skeptic. Attempts to correspond with the reporter were fruitless.

Germain's statement that she knows the name of the man who cried "Fire" is from Germain, *False Alarm* (2005), p. 119.

The Memorial

Description of the building from Harrington's report. The cost of refurbishing the Hall from Dan McCormick, interviewed by author on October 25, 2005.

"Wood from Italian Hall," souvenir block. Gift to author from Janet Larson.

Peggy Germain, interviewed by author, November 16, 2005.

EPILOGUE

As for the meaning of the word Calumet: Thurner, *Calumet Copper and People* (1974), p 9.

NOTES AND SOURCES

I exchanged correspondence for a while with Arthur Thurner in 2005 on the subject of Italian Hall and his book, *Rebels on the Range.* When I told him I considered the coroner's inquest to be botched, he dismissed my criticism as a "rehash" of arguments made previously. I asked him if he could point to a source that had raised the same criticisms that I did (lack of interpreters, few follow-up questions and so on). He could point to none, other than to say that there was a general criticism of the inquest from day one. In the same letter, he suggested we end our correspondence.

Michigan Triumphs and Tragedies, by Dale Killingbeck (2005), pp. 113, 120, 123, 125.

Norma Vezzetti, interviewed by author, August 6, 2005.

About the Author

Steve Lehto is a writer and attorney who resides in southeast Michigan with his wife Amanda and two dogs, Milo and Wolfy. He obtained a B.A. in history from Oakland University and his J.D. from Southwestern University School of Law in Los Angeles. He is also an adjunct professor at the University of Detroit Mercy School of Law in Detroit, where he teaches consumer protection and trial practice. He previously wrote *Bobby Isaac: What Speed Looks Like* and *A Most Unusual Experiment: Chrysler's Turbine Car*, both published by Tarheel Press, LLC.